TORTURED
WONDERS

TORTURED WONDERS

Christian Spirituality
for People, Not Angels

RODNEY CLAPP

BrazosPress
Grand Rapids, Michigan

Published by Brazos Press
a division of Baker Publishing Group
P.O. Box 6287, Grand Rapids, MI 49516-6287
www.brazospress.com

Printed in the United States of America

Library of Congress Cataloging-in-Publication Data
Clapp, Rodney.
    Tortured wonders : Christian spirituality for people, not angels / Rodney Clapp.
        p.   cm.
    Includes bibliographical references and index.
    ISBN 1-58743-106-8 (pbk.)
    1. Spiritual life—Christianity. 2. Spirituality. I. Title.
BV4501.3.C52 2004
248.4—dc22   2004009658

Once a poor creature, now a wonder,
A wonder tortur'd in the space
Betwixt this world and that of grace.

—George Herbert,
"Affliction (IV)"

CONTENTS

PART ONE

CLASSICAL
CHRISTIAN
SPIRITUALITY

INTRODUCTION

Spirituality for Tortured Wonders

*S*piŕituality is a tricky word. We hear and use it commonly, and that may make it all the trickier. Like the next-door neighbor you've known on a first-name basis for years, but who turns out to be a spy or a terrorist, the word fools us by its apparent familiarity. In fact, it freights quite diverse meanings. A cursory visit to my web search engine scratches up literally hundreds of "spiritualities." There is the spirituality of work, the spirituality of simplicity, the spirituality of imperfection, the spirituality of food, the spirituality of letting go. There is herbal spirituality, neopagan spirituality, animal spirituality, plant spirituality, nudist spirituality, political spirituality, and private spirituality. We resort to the word avidly, even promiscuously. Clearly we, our society, like this word.

But as a beloved aunt said to me intently after I—a nephew, a male—had pierced my ear, "What does it mean?" What *spirituality* means is not at all easy to say, given its range of referents. I assume, however, that this much is clear: *spirituality* is a word we turn to in preference to certain other, less appealing alternatives. We would rather talk about spirituality than religion, which connotes institutional ties and hypocrisy and rigid impositions on freedom. Nor is piety something we want to think about or aspire to; *piety* is conservative, meek, bland, the color brown in a Technicolor world. It befits grandmothers but not the *Esquire* and *Cosmopolitan* demographics. And, to consider another alternative, we would certainly rather think of ourselves as "spiritual" than as "holy." In our day the crucial working meaning of *holy* and *holiness* is best captured by the dismissive epithet "holier-than-thou." Holy people are somber, can't stand the thought of anyone having fun, and presumptuously think they are better than the rest of us. In this semantic atmosphere, to strive for holiness denotes "I want to be an anal-retentive spoilsport." Small wonder, in such a climate, that a not-at-all crabby or inert theologian friend of mine admitted to covering a book with "holiness" in its title when he took it to the beach for reading.

What of other candidates to give *spirituality* a breather? There is at least one other word previous generations used in place of our *spirituality*. It is the word *purity*. But if we very much want purity in our water and tomatoes, we just as definitely don't want to be pure in our sexuality or heart or business dealings. Purity is thought akin to innocence and naïveté, and that in a culture where virginity beyond age eighteen is considered a potential indicator of mental illness.

With so many alternatives discredited and out of play, we turn to *spirituality* by default if nothing else. Yet whatever has ruined the vocabulary of former generations, many of us still want to have something to do with God, or with the ultimate as we know it. We want life, and something to live for. We want peace and wholeness in our lives and relationships. We want to grow and deepen as persons, and to know that our work has lasting significance. *Spirituality* permits us to name these aspirations, these hopes, while not implying that we are prudish or conformist or pretentious or naive.

So the word *spirituality* in the subtitle of this book. I admit at the outset that words such as *piety*, *religious*, *holiness*, and *purity* do not trip happily off my tongue. Some of these words (*holiness* is certainly one) need to be robustly recovered, but along with my beach-reading friend, I allow that these older words have some embarrassing and disconcerting connotations for me. Like desert island raft-builders, writers must always make do with the materials at hand. I am not at all content with the word *spirituality*, but it seems to be the sturdiest timber available at this time and this place. With some ingenuity and a lot of close work, I think I can make it float.

Identifying Christian Spirituality

The ingenuity and work of making *spirituality* do for my purposes begins with qualifying and specifying it. As I have already hinted, one reason the term is so popular is that *by itself* it is vague, amorphous. Or, to put it positively, it is an elastic and capacious word—it can contain multitudes. Such big, vague terms appeal partly because they grant their users the easy illusion of communication and communion. We think we are talking about, and perhaps expressing our love for, the same thing or something quite similar. This while in fact Jane's (vague, unspecified) "red" is Dick's (equally vague and unspecified) "blue"—both are colors, after all. But they are not the same color. I trust it requires little argument to state that, say, "nudist spirituality" is not synonymous with "Victorian spirituality." What thin and exceedingly general meaning does *spirituality* have that allows it to be used of both nudists and Victorians? I could never imagine anyone committing life and energies to such an abstraction. Consequently, against conventional grammar, *spirituality* appears to be a noun decisively determined by its adjective. The adjective determining *spirituality* as I want to consider it is *Christian*.

By insisting on a qualifying adjective, and especially the adjective pointing to a faith formerly and sometimes coercively and abusively dominant in much of the Western world, I realize I immediately divest the term *spirituality* of some of its luster. The warm, fuzzy feelings of embrace and inclusion begin to evaporate as soon as you or I specify the "spirituality" we actually have in mind. And to many eyes and ears—not without cause—*Christian* is synonymous with *exclusivist, narrow-minded, arrogant, belligerent*, and *interfering*. I will say more about this in the final chapter of this book, but for now I will only note that we Christians have to take the bad with the good. We are the inheritors of a two-thousand-year-old, continents-spanning faith tradition, and so of many and vast treasures. The forebears who carried these treasures to us across the bridge of time were fal-

lible and, by their own profession, sinful. A lot of pyrite has gotten
thrown in with the genuine gold, plenty of dingy coal with the bright
diamonds, but we can have or accept none of the treasure they bore
without shouldering the entire load. (Also, only time will tell how
much trash our own generations are adding to the load, and how
little gold.) I am eager to sort out the true gold from the fool's gold,
and to offer it up as compelling and clean as I can. I believe Christians
have much of genuine worth and importance to say to those who
embrace other (or no apparent) spiritualities. But I will not deny that
the tradition possessing me has its troubles and, like any tradition
older than a century (a decade? a year?), needs its sorting out to be
really attractive and convincing.

The adjective *Christian* presents a problem closer to home, among
those sympathetic to it. Christianity is not only an old but a many-
colored tradition, containing great variety and even conflict within
itself. No one person can speak for all of Christian spirituality. The
pope or Billy Graham or some Eastern Orthodox luminary can't. Even
a Texas Baptist can't. Far be it from me, a mere Oklahoma Methodist-
cum-Illinois Episcopalian, to think I can. Yet there is a coherent and
dynamic (which is to say, living and fighting) tradition of orthodox
Christianity. It is a tradition conceived of the Jews, built on a biblical
canon roughly hammered out by the end of the second century, and
clarified and crystallized in the fourth- and fifth-century Nicene and
Chalcedonian creeds. From there the tradition grows more complicated and even convoluted, especially with the eleventh-century split
of the church into east and west (basically, Eastern Orthodoxy and
Roman Catholicism) and exponentially with the sixteenth-century
Reformation and birth of Protestantism. Still and all, inasmuch as
these later developments and complications hope to be evangelical
(based on the *evangel*, the gospel of Christ), catholic (related to the
church universal and whole), and orthodox (rooted in ancient apostolic worship and faith), they all hark back to and try to measure or
index their faithfulness out of the Great Tradition grounded in the
first five centuries of the church's history.

So the terms *evangelical, catholic,* and *orthodox* further specify
the "Christian spirituality" of this book's subtitle. There is at present
no single office that can speak magisterially for this tradition, and

I in any event would not be worthy of such an office. But the tradition itself invites and expects many voices, minor as well as major, to testify. And it calls all voices, greater or lesser, to be responsible to and so variously manifest the church evangelical, catholic, and orthodox. This, then, maps out the soil from which I will try to represent and fit out Christian spirituality for a twenty-first-century Western setting.

Orthodox Christian Spirituality Defined

How can we further specify spirituality on these orthodox Christian terms, especially as it bears on the concerns of this book? Out of this tradition, we can say clearly what spirituality is not. It is not opposed to the body, it is not nonphysical. It is not removed from history, the ongoing flow of time. It is not asocial, a solitary activity or state of being. It is not primarily inward and invisible, a hidden affair of the private heart. In all these ways it is unlike a common conception of "spirituality" in our day as a compartmentalized experience, customized by and for the lone individual, removed from any pesky, constraining traditions or social bodies (institutions). There certainly are private spiritualities of this sort about; there are even quite a number of spiritualities considered Christian which are marked by these characteristics. I will not insist they have nothing going for them. I do insist that in their very nonphysicality, privacy, and denial of history they are *not* orthodox, or catholic and evangelical, Christian spirituality.

Orthodox Christian spirituality is participation and formation in the life of the church that is created and sustained by the Holy Spirit. The God shaping and enlivening this Christian spirituality is the trinitarian God, Father, Son, and Holy Spirit—the Three in One and no less the One in Three. The *spirit*-uality of Christian spirituality draws its life and definition precisely from the Holy *Spirit* who is a Person or member of the Trinity. The Holy Spirit shares in the perfect communion of Jesus the Son and God the Father. Jesus prays to the Father that his followers, the church, will "all be one" just "as you are in me and I am in you" (John 17:21). It is through the Holy

Spirit, who, as the Nicene Creed has it, "proceeds from the Father and the Son," that the people are made one in the church and made to partake of, to participate in, the communion of the Triune God. As such, Christian spirituality thoroughly has to do with physical bodies and history and social institutions. Here is what I, answering to the orthodox tradition, mean by that:

God the Father created and gave humanity life by God's Spirit, the very "breath of life" which inspirited and animated Adam, the prototypical human creature (Gen. 2:7). It was God's Spirit that spoke through the prophets of Israel, such as Moses and Jonah and Isaiah. Through the Spirit the people Israel—a community, a nation, a social, cultural, and political institution—was brought to the love and knowledge of the particular God who created humanity, hustled Abraham and Sarah out of their homeland, and called Moses to spur a revolt and lead his people out of Egyptian slavery. It was this Spirit that the Israelite Joel prophesied would one day be poured out "on all flesh," all nations and classes, male and female (Joel 2:28–29).

The Christian church confesses that Joel's prophecy has come to pass via Jesus the Christ (the Messiah, the Anointed One). Like the water and blood issuing from his pierced side while he hung on the cross, from Jesus God's Spirit has flowed over and into all the nations. Through Jesus, himself a Jew, the God who first revealed God's self to the Jews is made known and inviting to all peoples. It was by the power of the Holy Spirit that Jesus was conceived and came into the world (Matt. 1:20). By the Spirit he uncovered and embodied the character of his Father, healed the sick, routed demons, confronted rulers and those calloused by their wealth, and otherwise brought good news to the poor. When the powers of this world were overrun by their darkest impulses and crucified Jesus, it was by the strength and life of the Spirit that Jesus was raised from the dead (Rom. 8:11). And so, some fifty days after Jesus' resurrection, Joel's prophecy was fulfilled.

At the time called Pentecost, "devout Jews from every nation under heaven [were] living in Jerusalem" (Acts 2:5). The disciples of Jesus were "filled with the Holy Spirit," and suddenly listeners from various foreign, Gentile nations could all understand what the disciples spoke in their Galilean tongue (Acts 2:5–13). In Jesus and visited by the Spirit, these former strangers and enemies were able to break bread and pray together, even to hold "all things in common" and sell superfluous possessions to help the needy (Acts 2:42–45). So was the church born, in the lineage of foremothers and forefathers who had been confronted and guided by the Spirit for centuries, and now that same Spirit midwifed and thrust into the world a new people, a third race (neither entirely Jewish nor merely Gentile).

It is clear, then, that the Spirit from which Christian spirituality takes its shape, its name, and its very life is not altogether removed from time and place, from the day-to-day doings of slaves and masters of empires, from mortal bodies that shed sweat and tears and give birth in a rush of blood and mucus. Nor is the Spirit, once having worked so thoroughly in space, time, and society, now withdrawn and hidden from the public eye. It is the Spirit who testifies and opens eyes and ears on Christ's behalf (John 15:26). The Spirit who raised Christ from the dead now "dwells" among those who say and mean to take Christ as their Lord (Rom. 8:11; 1 Cor. 12:3). Christians simply are those baptized into Christ's body, the church, led and guided into the fullness of faith by the Holy Spirit (Gal. 5:18, 21) and enabled by the Spirit to discern the ways that open to life rather than death (1 Cor. 2:14–15).

So Christian spirituality cannot be pitted against physical bodies. Through the Spirit bodies are made, and one has been resurrected (with others to follow). Christian spirituality also cannot be pitted against time or history. The Spirit initiated history and constantly works in it. Finally, Christian spirituality cannot be pitted against the church, even if it is a "religious institution." The Spirit enables us to see beyond the church's flaws and recognize it as Christ's body. The gifts of the Spirit, which help Christians to deepen in spirituality, are given "to each" for "the common good" of the body (1 Cor. 12:7), so that in its words and practice it might vouch to the world of Jesus as the way, the truth, and the life. This was Jesus' prayer and expectation: that the oneness of the church, the integrity of Christ's corporate body, would verify to the world that Jesus was the Son, sent by the Maker and King of the universe (John 17:21, again). The church, we might say, is the Spirit in public, or simply the Spirit's public.

Thus classical Christian spirituality is not, in a word, angelic. It's easy to see how spirituality is confused with angels. After all, angels have spirits but no bodies—so the very word *spirituality*, severed from connection to the Holy Spirit, can make us think we are somehow called to be angels, or at least as much like angels as we can manage. Angels are bodiless, so we intuit that spirituality must not have anything to do with our physical bodies. Angels are beyond the messiness and confusion of unfolding time, of history, in direct contact with God, and we intuit that our spirituality too should escape history. We may also think that angels, each gazing immediately on God, don't need one another, that they aren't social creatures—the Source of all life and being is right in front of each angel, so why would any one of them turn to angelic companions on the left or right? And again we may intuit that our spirituality should be similar, that it is first and foremost a matter of the hermetic heart "come to the garden alone," to commune only with God.

But notice how quickly all these intuitions remove us and our spirituality from God's work and the story told of it in Scripture. The earliest followers of the Christian tradition took more careful account of a startling, world-changing reality. God, in Christ, became one of God's creatures—Jesus was both God and human. However high and special the angels are, Jesus did not take on or assume angel-spirit; he took on or assumed human flesh. So we see in the Christ not only God as true God is but the human as true human—humanity as it ought to be. Jesus reconciles humanity to God and so restores humanity to its fullness, redirects it to its true end and purpose. He does this in and as a physical body, within history and in public, through a social body called the church.

Christian spirituality is for people, not angels. Christian spirituality is the whole person's participation and formation in the church—Christ's body, the Spirit's public—which exists to entice and call the world back to its Creator, its true purpose, and its only real hope. All this was recognized and affirmed from the church's earliest days. This is reflected in the Scriptures cited above and encapsulated nicely by the second-century church father Irenaeus. Christianly spiritual persons, said Irenaeus, "are not bodiless spirits, but our very substance, that is, the union of soul and flesh, . . . receives the Spirit of God." The

Spirit constitutes this human union of soul and flesh as a "spiritual person." And this constituting Spirit is the Spirit that acts in earthly, worldly history, through various ages or dispensations. "The truly 'spiritual' disciple is the one who has received the Spirit of God, the Spirit who, from the beginning, in all the dispensations of God, has been present to men, who announced things future, revealed things present, and explained things past."

Sin: Self-Destruction and Addiction

Now you may have noticed a skip, a gap, in the tradition's story of the world and the human condition as I have just sketched it. My sketch began with God's creation of the world and the Spirit's animation of humanity. Then it moved directly to Israelite prophets' calling the nations to God and finally Jesus' reconciliation and restoration of humanity with God. But if God created the world and gave humans our existence, why were prophets needed to call humanity *back* to God? Why did Jesus need to restore or reconcile a creation existing perfectly in and from the perfect communion of the Triune God?

Of course, what I skipped was the Christian tradition's teaching that though created by God, humanity has strayed from and even rebelled against God. Most people do not think creation as we now know it is perfect. Every human culture, so far as I know, has thought the world has its problems. Some cultures, in their religions and philosophies, have sought to turn their back on the world, to escape imperfection by abandoning the world. Other cultures, such as the ancient Greek Cynics or modern "realists," have simply said this is the way it is: not perfect, in fact often ugly and mean, but beyond basic change. Expect the worst and at least you won't be surprised. The Christian tradition, as a culture, follows a third route. The world was created perfect, or happy, and it *ought to be* happy. But clearly it and we are not. The world has turned from God. It is lost.

Once my family hoteled in the Foggy Bottom precincts of the District of Columbia. One night we set out by car to go downtown, to the Jefferson Memorial. Suddenly (or so it seemed to me, the driver) we were on a freeway bridge, hurtling inexorably into Virginia. It

was dark, we could not turn around, we were stuck on a trajectory
into another state, not even sure our crisp new Washington map
encompassed the treacherous, baffling roadways of this prematurely
visited province. Furthermore, once we passed over the bridge and
exited the freeway, we were far removed from our planned route.
My sense of geography, dim even in the daylight, ensured tourist's
panic. We needed to retrace our progress, find our planned route
or at least our hotel (food, drink, a room with our number on it!),
but who knew what traps lay back that way? My wife and daughter
wondered if we would enjoy Virginian hospitality a day earlier than
the vacation itinerary had it scheduled. We were lost.

Of course, the map did help and a gas station attendant got us
oriented. Within an hour we were under the floodlit rotunda of
the Jefferson Memorial, staring up the great bronze nostrils of our
country's third president. But my sense of frustration and panic had
been real, born largely of my rearing as an Oklahoma farm boy who
should have a sure sense of direction and always be able to find his
way. My wife and daughter, differently enculturated, were never so
frightened or frustrated. We weren't, after all, driving in a trackless
and empty desert. All we had to do was stop at one of many visible
gas stations or convenience stores and ask directions. That is exactly
what we eventually did, but not before I tried to rescue my pride and
by myself get us back on the right route.

According to the Christian tradition, humanity was once securely
located—little danger of starvation in a garden, as in a hotel—but
then got lost. And humanity has pretty much insisted on finding its
own way back to the garden. In fact, we could not. We were and are,
despite our best efforts, hopelessly lost, and the conventional roads
back into the garden are blocked. So God had to go looking for us
and call us back and beyond ourselves.

Yet our human plight is much worse, and even of a different kind,
than my family's unplanned foray into Virginia. As the Christian tradition tells it, once humanity got lost we remained intent on not being
directed back home. We wanted to find our way, even make our own
way, create a new garden in our own image and call that henceforth
and really home. It is as if, proud and bewildered in Virginia, I had
absolutely insisted we would take no directions, as if at any cost I

would deny I was lost. If it came to it, I would poke my eyes out to prevent finding my way back by someone else's knowledge, ability, and generosity. Now, if I were ever to see home (or the Jefferson Memorial) again, someone would have to not only lead or carry me there but restore my eyesight.

This headlong self-destruction is what the Christian tradition calls sin. God's judgment is what befalls us when God, to some degree, leaves us to ourselves and our own devices. In our sinfulness, the psalmist says, we shovel a pit and fall into the hole we have dug. Our "mischief returns upon [our] own heads, and on [our] own heads [our] violence descends" (Ps. 7:15–16). St. Augustine presents sin in this light repeatedly in his fourth-century *Confessions*. He notes that sins against God are simultaneously sins "against myself." He prays to God, "What you take vengeance on is what men inflict on themselves, for even when they sin against you, they do evil to their souls." He cries, "For without you, what am I to myself but the leader of my own destruction?" In his masterwork, *The City of God*, Augustine summarizes this same dynamic: "For it is certain that if man ignores God's will he can only employ his own powers to his own destruction; and thus he learns what a difference it makes whether he gives his adherence to the good that is shared by all, or finds pleasure only in his own selfish good." Sin is the drive to separate ourselves from the Creator and Sustainer of our being and our own true good, insisting on seeking pleasure, honors, and life not in God but in ourselves and other creatures apart from God.

Yet God, on the Christian account, will not leave us alone. God will not force it (love compelled is no longer love), but God profoundly wants to lead us home and restore our eyesight, our full health and goodness. So God gathered Israel and sent it prophets. God sent God's Son to assume our sickness, our blind eyes, and to heal us. Jesus stood against and revealed the futility of the powers to which we, in our blind struggle for autonomy, entrust ourselves. Jesus comes, said Augustine, "to protect from themselves those ready to become submissive to him." Jesus has come, rescue and the potential of restoration is at hand.

But of course we still resist, to one degree or another, even (sometimes especially) those of us on whom the healing light of the Holy

Spirit has shined. When the Holy Spirit began to give Augustine sight, Augustine confessed, "I was sure that it was better for me to give myself up to your love than to give in to my own [misguided] desires. However, although one way appealed to me and was gaining mastery, the other still afforded me pleasure and kept me victim."

More famously, the apostle Paul observed the same tendency. On the one hand he delighted in God and God's way, leading to life. But on the other hand he was at war with himself, "captive to the law of sin" (Rom. 7:21–25). *Sin* is not a highly popular or attractive word in our modern or postmodern world. It remains a necessary and irreplaceable Christian word, and a term that is pervasive in our day can help us understand it. Once we used *addiction* to refer only to a compulsive physiological attraction to a substance such as alcohol or opium. Now we also speak of addiction to experiences: the daredevil is addicted to speed and risk; some people are addicted to gambling, others to shopping or even shoplifting. We label "codependent" people we think are addicted to relationships. In themselves the things or experiences to which we may be addicted are not necessarily bad. God gave wine to warm and lift human hearts (Ps. 104:15). Shopping to clothe the body is not an evil act. It may not be good to be addicted to a spouse or a friend, but surely it is a good to have a spouse or a friend. We call people addicted not necessarily because they are drawn to something evil but because they center too much of themselves, maybe even their entire life, on a certain good. They separate the good from its proper context and ordering in the whole and try to make it the whole itself. And since no creaturely good is or can be the source of all life, the world of addicts shrinks to the eventually cramping and crippling dimensions of the part they would make the whole—the creature they would make god. By the time addicts recognize how small and cramped their world has become, they are already stuck, enslaved. Their liberation will be possible only when they painfully break out of the puny, constraining world to which their self has molded. Then addicts are, for a while, in between. They see that they must for their own good break out, and they want to return to the real world, so much bigger than their addiction. A new and restorative way appeals to them, but the addiction still affords some pleasure and security and clutches to keep them victim.

Again, Christian spirituality is not for the angels. The angels do not know the addiction of sin. Christian spirituality is for people: bodily, social, embedded in time. It is for men and women who are creatures of God but who also are (as we all are) sinners. God has not abandoned us but has come after us in Jesus Christ and in the Holy Spirit reaches out a lifesaving hand now. The restoration has begun; it is available, but it is not yet complete.

So the Anglican poet George Herbert, in his eloquent way, got it just right. We are together and each of us "once a poor creature" simply lost and self-destructing, yet also "now a wonder" remembered and revisited by the Spirit. We are a "wonder tortur'd in the space / Betwixt this world and that of grace," the grace of a new heaven and a new earth, of creation whole in all its parts. Christian spirituality, then, is spirituality for tortured wonders.

A Spirituality for the Road

The Christian tradition sees human beings as tortured creatures primarily because we are "in-between" creatures. We are in between angels and brute animals, sharing some characteristics (such as self-consciousness, reason, and imagination) with the angels and some characteristics (bodies that will die, the urge to procreate) with dogs, cats, apes, horses, cattle, and other animals. We are in between abject sin and our full salvation. We are in between our passions and appetites as they should be (centered on and ordered to the Triune God), and our passions and appetites as they often are (scattershot, gluttonous, lustful, and self-destructive). All of creation, in fact, is in between: in between Jesus' inauguration of the kingdom of God and the consummation or perfection of that kingdom in a new heaven and a new earth. So spirituality is a journey and a struggle. We have not yet arrived at our destination, and we must constantly wrestle with tendencies to leave the path leading us toward our true end. It is a journey with joy, certainly. There is hope, there will be fulfillment, and even now along the way there are sweet snatches and glimpses of that final fulfillment. But it is just as certainly a journey with hardships, challenge, and bitter surprises and disappointments. "You stand before God and would like to enjoy yourself and you may enjoy yourself," theologian Karl Barth wrote, "and yet you must experience every day how your sin is new every morning. There is peace, and yet only peace which can be confirmed among struggle. . . . There is life, and yet but life in the shadow of death."

This unfolding dynamic of struggle is what I am trying to capture when I say Christian spirituality is participation *and formation* in the church, the community created and sustained by the Spirit. To say that spirituality includes formation is to recognize that the church, and each of its members, has not arrived, that it (and each of us) is not at all entirely as it should be in its practices and behaviors. We are in that sense babes or children, still being formed into adults by stories, disciplines, exemplars, and the rehearsal of creation-as-it-should-and-will-be called worship. Christian spirituality is about our being fitted to live as the creatures we are and are meant to be, with and as bodies, in society and in history.

If there is an epitome or encapsulation of this spirituality, it is the Lord's Prayer. Jesus' prayer, which he taught his followers to practice, is a prayer for physical creatures. In it we boldly ask for—even demand—the "daily bread" our bodies need. We learn in it to pray for this world, that the Father's will be done "on earth, as it is in heaven." The Lord's Prayer teaches us to pray as creatures within history and time, for bread and God's will "this day." It also reminds us that we will face temptation and evil. And by this prayer we are taught that we pray, hope, and live first and foremost as a community: "*Our* Father . . . , Give *us* . . ."

"Amen," the prayer ends, or, "So be it." But how can it begin to be so? How do we grow and advance in Christian spirituality? What can it mean to live and practice a spirituality that it is not merely spiritual (as in nonmaterial or ethereal) but bodily?

1

AFFIRMING THE FLESH

*Christian Spirituality
and the Necessity
of the Body*

A few years ago I took on a new physician. Concerned to do his job right, he made his first item of business with me a physical examination. So our budding acquaintance was literally fostered hands-on. Not long after I had, at the nurse's behest, stripped down to my undershorts, the doctor entered our small sanctum and shook my hand. There were a few words of salutation about how long I'd lived in the area and whether I was following the pro basketball playoffs. Even as I set about answering, the doc went to work. He pressed at my neck and throat like a potter molding clay. He rubbed his stethoscope on his coat to warm it, then listened to my heart and lungs (and not so much to my remarks about the Chicago Bulls). The physical progressed with his occasional perfunctory comments. Then he asked me to stand up and lower my shorts for a hernial exam. It was then, as I tried in futility not to be self-conscious, that he chose to ask about my occupation. I told him I was an editor and writer.

"So what do you write about?" he said. "Please turn your head and cough."

"I write [cough] . . ."

He moved his hand to the other side of my groin and interrupted—"Turn the other way and cough."

". . . I write about [cough, cough] theology."

"Oh," he said noncommittally, almost absentmindedly. "Now please bend over and put your elbows on the table, so I can check your prostate."

Theology, or thinking about God, who by definition has no physical body, usually is a highly disembodied practice. It links to textual artifacts (especially the Scriptures) and occasionally to archaeological artifacts. But it is not hard, when one is doing theology, to forget about the body. Maybe thinking and writing about theology, and spirituality, should be done in the course of physical examinations (although it would be hard to concentrate). That would keep us down to earth and aware of the bodies that we possess, that we *are*, as human creatures. There are, I learned that day in the doctor's office, few pretensions to angelic, ethereal spirituality when your elbows are on the cold plastic of the examination table and you hear rubber gloves being snapped on behind you.

The Morbid Anarchy of Decay

In no small part, the human condition is about the constant sheddings and emissions of the body. Every day hairs fall from our heads. Skin dries and flakes away. Fingernails break or are clipped and tossed. We blow our noses, we emit urine and feces, menstrual blood or semen. All this is messy, and we do our best to hide and tidy it. It is impolite to groom ourselves in public. We use handkerchiefs or tissues as discreetly as possible and conceal the results of their usage. Bathrooms, with their toilets and showers, entail solitude.

The tendency to contain and conceal bodily emissions appears inherent to human civilization and enculturation. The ancient Hebrews, for instance, had rules about how to become "clean" again after the "uncleanness" of seminal emission, menstruation, and the infected discharges of illness. Until cleanliness was restored, entrance into the sacred precincts of the temple was barred. "Thus you shall keep the people of Israel separate from their uncleanness," the Levitical writer quotes God, "so that that they do not die in their uncleanness by defiling my tabernacle that is in their midst" (Lev. 15:31). Bodily discharges, after all, are not found among God and the angels.

We denizens of the complex and technologized twenty-first century may think ourselves beyond the strange ideas of the Israelites. Our worries about uncleanness, we think, have nothing to do with murky religious taboos. Our concern and practice is scientific; it is about hygiene and the prevention of disease. But are our hygienic obsessions entirely and simply rational? Running water, we know, has indeed been crucial to controlling and almost eradicating many infectious viruses and bacteria. Staying reasonably clean does have something to do with staying reasonably healthy. Yet our hygienic concerns are often obsessive. Soap and disinfectant manufacturers play on our unceasing fears by endlessly introducing new and purportedly more effective products. With these, we are told, all germs will be routed from our kitchens and bathrooms. Though, so far as I know, dandruff, ring around the collar, and halitosis have never yet killed anyone, we hustle to buy and use a succession of products promising to free us of such plagues. Medical studies are reported breathlessly, scaring us out of the woods where we may contract Lyme's disease; warning us to keep our children's hands off bird feathers lest they contract a newly discovered, fowl-transmitted disease; sounding the alarms as mosquitoes carry the West Nile virus into our neighborhood. Television news programs microscopically scrutinize hotel bed sheets and dentists' offices and reveal all manner of dreadful dirtiness. Lost amid all the hysteria is the simple recognition that the odds of contracting life-threatening diseases in the woods or a hotel room or a dentist's office are exceedingly small, and that the logical conclusion of eliminating absolutely all chance of contamination is to lock ourselves away in our immaculate home and never venture outdoors or into the public. Where the ancients fretted about God and the angels, we can dread viruses and bacteria with something quite like religious awe or terror.

My point is not that we should ignore reasonable precautions against contamination; it is that our precautions and hygienic practices often exceed the strictly reasonable. (In fact, researchers now suggest our mania for spotlessness is making some children sick. Excessively clean environments allow no flexing and exercising of the developing immune system, and sensitive children become especially vulnerable to even the mildest allergens.) So for us moderns as well as for the ancients, there is something profoundly unsettling about our bodies and their susceptibility to contamination. It is this: mortal bodies are corruptible, and the ultimate corruption is death. The constant changes and emissions of our bodies remind us that we will die.

When we die, our bodies corrupt. Compared to earlier ages, our modern setting sterilizes and glosses over this brutal reality. Moderns are more apt to die in a hospital than at home. And at death we whisk bodies from the hospital to the undertakers, who, with all their tricks of embalming and cosmetics, go to great lengths to make corpses as lifelike and attractive as possible. The irony is that embalming, in the service of rendering the corpses apparently alive (and "just sleeping"), actually makes the deceased beloved even less like himself or herself, even more dead, so to speak. Morticians drain blood, the fluid of life. They stuff or sew shut bodily cavities.

The body, while living, constantly pulses—absorbing, shedding, taking in nourishment, emitting waste. But with death, the change goes in only one direction. No more will rejuvenation follow deterioration. The circle of life breaks and unravels into a plummeting angle of decomposition. Still, hours and even days pass before all cells suffocate, all neural discharges fire and go cold. Former generations were not as effective as ours at immobilizing corpses, robbing the body of its lingering, final organic alterations. They had occasions when corpses spasmed and suddenly sat up in coffins, when lifeless eyes or mouths popped open, when intestinal fluids leaked out and stank up the family parlor. We are better at hiding from ourselves the terrifying reality that when we die our body is no longer ours, our eyes and mouths and limbs are no longer under our control, that now all of the body's changes are beyond our ministrations and against any desires we may have had. There is only the process, or the morbid anarchy, of decay.

And this is a terrifying reality. For years after my father died prematurely, at age forty-five, I would sometimes awaken with a start just as I was drifting to sleep, suddenly remembering Dad. I would remember that he was gone, that his body was in the ground, and then think, *Someday, me too.* I listen to a lot of music, the best of it far from sentimental, but among the scariest lines I've ever heard come from Jimmie Rodgers, the oft-declared father of country music, when he was dying of tuberculosis in 1931:

> Gee, but the graveyard is a lonesome place;
> They put you on your back,
> Throw that mud down in your face.

It is hard enough to think of a father and aunts and grandfathers gone, their bodies given up to the soil, yet that barely compares to realizing in the marrow that my case is the same, that the only difference is time. Someday I'll be on my back, the mud flying down in my face.

I am not obsessed with death, but occasionally the stark chill of its inevitability will linger and haunt. That was true when, one summer vacation, I lay contentedly reading on a porch lounge and came across the statement that sometimes, on hot late-summer days, people walking through cemeteries have heard swollen, gaseous corpses explode beneath their feet. So much for idle relaxation that afternoon. When we die, I thought, our bodies respond like other decaying organic matter. When we die, we rot.

When Death Visited Daily

In that brute reality, and in our aversion to it, we are at one with our Christian predecessors. We err when we think the early church's qualms about the body had primarily to do with sexuality. It is true that church fathers and mothers often referred to the body as a burden. But they thought of it as a burden in relation to its mortality and perishability, its susceptibility to literal physical corruption. In this regard St. Augustine quoted the apocryphal Wisdom of Solomon, "The body which is perishing weights down the soul." The body's constant changes reminded Augustine and others of its propensity toward the ultimate, one-directional change of death and decay. The flaking, eating, digesting, excreting body, they correctly saw, is constantly in process and never, from one day to the next, identical with itself in composition. So the third-century theologian Origen averred that "river is not a bad name for the body since, strictly speaking, the initial substratum in our bodies is perhaps not the same for even two days."

Philosophically, early Christians argued that the only possible alteration from perfection was adulteration or defection. Since you cannot improve on perfection, anything in a state of perfection could by definition change only for the worse. So the chronic changeability of the body reflected its imperfect condition. More mundanely, the body's undeniable weakness—its vulnerability to illness or injury, the inevitable depredations of aging—was in each concrete instance a foreshadowing of death and its finalizing decay. Each fever or flu or loss of a finger or eye was a little death, a happening in degree or in part that would eventually come to pass completely, for the whole. Aging was, and remains, a decline that ends only in death.

Now that I am past age forty-five and rolling toward fifty, my bladder no longer holds quietly all night long, my stomach can no longer peacefully abide late-night consumption of jalapeño-studded nachos. I can no longer threaten, with any realism, to run a mile in under five minutes. I've long needed corrective lenses for my eyes, but recently the optometrist fitted me for bifocals. In high school I played football, and bruises and cuts healed from one Friday night to the next. At middle age the bruises and cuts linger for weeks; I'm sore for days after moving boxes into a new home. Through my twenties, I could imagine my body indestructible. As I age, illusions of indestructibility are transparent as exactly that—illusions—and death seems less distant and theoretical.

Mortality was much more visible and pervasive for premodern Christians. We can justly be glad we do not have to dwell on the weakness of the body as much, and as often, as they did. The average life expectancy in the Roman world was under thirty years. A common cause of death was malnutrition pursuant to loss of the teeth and the inability to chew foodstuffs. Cities were excessively crowded and dirty. Antioch, the fourth largest city in the Roman era, hosted 150,000 inhabitants in an area two miles long and one mile wide, or roughly 117 people per acre. By comparison modern Manhattan Island houses 100 inhabitants per acre, and that with skyscrapers providing considerably more space to each inhabitant. Occupying airspace hardly helped in the ancient world. The highest buildings had about five stories, and these often lethally collapsed because the poor crowded many people onto the upper floors. Living spaces, usually one room to an entire family, were shared with livestock. Streets were either muddy or choked with dust and were soiled by horse and ox traffic as well as human sewage. Cooking was done hazardously over open fires, and buildings frequently burned. Crime rates exceeded those of even the most lawless modern cities. So in overcrowded buildings we would today regard as fire hazards, well beneath minimal building-code requirements, the ancients sought insufficient shelter in the face of epidemics and a numbing array of social and natural disasters.

During Antioch's six hundred years of intermittent Roman rule, the city burned entirely or in large part four times; six major riots racked the city; eight earthquakes shook it to its paltry foundations; three devastating epidemics, with mortality rates over 25 percent, savaged it; and five horrific famines spread starvation. In Antioch, as in other ancient cities, the mortally ill were seen daily. Missing body parts were so common that individuals were identified in public records by their disfigurements and scars. And both infant and adult corpses were routinely dumped in the street.

With such realities remembered, we may perhaps better understand why early Christians paid more attention to death and to the fragility and perishability of the body than do we. They saw evidence of mortality and bodily vulnerability daily and vividly. Our improved living conditions triple and nearly quadruple our life spans and make early death by disease, accident, or the ravages of nature comparatively rare. But still, as I have said and as we all know, our bodies remain weak and susceptible. Still we die and our bodies rot. If for us the ancient Christians are a bit too fixated on death and the corruptibility of the body, the wisdom of their spiritual experience and ruminations is not entirely beyond or behind us. In fact, the shortness, nastiness, and brutishness of bodily life in the world of Christianity at its beginnings makes it all the more remarkable that—whatever the sometimes deprecating comments about the body as a burden—Christian spirituality has from its origins been an embodied spirituality, insisting on the goodness of body as well as soul.

Bodily Discontent

It is commonly supposed that classical Christian spirituality despises the body. There is some inherent basis for that supposition, especially, as we will see later, when the faith is misconstrued and malpracticed as a kind of angelic spirituality. (Then it is assumed that Christian spirituality is ultimately about escaping or shedding the limitations of the physical body.) But much of the criticism of orthodox Christian spirituality arises out of anachronistic judgments. As I have said, in the premodern world, with much shorter life spans and greater vulnerability to disease and accident, the weakness of the human body was glaring. Looking to a surer source of some stability and permanence, ancient faiths and philosophies in general shied away from idealizing the body. When the New Testament was written, celibacy was considered the proper deportment of any philosopher, Christian or pagan. Sexual passion disrupted the serene, contemplative work of the intellect. Followers of Plato were notoriously dualistic, seeing the body as a tomb imprisoning the soul. One such Platonic philosopher, Plotinus, was so dismissive of bodily existence that he would admit to no parents or birthday and would allow no one to paint his portrait. Well before the inception of Christianity, Roman doctors thought avoidance of sexual activity left the body healthier and stronger. What about non-Western faiths and philosophies? Scholars tell us that throughout Asian religions there has been a notion of the soul's departing the body at death, then being purified of bodily and earthly taints before being liberated into the heavens. Buddhists have variously referred to the body as an abscess, a prison, and "an ornamented pot of filth." Sufi Muslims feared that sexual activity hindered the pure submission of the soul to God. Sikhism thought attention to women distracted and diverted men from clean and true spirituality.

Put in their proper chronological context, then, early Christian worries about the body as a burden and wariness of sexual desire do not appear so unusual or quite so negative. Delaying gratification, so to speak, I will turn to sexuality and bodily desire in the next chapter. Here I note that traditional philosophies and religions, however misguided we may consider them in many particulars, built off basic and reliable human observation in their concerns about bodily weakness. Even in a state of health, the body constantly tires and needs nourishing. The body grows tired standing and must sit. But soon it tires of sitting and must stand again. The body eats and fills up but in a few hours is hungry and must eat again. St. Augustine spoke of simple and undeniable human experience when he wrote, "Whatever you take, after all, to refresh yourself when you are tired, is simply the start of another form of tiredness, because if you persist in the thing you've taken for relief, you will grow tired of that too—so in this weak and perishable body, what does this health, such as it is, amount to, after all? In any case, what's called health in weak and perishable flesh is in no way to be compared with the health of the angels."

Witnessing the body's perishability and constant need for renewal, some faiths and philosophies sought to dismiss it as much as possible, or saw it as originating in or because of evil—as in the widespread Greco-Roman belief that souls preexisted the body in bliss, then got trapped in flesh molded by demiurges or lesser (even evil) gods. For that matter, modern secular naturalism not only dismisses the soul but sees the human body—in all its complexity and apparent wonder—as the result of brute evolutionary accidents. Under the aegis of this modern secular view, the body is easily imagined as nothing more than a machine of interlocking fleshly parts. The body then is not seen as necessarily integral to personal identity, as shown in scientific dreams of downloading human consciousness into a hypersophisticated computer. In this scenario the "real" or core person is not found in the body as a whole, or even in the brain, but in consciousness as "information" separable from the body.

It turns out that the modern and postmodern esteem for the body is a thin veneer punctured by the gentlest examination. We readily and regularly flee bodily limits into realms of virtual reality (where the represented body, as in video games, never really and finally dies). Facelifts that stretch skin like rawhide on a tanner's rack and botox treatments that smooth wrinkles by paralyzing the flesh express not so much love for the body as desperate dissatisfaction with it as it is. Medieval flagellants parading through city streets, lashing their backs with leather whips, strike us as morbid. But the hordes of marathoners struggling through the streets of contemporary Boston, Chicago, New York, and other cities, dehydrating and pushing their bodies past exhaustion, will appear no less bizarre to future generations. We are still trying to whip our bodies into shape.

In the light of both traditional and modern practices, then, what requires explanation is not so much orthodox Christianity's acknowledgment of bodily weakness as its stubborn and profound affirmation of the body—whatever its weaknesses. Classical Christian spirituality never rejects and never gives up on the body because of three key features of its basic story and logic: creation, incarnation, and resurrection. We will take each up in turn.

Creation as Body No Less Than Soul

Like the Judaism that birthed it, the church sees the body (not just the soul) as the creation of a good God. Neither lesser deities nor brute, purely random and accidental evolution created the body. Its making, like that of the soul, is an act of the highest and only true God. So the church sees all of creation as "good." In Genesis the Creator God directly makes sky and land, plants and animals, stars and seasons, and humans body and soul. After each act of creation, the text tells us, the Creator steps back to admire the handiwork: "And God saw that it was good." Modern Christians need not (and most do not) deny evolution as a means of creation, but do profess a loving Creator who is working behind, in, and through all means of creation. All of human being—flesh and bones as well as informational consciousness—is sourced in the blessed Creator, and none of it is finally or simply disposable.

To put it another way, our entire human nature and personhood is a gift from God. As a twelve-year-old, I bartered away to a friend a pocketknife given to me by my grandfather. I'd had Granddad's knife for months, and my friend's stamp collection then looked much more exotic and interesting. I still remember my parents' disappointment and anger when they found out I had traded Granddad's gift. It was, they said in no uncertain terms, a gift from my grandfather, one of special meaning that he meant particularly for me. How could my capricious disposal of that gift reflect love and respect for its giver? As it turned out, my friend's parents emphatically agreed, and our transaction was canceled. I learned that no gift really belonged to me—not in the sense that I could blithely do with it whatever I wanted, such as getting rid of it. The church likewise views the body as a gift, one of the most precious imaginable. Says the apostle Paul: "Do you not know that your body is a temple of the Holy Spirit within you, which you have from God, and that you are not your own?" (1 Cor. 6:19).

But how is the body related to the soul? At the broadest level in biblical thinking, the soul is life. This is directly reflected in the Latin translations of biblical terms for "soul." There it is rendered *anima*, as in the English *animal*, a sentient creature, and *animation*, the giving or imparting of sentient life. In human beings the soul not only vivifies the body but is rational and the source of a person's thinking and willing. The soul then both vitalizes and directs the body. Note, accordingly, that the soul in human beings is not just a raw, amorphous, and all-pervasive life force. The "soul" of plants (*vita* to the ancients) is something like that. But the human soul is sentient and rational—it is the source of thinking and willing. Each of us becomes the person we are through our relationships and our thinking and willing in response to them. So the soul is distinctive to each person; it is the particular and unduplicated life-identity of the individual. Note also that the soul ideally directs the body. This in a sense puts the soul "over" the body, making it the head or chief of the person's life and actions. But the traditional Christian anthropology—or understand-

ing of personhood—does not succumb to a dualism that glorifies the
soul and denigrates the body. The soul as vitalizer and director of
the body no more makes the body unimportant or disposable than
does a parent's procreation and direction of offspring make children
unimportant or disposable. In Christian spirituality soul and body
are integral—no person is whole without both.

So in the Old Testament the dead, separated from their bodies,
may continue some form of existence, but only as pale shadows of
themselves. They linger almost comatose in Sheol, as in a hospital
or jail, and are referred to as mere "shades" (see Ps. 88:10). By New
Testament times Jews and Christians had more highly developed
expectations of the afterlife. But still the body and soul were integral, and emphasis clearly fell on their reintegration at the resurrection of the body. The soul might "sleep" in the interim between
the individual's death and the corporate resurrection of all the dead
at the last judgment (as in 1 Thess. 4:14). Or the soul might linger
consciously in a weakened condition—St. Augustine thought the
soul "persisted" after death, "in however low a degree." Biblically,
the soul's state in the interim between death and resurrection is not
terribly clear and receives little attention. The focus instead rests on
the ultimate hope of the body's resurrection and reintegration with
the soul, and the renewal of all creation in a new heaven and a new
earth, as in 1 Corinthians 15 and Revelation 21.

In light of the biblical witness, then, Karl Barth correctly identifies
human persons as both ensouled bodies and embodied souls. The soul
vitalizes and directs the body, but the body also in some sense informs
and shapes the soul. This is displayed in the biblical penchant for
personal names that reflect physical characteristics. For the Hebrews
names encapsulated personal character and identity, which is why the
pious yearned to know the name of God (Ps. 9:11; 91:14). In relation
to mortals, to remember and carry on someone's name was to keep
his essential nature and character, his soul, alive. The father lived
on in the son, not least in the son's bearing of his name, so that for
the Hebrew nothing was worse than the extermination of the family
name through a failure to bear children (Num. 27:4; 1 Sam. 24:22;
2 Sam 14:7; Ruth 4:10). If names captured and expressed the unique
life and identity (the soul) of their bearer, it is worthwhile to note

biblical names that reflect bodily features, inclinations, or behaviors. The hirsute twin brother of Jacob was Esau, denoting his hairiness. The jawbone-wielding slayer of lions and Philistines was Samson, meaning "strong." Zoheth means "fat." Paul means "little." Edom, borne by the patriarchal lover of red stew, denotes "red." Abraham is by name and in fact "father of a multitude."

Such names indicate that we are shaped and formed in our very souls (our deepest, most vital and animating selves) by our bodies. In our day we give less care and attention to names per se, yet we can still see how body shapes self. Many of our abilities and loves grow out of our bodily limitations and potentials. No 140-pounder will be an NFL lineman, but an agile 320-pounder might. Usually an excellent pianist has long fingers. A painter needs extraordinary eye-hand coordination. In such ways the young person's body informs his or her developing identity and aspirations. Bodily characteristics such as race also shape the soul—we can talk after W. E. B. DuBois of "the soul of black folk," so that the "soul" here is indelibly marked by the "black" body. More elementally, it is a commonplace that males and females typically have different identities because of their bodies. The feminine soul and the masculine soul are distinctive to their embodied genders.

Of course, the meaning and possibilities of many bodily characteristics can change over time and from culture to culture. No longer, for example, do we assume that the African-American body means "slave," or the female body a male subordinate. Yet bodies always mean something, always delineate distinctive ranges of potential and opportunities. In any given time or place, the person you or I will become has much to do with the bodies in and through which we move and have our being. Over the course of a lifetime and its various struggles and achievements, the body reflects the soul and the soul reflects the body. So when we remember the essential Winston Churchill, we picture an older, balding, rotund man—not the dashing young figure Churchill once was, but who he was after the soul-making ravages and challenges of World War II.

Some spiritualities or ways of life are uncomfortable with embodiment. For instance, the extreme modern individualism that tells a child "you can be whatever you want to be" downplays or ignores how embodiment brings limitations as well as possibilities. But Christian spirituality cannot overlook the body. Orthodox Christian spirituality *essentially* and *necessarily* links the formation of the soul and spirit to the givens of the body and to the teaching and formation of the body. Such is what it means to be created wholly—body and soul—by a good and loving Creator.

Incarnation and the Saving of the Whole Wreck

In the grammar of Christian spirituality, creation means that from the start both soul and body are of inestimable worth. But we can imagine things of great worth that are ruined and must be forgotten. For example, a Rolls Royce in a serious accident may be destroyed, rendered so broken that—even though it was once valued at many thousands of dollars—the best that can now be done for it is to tow it to the junkyard. Or it is sometimes the case that a part of the car is destroyed and must be trashed. A rear-ended Rolls may demand a new back end while the rest of the car is fine. So once possessing worth is not a guarantee of always possessing worth. The whole or at least a part of something valuable may be rejected and jettisoned. The next feature of the Christian story under our consideration, the incarnation, acknowledges that the human being is a creature of great value that has been seriously wrecked—but insists that (unlike a wrecked automobile) neither the whole nor any part of it can be rejected and forgotten. Even damaged, bent, and distorted, the human being retains inestimable worth: as a whole and in its parts.

As is well known, the most persistent heresy battled by the early church was one or another form of gnosticism, the belief that the physical world is evil and deficient and that salvation (for the soul alone) can be achieved through grasping the right *gnosis* or knowledge. The late modern fetishism of information (i.e., knowledge), along with imaginings of the consciousness escaping into virtual reality or a sophisticated computer, is a contemporary form of gnosticism. For gnosticism, sin is a "fall" of the soul or consciousness into the imprisoning body. In this view the body is a cage of mere "meat" that might be jettisoned, to great advantage. The body and soul are not integral; the body is not essential to personhood.

For classical Christian spirituality, on the other hand, the body cannot be jettisoned if there is to be any salvaging of the person. The body as well as the soul must be saved. Furthermore, Christian spirituality insists that the fall into sin is as much (or even more) the fault of the soul as of the body. The fourth-century desert fathers, for instance, did not imagine Adam's and Eve's trespass in the Garden was sexual sin, a result of nonrational drives and urges of the body. Adam and Eve rebelled and fell in an act of eating, grasping and gobbling a fruit forbidden to them. Do we then blame their fall on bodily hunger? No—they had plenty to eat and were no hungrier than I need to be in a cafeteria replete with food even if my doctor has forbidden me the high-cholesterol desserts. The first and original sin, then, was a sin first and foremost of the soul, not the body. It was sin prompted not by the physical quality of hunger (or sex) but by the spiritual qualities of greed and avarice. As St. Augustine put it, "It was not the corruptible flesh that made the soul sinful; it was the sinful soul that made the flesh corruptible."

Casual readers of the New Testament are sometimes confused by references to sinful flesh, especially in the writings of the apostle Paul. But an only slightly closer reading reveals that *flesh* is a technical term for Paul, not designating simply the body but the body and soul together as fallen, or separated from and rebelling against God. Conversely, for Paul the "spirit" is the integral person—body and soul—living in communion with and obedient to the Creator. So for Paul the mind can be fleshly or carnal (as in Col. 2:18) and the body can be spiritual (as in 1 Cor. 15:44). The "works of the flesh" include such attitudes and behaviors as quarreling and envy, matters more of the spirit than of the physical body. Thus Paul's terminology echoes the created wholeness or integrality of the human person we have noted. The fall and sin in general affect the whole person, flesh and spirit, body and soul.

In traditional Christianity, the fall brings death for both body and soul. Sin is synonymous with self-destruction and mortality. Death for the body is apparent enough: aging, illness, weakness, and the eventual transformation of the living body into a cold and lifeless corpse. Death for the soul is not so visible but is no less deadly. It is separation and alienation from God, the source of all true life. Death to one (the body or the soul) comes with death to the other, so no part of the person can be saved or healed without the salvation and healing of the whole. Neither soul nor body will be forgotten or rejected; both, together, will be made new.

Thus the incarnation, the coming of the Christ in whom "the whole fullness of deity dwells bodily" (Col. 2:9). Christ is the creating and redeeming Word who "became flesh and lived among us" (John 1:14). As the fourth-century church father St. Athanasius explained,

> It is we [in our sin] who were the cause of his taking human form, and for our salvation that in his great love he was both born and manifested in a human body. For God made man thus (that is, an embodied spirit), and had willed that he should remain in incorruption. But men, having turned from the contemplation of God to evil of their own devising, had come inevitably under the law of death. Instead of remaining in the state in which God had created them, they were in the process of becoming corrupted entirely, and death had them completely under its dominion.

In Christ God assumes or takes humanity into God's self. Orthodox Christian spirituality denies that humanity, whatever its powers and aspirations, can save itself from its own wreckage, its own self-destruction. Yet it is true humanity, or humanness, that will be saved. The original creation, though marred in and by sin, will not be tossed away and forgotten, as a potter might trash inferior clay and move to a new and different clay pit. Nor will God forget about the human project altogether. The story of Noah and the flood, with God's rainbowed promise never to relinquish or destroy humanity, however violent or lost it may become, is emblematic of this point (Gen. 9:12–17). Humanity will be assumed and *resumed*, restored to its pristine wholeness and reset on the path to the maturation and fullness of that wholeness. The great and saving mystery of the Trinity is that Jesus is human as well as divine. He is one person, not schizophrenic, but somehow in that one person both "perfect God and perfect Man," as the so-called Athanasian Creed puts it. And in taking on human brokenness and weakness, God is not broken or weakened by it. "Rather," said St. Athanasius,

> he sanctified the body by being in it. For his being in everything does not mean that he shares the nature of everything, only that he gives all things their being and sustains them in it. Just as the sun is not defiled by contact of its rays with earthly objects, but rather enlightens and purifies them, so he who made the sun is not defiled by being made known in a body, but rather the body is cleansed and quickened by his indwelling.

So in (as) this embodied, perfectly divine and perfectly human life, Jesus the Christ confronts and overcomes sin and death through the cross and resurrection. In the story and logic of Christian spirituality, incarnation cannot be separated from redemption, the work of the cross. It is not as if salvation might be accomplished simply by the birth of the baby Jesus. The helpless, crying baby is divine as well as human. But the human will not only be saved exactly as the human; it must also be saved in and toward its maturity, its perfection or completion. In the orthodox reading, Adam and Eve did not reach maturity or perfection before they damaged human nature in their rebellious and alienating sin. In Christ, then, God assumes and resumes the human project, now to take it from its originally intended but interrupted growth to maturity. So with great insight the apostle Paul saw Christ as the second Adam. The second Adam will succeed where the first failed, will proceed to the true human end or maturity. Where the first Adam succumbed to sin and separated humanity from God, the second Adam will overcome sin and reconcile humanity to God; where the first Adam brought death into life, the second Adam will bring life into death.

Building on the insights of Paul, Irenaeus in the second century suggested his marvelous teaching called recapitulation. In Christ God refused to abandon the human project, refused even to abandon the original material (so to speak) of the human project. The human is a physical and spiritual creature and is restored in all its parts. Since the human is a creature living in time and space, Irenaeus said, God enters time and space and is crucified in time and space, so that God "has imprinted the form of the Cross on the universe. In becoming visible, he had to reveal the participation of the universe in his cross." And the human is a creature born in the weakness and incompleteness of infancy, achieving maturity only with time and experience. So "Christ passed through all the ages of human life, restoring to all men communion with God."

The human story is reenacted or recapitulated in Christ, but this time to its true and intended end. Where the first Eve wandered and brought sin, Mary the second Eve stayed on track and brought redemption. "The knot of Eve's disobedience was untied through the obedience of Mary. For what the virgin Eve tied through unbelief, the Virgin Mary set free through faith." Born of Mary, Jesus assumed real flesh. Irenaeus noted that Jesus could hunger and get tired, that he suffered and died. In this real flesh Jesus passed from infancy into childhood and finally adulthood. In the classical world, persons were believed to reach their peak or perfection around the age of thirty—the age, of course, of Jesus at his crucifixion. So Christ lived through and sanctified all the stages, seasons, or chapters of human life, bringing it to its fullness or ripeness. Doing so, he enabled humanity's potential for true maturity. Babies can eat and swallow only soft foods, but Christ made us capable of consuming "stronger nourishment," said Irenaeus: "the bread of immortality, which is the Spirit of the Father." Accordingly, "the truly 'spiritual' disciple is one who has received the Spirit of God who, from the beginning, in all the dispensations of God, has been present to men." As I said earlier, Christian spirituality is undergirded, sustained, and directed by the Holy Spirit who brought life at creation, spoke through the prophets, worked in the works of Christ, and now enlivens the faith of the church.

And it is that same Spirit, Irenaeus said, that will lead creation to its ultimate fulfillment and wholeness. We live now after the beginning of that fulfillment (in the kingdom inaugurated by Christ) but before its end or completion. At its completion, sin will be defeated, death vanquished, and all creation will achieve its God-intended purpose, maturity, and ripeness—a richness beyond the current capacity of imagination. For instance, with others in the early church, Irenaeus suggested that in the fully renewed creation each cluster of grapes would produce 10,000 grapes and each grape nearly 230 gallons of wine, and that each grain of wheat would produce 10 pounds of flour. Whatever the fancifulness of these specifics, it will be a world without hunger or desperate need of any kind, full in and of the Spirit that gives, sustains, and fulfills all life—a world made possible through the incarnation and recapitulatory life of Jesus Christ.

Forays on the Resurrection of the Body

The anticipation of a fully restored and perfected human body takes us to the third key feature of the orthodox story bearing on the extraordinarily robust Christian valuation of the body. Other philosophies and ways of life may affirm the goodness of the body to a point, but only a handful (Judaism, Christianity, Islam, and Zoroastrianism) posit the resurrection of each and every body as we know or have known it, and so refuse ever to give up on the body, even at death. For Christians, Jesus bore the "firstfruits" of the harvest of his work when he was resurrected, in the same (though now transformed) body, right down to the scars of wounds sustained in the crucifixion. The greatest and most blessed Christian hope, accordingly, is not the escape of the individual soul from the body to heaven; it is the bodily resurrection to life everlasting as an integral human whole.

The capstone text on bodily resurrection is the fifteenth chapter of the apostle Paul's first letter to the Corinthians. There Paul declares that when Christ's work is consummated, brought to the fullness of its end, all things will be subjected to him. "The last enemy to be destroyed is death" (v. 26). Then the dead will be raised. Just as the acorn is seed to its own oak tree, the animal bodies we now know and are will be seed to their own mature and ripened spiritual bodies. "What is sown is perishable, what is raised is imperishable. It is sown in dishonor, it is raised in glory. It is sown in weakness, it is raised in power. It is sown a physical body, it is raised a spiritual body" (vv. 42–44).

To our modern eyes, "spiritual body" appears an oxymoron. We think of bodies as physical and material, of the spiritual as ethereal and nonmaterial. A "spiritual body" then is as self-contradictory as a "black whiteness" or a "happy depression." The "spiritual" cancels out the "bodily," or vice versa. We may then, if we are people of faith, assume this is a reverent paradox—if the Trinity is three and yet one, if Christ is fully God and fully human, so then can there be a "spiritual body." But Paul here is dealing in no paradoxes. To the ancients, a soul or spirit could be incorporeal and still be made of "stuff." Even Plato, sometimes regarded as among the most sharply dualistic of ancient philosophers, did not see the soul as immaterial in our sense of the word. The soul in his view had at its strongest something to do with the divine, but he suspected the gods were made of fire (a physical substance, in our modern parlance) and were spherical (taking up some kind of space or place). Likewise the resurrected Christ has a kind of physicality: he can be seen with physical eyes, he consumes fish and bread, the wound in his side can be touched. So the resurrected body for Paul is not nonphysical, in our sense. It is stripped of its *merely* earthly or animal qualities. Inasmuch as the human *animal*/animal composed integrally of body and soul could be separated from life in God, and consequently die both body and soul, so the resurrected person will dwell entirely in the Spirit and be reunited body and soul with God.

As St. Augustine glossed this wondrous mystery, human bodies even before the fall were bodies "not yet spiritual but animal, still [simply] bodies of earth." Following the resurrection bodies will be bodies, yet bodies not simply of the earth—they will be bodies living altogether in the Spirit, in free and perfected communion with the Triune God. Their sole source of energy and nourishment, of life in unimpeded fullness, will be the Spirit: life, vitality, relationship in the overabundant fellowship shared by the Father and the Son. At the resurrection of the denizens of the new heaven and new earth, spiritual flesh will be subject to the spirit of the Spirit, "just as carnal spirit was subject to the flesh, and yet was spirit, not flesh."

Augustine, like the apostle Paul, struggled to make sense of this unplumbable mystery. We moderns and postmoderns can hardly expect to be any less stymied, to find our own language and imagination stretching and failing any less to embrace this marvelous hope. Ultimately, like our predecessors in faith, we must trust that a God great enough to create all and to resurrect the Son is great enough to accomplish this final, glorious mystery. The details or strict how-to would expectedly surpass human understanding: the Christian confession is that God is God, not merely human. But I think we can make some rough (and admittedly speculative) sense of the mystery in analogy with our contemporary scientific terms.

Modern science has long understood that inert matter can convert into energy (as when gasoline fires in an internal combustion engine) and energy into matter (as when the living flesh of dinosaurs transformed over time into petroleum products). And certainly after Einstein matter and energy are no longer understood as two utterly distinct entities. Along such lines, and only analogously, we may understand the transformation of the earthly body into a heavenly or spiritual body as conversion of matter into energy. The spiritual body is the human fully alive, burning (but never burning out) in the Spirit. Here we can think of the frequent symbolizations of the Spirit as fire in the Christian tradition, as with the "tongues of fire" flickering over the heads of the first Pentecostal believers (Acts 2). In a striking tale of the desert fathers, one holy man grew so profoundly in holiness—in communion with the hot Spirit of all life—that flames flickered from his fingertips. Just as fire is physical, the spiritual body is bodily, now absolutely blazing with life.

But this is, I say it again, nothing more than an analogy. Like all analogies it breaks at some point. A key limitation to this analogy is that it might be taken as suggesting the simple conversion of the human into the Holy Spirit itself, one more drop of water added to the ocean of Being. But classical Christian spirituality never expects us humans to become God, the creature becoming the Creator. Instead, Christian spirituality expects only (only!) that we will come more fully and really to participate in the life and communion of God.

To avoid grossly identifying the human with the divine, we might adjust the analogy to think of the spiritual body as a transformed matter that can now be fueled and vitalized by a different and greater kind of energy. The remains of dinosaurs lay inert until a capacity (the internal combustion engine) was invented to convert them into energy. Similarly, the human alienated from God cannot attain intended human potential; the human is "dead" or inert matter and can sustain itself only for a while with the consumption of other "dead" matter. Regular, earthly food is a source of energy, but it is needed again and again, until the body weakens and cannot be sustained past bodily death by any earthly food. Resurrection and transformation into a spiritual body, then, is the divine equivalent of inventing the internal combustion engine. Now, through grace, new and higher forms of energy can be tapped. So St. Augustine observed that after the resurrection the righteous will not need "material nourishment to prevent any kind of distress from hunger or thirst." They will eat only if and when they wish; eating will be "a possibility, not a necessity." With the resurrection, our spiritual bodies can burn with the fuel, live in and through the life, of the Spirit.

However adequate any of these analogies may be, they point toward hopes grounded in Christian revelation and not in modern science. Modern science has no capacity and (at its strictest) makes no pretense of discovering or scrutinizing God. As the British physicist Arthur Eddington once parabled, science is like a fisherman fishing with a net woven with six-inch openings. That net will never bring in a fish shorter than six inches, but it would be a mistake to assume, accordingly, that no fishes shorter than six inches exist. Science's net is not made or equipped to capture spiritual fish, let alone be the fisher of men and women. Or, to change the metaphor, science focuses on a three-dimensional world; dimensions beyond the three necessarily escape notice. That makes a fourth or fifth or sixth dimension—a dimension of the Spirit—different from the world of scientific purview, but not necessarily incongruent with or utterly unimaginable in light of the world science discovers. Linkage with the classical Christian tradition of bodily resurrection is possible, even for twenty-first-century disciples.

That linkage may be further apparent in response to an obvious objection to the resurrection of the body. (It was obvious not only to us but to Christians and church detractors of the early centuries.) If the particular bodies of particular persons—of "individuals," in modern parlance—are integral to their personhood, and if it is these bodies that are raised (albeit transformed), what of people cremated, or oxidized by a bomb, or swallowed and digested by a lion or shark, or simply dissolved and scattered over centuries after their deposit in the grave? Classical Christians went to great lengths to answer such questions, and frankly, many of their answers can only be incredible to us. Yet, in a way we might read now as prescient of the science of genetics, St. Augustine noted that in physical or bodily terms perfection and maturity are "already latent in the seed." Even as a seed or embryo, "a kind of pattern [is] already imposed potentially on the material substance of the individual." Though Augustine certainly had no possession of a modern understanding of genetics, the arc or trajectory of his comment is easily extended to our current understanding of DNA. Whatever may happen to the original physical body, we can trust that its DNA (and much more) is never lost to the memory of God. And so the "seed" or "pattern" of the physical body will never be entirely lost but can be recovered and in the spiritual body realize its full and true potential.

At the Heart of Christian Spirituality

The insistence on the resurrection and the spiritual body underscores just how much orthodox Christian spirituality esteems the body. From creation to and beyond the final judgment, Christian spirituality values the body. From conception to and beyond death, Christian spirituality never relinquishes the body—however strange or apparently incredible its hopes of bodily life after death may be. The body as we now know it is weak: yes. The body is perishable: yes. It is corruptible and will rot: oh, yes. As such it can be a lot of trouble and bring disappointment: yes, again. Christian spirituality affirms all these possibilities as realities, but even more vigorously it refuses to give up on the body. The body, like the soul, can be taught. It can be formed and molded. Even now, to some degree, it can live in the Spirit. So we embodied souls, ensouled bodies, are wonders. But we are until the resurrection *tortured* wonders. We live in between, in and as bodies that before the resurrection can only slightly anticipate their full and grace-ripened spiritual capacities.

For now, then, we must—we necessarily will—wrestle with limitations and bodily failures. We wrestle with the specter of death, of the grave, of mud in the face, and with every thought or event that foreshadows it. We wrestle too with lust, with sexual urges that at least sometimes are awkward or ill-timed, precursors to frustration and betrayal as well as bliss and union. The body, untaught, may lead us into all kinds of traps and self-destruction. The body, like a child of great potential, is too precious to be left untaught. So the formation of the whole person, body as well as soul, is at the heart of Christian spirituality.

2

AGAINST IMITATING
THE ANGELS

*Christian Spirituality
and Sex*

C an we agree on this much? Sex is trouble. I do not (as a Christian I cannot) say it is evil. And sex is not *only* trouble. But it is trouble. Traditional and modern narratives alike, when they turn to sex, always at points turn to trouble. Sexual attraction to another can be and often is wonderful, the site of ecstasy. Read the Song of Songs and see that the Bible is quite aware of the joyous wonders of sex and sexuality. But of course the Bible, and Christian tradition after it, also worries about sex and its potential for trouble. So too do modern, secular narratives of romantic love. Lovers fall in but also out of love. Lovers can and often do disappoint and betray one another. Wives and husbands grow tired of each other, and when sexual sparks fly anew with others rather than spouses, there can be trouble. Even outside actual infidelities, we moderns struggle with sex. Our physicians and therapists help us worry about whether or

not we are getting enough sex—in a hectic, over-busy society professional brows are now furrowed over "low-sex" marriages. Frequency
is not our only concern. Our media indicate that we constantly worry
whether we, well, measure up in bed. The spam within my e-mail
day after day offers new and renewing sexual opportunities and
enhanced sexual equipment ("More length! More girth!"). My wife
and other women tell me in their e-mailboxes they meet their own
"opportunities" with constant promises of larger breasts. Ads in
newspapers promise someone who must be concerned (could it be you
or I?) that sexual passion need never cool or die, even into old age.
Apparently—no, clearly—human sexuality is now as it has always
been the site of great joy but also of ongoing insecurity, frustration,
and threat of failure.

I have promised that this book's account of spirituality will be
grounded in Christian orthodoxy. To keep that promise, I need to
honestly rehearse the Christian tradition's quite real wariness and
suspicion of human sexuality. Without backing off an inch from
the previous chapter's argument that Christian spirituality robustly
affirms the body, I must take account of the fact that it has not so
robustly affirmed that aspect of bodily existence we call sex. It is
true that orthodoxy, up to and through the Protestant Reformation, has doubted that sexual pleasure can be spiritually edifying.
I believe (along with most modern Christians, including those who
style themselves profoundly conservative) that there is a place for
sexual pleasure in Christian spirituality. But let us be frank. That
argument calls for adjustments, for winnowings and extensions, in
the tradition.

That in itself is no surprise or scandal. As a *living* tradition, rather
than a dead and static museum piece, Christian spirituality is open
to change. The only tradition done and settled once and for all is the
dead tradition. Thus the Christian orthodoxy of today is not identical in all particulars to that of the past. To take just three examples,
it no longer condones slavery, rigorously questions the charging of
interest on loans, or assumes that women are defective men. These
are alterations we now accept as maturations and proper developments of and within the tradition. Just as we say a child becomes
"more herself" as she grows (and changes) into an adult, so regarding

slavery, for example, we say the Christian tradition has "come into its own" by eventually and flatly condemning ownership of another human being.

Of course, not just any change is truly growth, not every alteration is necessarily a maturation of the tradition. So the question is always how those of us in the tradition can be true to its richest impulses and purposes even as the tradition meets new challenges, sees further than before by its own light, and stretches forward in unanticipated directions. The first step in fidelity to the living tradition is to pay real attention to what the tradition once held, as concerns any given matter, and resist temptations to make it what we now might wish it had always been. It is exactly because the tradition to some degree stands outside us, can differ from us on a given point, that we can learn from it and be guided by it. Otherwise we are simply and solipsistically staring into a mirror of our own imaginings.

The Early Church: Suspicious of Sex

Some faith traditions offer more or less elaborate guidance for the enjoyable sexual behaviors of at least some of their practitioners. Hinduism's *Kama Sutra,* for instance, graphically and extensively coaches its readers in a variety of sexual positions and techniques, unabashedly intending to enhance their sexual pleasure. The New Testament stands in stark contrast to such texts. It says relatively little about sex. Its main characters and teachers are celibate or, if married, are depicted outside of or apart from their marriages. Jesus is an abstinent bachelor. Mary, the mother of Jesus, is remembered mainly for her *virginal* conception of the Lord. Married disciples are called away from their wives and families, to join Jesus in the new family composed of those striving first and foremost to do the will of God (Mark 3:31–35). Far from mouthing late-modern "family values," Jesus can say, "I have come to set a man against his father, and a daughter against her mother, . . . and one's foes will be members of one's own household" (Matt. 10:35–36). He calls a son to skip his father's funeral and depart immediately with Jesus (Luke 9:57–62). He admires those who make themselves "eunuchs for the sake of the kingdom of heaven" (Matt. 19:12) and says there will be no marriage after the resurrection (Matt. 22:29–33).

Most other New Testament texts address sex only to proscribe certain forms of it, such as fornication and adultery. The apostle Paul (whose own marital status is so marginal to the New Testament that it cannot even be determined) does discuss married sex at some length, but if we take him strictly at his word we hear him allowing sex in marriage as second best to the life of singleness and celibacy. The married life is one of "divided" interests, while the single disciple can focus altogether on the "affairs of the Lord" (1 Cor. 7:32–34). Paul is clear that marriage is not a sin, and expects that marriage will include intercourse, but just as clearly regards marriage as a lesser good than celibacy. "By way of concession," he allows that any lacking "self-control" should marry rather than "be aflame with passion" (1 Cor. 7:28, 6–9).

Of course there is much more to be said about the Bible and sex—and we cannot gainsay the Old Testament, which is also Christian Scripture. But in this short compass we have touched on the New Testament's most explicit teachings about marriage and sexual practice. It is enough to indicate that the early church was not simply ignoring or denying Scripture when it evinced frequent suspicions and worries about sexuality and in fact idealized virginity as the highest spiritual condition.

Early Christian apologists such as Athenagoras boasted to the pagans that Christians renounce marriage in order to draw closer to God. By some accounts, the third-century theologian Origen castrated himself to literally become a eunuch for the kingdom of heaven. Such radical surgery, though unusual in its actual execution, was no wild aberration. The second-century church father Justin Martyr wrote with praise of a youth seeking castration, yearning to become a eunuch for God's sake.

The attitudes behind such idealization of celibacy are elaborated in the writing of Clement of Alexandria, a teacher of Origen. In *Christ the Educator,* Clement counsels against "sense-pleasure" of all sorts. He fears spiritual catastrophe for those who partake of any but plain meals and dare to enjoy "pastries and honey-cakes and desserts." A little wine in the evening is okay, but water is the "natural

and pure drink for ordinary thirst." Music can "insidiously inflame
the passions" with its "exciting rhythms." Flutes, harps, castanets,
choruses, and dances easily "get out of control and become indecent
and burlesque, especially when they are reinforced by cymbals and
drums." Laughter "should be kept under restraint." Perfume is not
necessary and "shipwrecks us upon pleasure." Even bathing must
be undertaken soberly and in moderation: "We must not think of
bathing for pleasure."

For all his concerns about other sensual pleasures, it is sex that
especially puts Clement on guard. "We must keep a firm control
over the pleasures of the stomach," he says, "and an absolutely
uncompromising control over the organs beneath the stomach." He
allows married intercourse only with the intention of procreation.
"Pleasure sought for its own sake, even within the marriage bonds,
is a sin and contrary to both law and to reason." Indeed, "To indulge
in intercourse without intending children is to outrage nature."

Two centuries later St. Augustine addresses marriage and sex
more carefully. In due course, as with so many topics, we will find
in Augustine help to enrich a Christian spirituality of sexuality. But
here it is necessary to acknowledge that like Clement and others
before him, Augustine approaches even married sex with what will
strike moderns as severe caution and reserve. In his short piece *On
the Good of Marriage*, Augustine is true to his title. He unequivocally
declares marriage a good. But he is equally clear that it is a lesser
good than sanctified virginity. It is good to marry, he says, since it is
good to beget children and since marriage provides for "the natural
companionship between the sexes." Even so, "it is better not to
marry." And again: "Marriage and virginity are, it is true, two goods;
the second of them is the greater." Augustine does not flinch from
the ultimate logical outcome of a world filled with celibates. Such an
all-encompassing outbreak of holiness is not likely, but if it came to
pass, then "much more quickly would the City of God be filled and
the end of time hastened."

So marriage is a proximate earthly good, as is procreation, but
Augustine cannot allow pitched sexual desire (lust) to be anything
but an evil. The intensity and abandon of lust came with humanity's
fall into sin. Had Adam and Eve not fallen, it is possible they might

have birthed children "without physical coition"—after all, God had Christ born of a virgin. However that may have been, St. Augustine is sure that if Adam and Eve had not fallen and had in fact required sexual intercourse for procreation, they would have been able to do so with rational control and intention. They would have desired intercourse only when they intended it. The sexual organs would have responded only to the conscious direction of the will. And Adam and Eve would have mated infrequently, only on those occasions when they intended to produce offspring.

Accordingly, Augustine is straightforward about the "evil of lust." It is "disgraceful" for a spouse to demand sex for pleasure rather than strictly for procreation. It is of course better to marry and confine sexual intercourse than to fornicate or commit adultery. By channeling youthful lust toward procreation, "marital intercourse makes something good out of the evil of lust." But as the couple begets children, and age dampens the rages of passion, they should hasten to think foremost of "themselves as mother and father." The sooner intercourse ceases "by mutual consent" of the spouses, the better.

These are heavy words against sexual desire. Married sex without the purpose of procreation is a lustful indulgence, and lust is always sinful. But to fairly represent St. Augustine's views, we must also note that he regarded enjoyable married sex as a venial or excusable sin, not a mortal sin such as fornication or adultery. In one of his sermons he lists nonprocreative married intercourse alongside other comparatively minor, mundane sins such as speaking harshly or laughing raucously. For Augustine, you need not severely worry about your salvation if you indulge in marital sex for pleasure. At the same time, if you want to pursue obedience and faithfulness to God diligently, it is clear you should resist sexual pleasure; and if you want to pursue faithfulness as diligently as possible, you will not marry but undertake a life of "holy virginity."

Celibacy as the higher good is reflected through the medieval period in monastic vows, and even today in the total chastity embraced by Roman Catholicism's priests, monks, and nuns. It is widely supposed that Protestantism, as early as its sixteenth-century Reformational founding, shucked off all hints of married, pleasurable sex as evil, or of marriage as a lesser spiritual state than virginity. But did it?

Adultery within Marriage and Protestant Reluctance about Sex

The Reformer John Calvin is a famously close reader of St. Augustine. Calvin departs from Augustine in playing down the unique or premium holiness of virginity. He will have nothing to do with differing standards of Christian behavior for monks and laity. He sees sustained celibacy as enabled by a special gift of God, given to only a few. But, echoing Augustine, Calvin continues to describe nonprocreative married sex as an evil. Succumbing to sexual pleasure at all is a "vice." Most people are subject to this vice, and marriage is the sole and necessary "remedy" for their weakness. Married sex is a kind of inoculation that keeps us from "plunging into unbridled lust." Even within marriage and its "covering" of sexual sin, lust is a powerful and destructive force which the couple must resist. The married are not to "pollute" marriage "with uncontrolled and dissolute lust. For even if the honorableness of matrimony covers the baseness of incontinence, it ought not for that reason be a provocation thereto." Citing Ambrose (Augustine's teacher), Calvin avers that a husband who expects sex for pleasure is "an adulterer toward his own wife."

In these regards Calvin practiced what he preached. He was married for only seven years of his life—to a widow he found after circulating a deliberate description of the qualities he sought in a wife. After her early death he did not remarry, apparently judging himself able to resist the "vice of incontinence" and so no longer in need of the "remedy" of marriage.

The other major Protestant Reformer, Martin Luther, is more ambiguous on married sexuality. Surely the earthiest of all traditional theologians, he left behind his own monastic vows for marriage and (eventually) a family of five children. Writing in 1530, he declared, "God has created man and woman so that they are to come together with pleasure [in his original German, *lust*], willingly and gladly with all their hearts." Repeatedly plagued by depression, the crusty Reformer said one of his best cures was embracing his wife naked in bed. With his vigorous and sometimes raw polemic, Luther often attacked the corruptions of monasticism. Yet he never condemns the notion of celibacy as the highest spiritual ideal. And alluding to the apostle Paul's comments in 1 Corinthians 7, he agrees that "the necessities of this life, the Christian life particularly, are carried more comfortably by those who are unmarried and free than by those who are married and bound."

Moreover, at least early in his work as a Reformer, Luther continued the classical Christian line that sexual pleasure is always sinful. In "A Sermon on the Estate of Marriage," he declared that "since the fall marriage has been adulterated with wicked lust." In marriage as we now know it, each spouse "seeks to satisfy his desire with the other, and it is this desire which corrupts this kind of love. Therefore, the married state is no longer pure and free from sin." Like Calvin, Luther sees marriage as a kind of remedy for the ravaging sickness of lust. "The temptation of the flesh has become so strong and consuming that marriage may be likened to a hospital for incurables which prevents inmates from falling into graver sin." So he spoke in 1519—how then do we reconcile his 1530 coaching of spouses to "come together with pleasure"? Had he decided there can be married "pleasure" without sin? Or was he in 1530 merely emphasizing the comparative excusableness of married, nonprocreative sex, while not meaning to altogether deny that it is tainted? Unlike Calvin, Luther was never a strongly systematic thinker. It is impossible to say that he ever had an absolutely clear-cut and "final" position on the matter. In any event, the most mature (or at least the oldest) Luther never contradicts the classical position that celibacy is a higher spiritual condition than marriage.

Glances at the two most influential Reformers indicate that, with Protestantism, the intensity of the rhetoric idealizing singleness over marriage lessens. But if concern about married "lust" recedes in urgency and retreats toward the back of the (Protestant) Christian mind, it does not depart altogether. So in the late seventeenth century the Anglican divine Jeremy Taylor can praise sanctified virginity as "a life of angels, the enamel of the soul, the huge advantage of religion, the great opportunity for the retirements of devotion: and being empty of cares, it is full of prayers: being unmingled with the world, it is apt to converse with God; and by not feeling the warmth of a too-forward and indulgent nature, flames out with holy fires, till it be burning like the cherubim and the most ecstasied order of the holy and unpolluted spirits." Taylor appears to retain a sense of sexual behavior as a kind of pollution and unequivocally follows Paul in lifting up the practical devotional benefits of singleness. By the mid-eighteenth century, Methodism founder John Wesley (himself a lifelong bachelor) is reluctant to judge whether the married or single life is "the more perfect state" but will declare, "We may safely say, Blessed are 'they who have made themselves eunuchs for the kingdom of heaven's sake'; who abstain from things lawful in themselves, in order to be more devoted to God."

This hasty survey is by no stretch comprehensive, nor does it begin to do justice to the nuances of positions on sex and marriage taken by various Christian worthies of the past. But it does suggest how deep and strong runs the Christian tradition's hesitancies and reservations about sexual pleasure, even within wedlock. It is fair to say that in general terms the Christian tradition, before modernity and especially late modernity's wide acceptance of contraceptives, looked askance (or at best winked) at any sexual enjoyment.

Misgivings about sexual pleasure, linked in the tradition back to readings of Scripture itself, stand in stark contrast to modern Christian attitudes and practices. Today Christians, Protestant and Catholic alike, generally encourage the unqualified enjoyment of married sex. Of course, debates over issues such as homosexuality show that Christians are still quite capable of arguing, fiercely, about sexuality. And the Catholic Church in its official teaching still tightly connects intercourse to procreation. But even staunchly "traditional" Catholics endorse the pleasure of married procreative sex. Meanwhile, it is not liberal Protestants but conservative evangelicals who can write and buy in the millions a book that flatly declares married sex is *Intended for Pleasure*, imagine a panoply of seductive sexual teases to be enacted by the evangelical *Total Woman*, and represent monogamy as an aphrodisiac, intensifying sexual pleasure via the safety and security of commitment. One evangelical marriage seminar T-shirt sported the legend "I'm having a wonderful affair—with my wife."

We have heard enough from Calvin, Luther, and Wesley (let alone Augustine or other earlier figures) to know these attitudes do not reflect the older mainstream Christian tradition. Calvin, for instance, would have seen the "wonderful affair" mindset making a man an "adulterer toward his own wife." Yet even if we don't reconceive and justify Christian monogamy as the ultimate aphrodisiac, it will be hard for any modern Christian to censure sexual pleasure altogether. Questing after an orthodox Christian spirituality, how can we honor the tradition and yet differ with it on certain nontrivial specifics?

To say it again, we honor the tradition of orthodox Christian spirituality most vitally not by trying—by omission or distortion—to remake it in our image but by taking honest account of its specifics. Then we can know where particulars of the tradition push or challenge us, as well as where we, as the contemporary and living embodiments of the tradition, may want to flex or extend it. Accordingly, as we work to articulate and live a Christian spirituality of sex for our day, we will do well to dig further into the venerable tradition and ask why it was so reserved, even suspicious, about sexual pleasure. That may allow aspects of the tradition to guide us even as we return ourselves and it to its own taproot and ultimate measure of truth, the gospel of Jesus Christ.

To Be like the Angels

The strongest undercurrent feeding suspicion of sexual pleasure was uncovered in the previous chapter. Premodern cultures were profoundly aware of the body's susceptibility to change and corruption—not least the ultimate corruption of death. A world of mortals, in which every person dies, can be replenished only by procreation. Thus sex is integrally associated with death, and awareness of that association was surely all the more vivid in a world where parents routinely buried their children. To procreate was in one sense to admit and allow the overarching sway of death, whose onslaught is denied utter victory over humanity only by the desperate expedient of sending generation after generation like ranks of soldiers to crumple before it. Since every person born will certainly die someday, procreation only fleetingly beats back death. By contrast, confident Christian celibacy, based on the hope of the resurrection of a then undying body, was a bold witness to the total defeat of death. So the fourth-century Greek father Gregory of Nyssa could observe, "In every soul that surpasses fleshly life by virginity, the power of death is somewhat broken or dissolved."

In addition, sexual feelings and expression can be notoriously unstable and destabilizing. Who knows when fervent sexual desire will burn, or cool, and toward what objects? You may stop desiring your spouse and start intensely desiring your neighbor's spouse. Infidelity and jealousy still, in the affluent sectors of the modern world, can tear apart families and shake communities. But premodern communal life, bereft of the insurance companies, welfare policies, retirement provisions, and other societal safety nets by which modern individuals may be caught when they fall out of a family, depended entirely on the solidarity of families and communal clans. Because they cut so deeply and disastrously, the disruptive powers of sex were all the more keenly feared. So in ways both literal and figurative, the turbulent fluidity and instability of sexual desire mimicked and reinforced bodily (and social) vulnerability to corruption and chaos. When they felt the sexual urge, premodern Christians did not simply imagine it as the benign, surging flow of life and generation. For them the river of lust rolled with a dark undertow of death.

Since sexual desire suggested chaos and the precarious loss of control—in a word, death—to premoderns, they were wary and respectful of desire's great power. Greco-Romans tended to see desire as a fire, with all of fire's potential for destruction. They could speak of passionate desire as a "parching fever," piercing bones, melting the heart, burning under the skin. For ancient physicians like Galen, desire was an illness that violently disrupted bodily harmony. In like manner, Clement of Alexandria believed that sexual intercourse strained and stretched the nerves as if they were on a loom. Adopting a popular phrase of his day, he regarded orgasm as "a minor epilepsy." Accordingly, he observed, "it spreads a mist over the senses and tires the muscles." In this regard Clement praised the pagan dramatist Sophocles, "who replied to someone asking him his attitude toward the pleasures of sex, 'O man, quiet! I have been supremely happy in avoiding them as a fierce and wild tyrant.'" Similarly, St. Augustine noted that sexual desire can disrupt the entire body with physical craving and emotional disturbance. Orgasmic climax brings "an almost total extinction of mental alertness; the intellectual sentries are, as it were, overwhelmed."

Consider, then, how premodern Christian sexual attitudes were profoundly affected by Christ's resurrection and inauguration of the kingdom of God on earth. The Lord's bodily resurrection, and its concomitant promise of the resurrection to eternal life for all who trusted him, broke the desperate cycle of life and death. Ongoing life was possible even without offspring who would carry on the parental name and identity. Procreational sex might generate life, but never without the taint of death: every child is born to die. Christ created a spiritual family of disciples who could secure life without sex. Overwhelmed by God's vindicating resurrection of Christ, death lost its "sting" and relinquished its "victory" (1 Cor. 15:55). This much is inherent to orthodox Christianity, whether ancient or contemporary. Christ's life, death, and resurrection did shatter the power of death and turn the world upside down (Acts 17:6). The explosive revelation of God in Jesus Christ is apocalyptic—it ends the world as it was and redefines all life and existence on its own terms. No human institution, however estimable, including the biological family, stands utterly unaffected or unshaken by the coming of the kingdom. Orthodox Christian spirituality, in the present no less than the past, is participation in and formation by the community on which the Spirit has poured in a baptizing flood, and which sees the destiny of heaven and earth illuminated and determined by the resurrection of Christ.

This much, then, a contemporary Christian spirituality must affirm with its classical predecessors. But notice that our predecessors went further and unpacked storylines and expectations that need not necessarily be ours. The world has changed in Christ, and the inauguration of the kingdom has ramifications today, even before its fulfillment and perfection with the second coming of Christ. Again, that is orthodox belief and spirituality, modern as well as ancient. Yet exactly what the inauguration of the kingdom entails in our current epoch, the time between the times of Christ's advents, is not so clear. Does it entail that now, already, earthly Christians should ideally be as the angels in heaven, unmoved and unimpressed by bodily, sexual passion?

The premodern Christian tradition tended to think it did. Remember the words of the seventeenth-century Anglican worthy Jeremy Taylor. He saw celibacy as an earthly "life of angels," and the holy celibate hot not with sexual passion but instead "burning like the cherubim and the most ecstasied order of the holy and unpolluted spirits." Taylor's reading of virginity as a grasp of angelic life on earth was not at all his innovation. Much earlier Athanasius said that in the state of virginity "we possess upon earth" a kind of "picture of the holiness of angels." Ambrose had declared, "[A virgin, Mother Mary] has brought from heaven what is to be imitated on earth. . . . Passing beyond the clouds, air, angels, and stars, she has found the Word of God in the Father's breast, and she has drawn him into herself wholeheartedly." Ascetics and monastics explicitly sought to live their lives "in imitation of angels" and saw their celibacy as a key aspect of this imitation. So John Chrysostom sermonized, advising fathers worried by the agitations of lust in their adolescent sons to take them on Sunday walks. Stroll by the huts of monks, he said, and tell the sons, "These are our angels."

Looking to Christ the Man, Rather Than the Angels

This, I believe, is just the point at which we should begin respectfully questioning our forebears on the touchy matter of sexuality. Here I must resort to a bit of technical language. I suggest that when our forebears called for or praised an angelic (non)sexuality for earthly men and women, they lapsed into the theological fallacy of a realized eschatology. Eschatology has to do with the end of time, of history. Christian eschatology considers the end of history in two senses of the word *end*: it is the end in the sense of termination but also the end in the sense of goal or purpose—the destination point. In Christ, the New Testament professes, the flow of time and history has been definitively disrupted. The kingdom of God on earth has been initiated, so that the end (in the sense of "end" as the goal or purpose) of the world is now made clear. Yet, just as clearly, the world is not already utterly and completely changed. Evil and suffering remain all too pervasive. They may now be seen through—in Christ's victory

over death it is apparent that evil is not ultimate, that suffering will
not be the last word—but they will not vanish from sight altogether
until Christ's second advent. Only at Christ's return in glory and
judgment will the kingdom arrive in unabated fullness. The eschaton
(both as the termination of time and history and as the destination
toward which all things are headed) has already begun in Christ. But
it is has not yet come in its consummation and perfection.

Orthodox eschatology consequently indwells a tension. It walks
a narrow way, wary of ditches on both sides. To err on one side is to
deny the world-changing effect of Christ's first advent. To err on the
other is to presume too much and act as if the end has now, already,
come in its fullness—rather than awaiting the real ripening and full
bloom that will in fact come to pass only with Christ's second advent.
The latter ditch of error, presuming that the kingdom has already
arrived in its fullness, is what has been called realized eschatology.
It assumes that the end has been comprehensively realized, that the
kingdom is now and already with us in its completion.

In these terms, premodern Christians were correct (emphatically!)
to take seriously Jesus' resurrection and his words that in heaven
people, like angels, will no longer marry. But they were arguably
presumptuous to think that today, already, on this earth and at this
time, people should ideally live like angels, without marriage (and
sex). Whatever may be the case *when* the new heaven and earth arrive in their fullness, Christ's words in the gospel need not be read as
endorsement of or urging toward an angelic absence of sexuality *now*.
A spirituality striving against sex and sexual pleasure of all sorts may
be fit for angels, but it is not Christian spirituality fit for people. It is
a mistake, and a mistake of real consequence, to assume that people
should now (or even ultimately) be in every way like the angels. After
all, as Karl Barth reminds us, God through the incarnation "did not
become an angel but man. . . . This means that the service of God
to which the angels summon man and the Church is one which is
proper to them and different from [the angels']. Imitation of angels is
not what is demanded of man and the Church by the ministry of the
angels," since the angels themselves herald and witness to the God
revealed in and through the humanity of Jesus Christ. In trying to
imitate the angels we in fact dishonor them and their witness, since

our "false ascent" presumptuously "raises us past the God who in His Son came down to us men, and will come again."

Respecting the Mystery of Sex

What unfolds, then, if we take sexual desire's measure as Christian people and not as would-be angels? We can leave off an unremitting suspicion of sexual and bodily pleasure; this pleasure can have its place, which can be wholeheartedly affirmed and appreciated. Even if we (correctly, in my estimation) follow Paul in admiring singleness as well as marriage and in acknowledging certain *practical* advantages of singleness over marriage, we will let go of suspicions that all enjoyment of sexual pleasure itself necessarily detracts from one's *moral* or *spiritual* standing. We will turn from regarding sexual pleasure as innately polluting or debilitating. As people and creatures of the earth, we need not hanker after the spirituality of angels. We are embodied, and when our bodies operate and respond as God intends, we in and as our bodies know pleasure. This is as it should be.

This case may be bolstered if we also notice that our predecessors often suspected sexual pleasure because of what we can now regard only as physiological misperceptions. Clement of Alexandria, along with the ancients in general, believed that semen was heated and foaming blood. (Menstrual blood, then regarded as a kind of female semen, appeared to reinforce this inference.) Consequently, to lose semen was to lose blood, which in turn meant losing a portion of strength and life. Imagine how our own ambivalence about sexual activity would increase if we thought intercourse was equivalent to opening a vein and draining an ounce of blood. Even more significant, Clement like many other ancients thought that a whole, miniature person was nascent in the male seed. There was no notion of (male) sperm fusing with the (female) egg to achieve conception. Woman's womb was merely an incubator and carrier. So, Clement remarked, "a whole man is torn out when the seed is lost in intercourse." This contributes to an abhorrence of masturbation or intercourse for enjoyment, without the express intent of procreation. Every such act is then a kind of wanton, purely selfish abortion—wasting incipient persons merely for the sake of gratification. Modern science has more carefully and reliably scrutinized human reproductive physiology, and we need not ally our spirituality with ancient beliefs we can now regard only as mistakes.

That said, there are other, more theologically rooted, aspects of the Christian tradition that continue to repay our attention. Much of the traditional wariness of sexuality may suggest a fitting prudence about and truer estimation of sexuality for our day—a day marked and marred in its sexual attitudes by a romanticized and hedonistic individualism.

I have said that the Christian tradition has been aware of a linkage between sex and death. That linkage has not been altogether severed in modernity and postmodernity. In general, we present-day Christians with our contemporaries typically try to look on sex with rose-tinted glasses, to emphasize its associations with life, liberation, and fulfillment. Yet when we do fight and worry about sex, the specter of death often looms. The abortion debate is intense not least because it juxtaposes sex and death. AIDS all too vividly reminds the entire world that sex and death can sometimes come hand in hand. But even apart from such controversial cases, sex ordinarily and pervasively carries intimations of death. The French speak of orgasm as "la petite mort"—a little death. Sex, like death, brings with it breathlessness, forgetfulness, timelessness, and loss of control. This in and of itself is not an evil. After all, sleep too involves loss of conscious control and relaxation of what Augustine called our "intellectual sentries." With sex as with sleep, in places of peace and security, the sentries may justifiably stand down for a while.

Even as it good to repeatedly and temporarily relax the sentries, however, we can never permanently and altogether elude the negative potentials of sex's linkage with loss of control and death. We may most obviously think of sexual loss of control in terms of raging, irresistible passion. But St. Augustine noticed that the sexual loss of control is more comprehensive. It includes not only the rampant libido but impotence or frigidity. Sometimes "desire abandons the eager lover, and desire cools off in the body while it is at boiling heat in the mind. Thus strangely does lust refuse to be a servant not only to the will to beget but even to the lust for lascivious indulgence. . . .

It arouses the mind, but does not follow its own lead by arousing the body." We might, in our rebelliousness, attempt to enjoy sex apart from God's good designs for it. Yet even (or especially) in our grasping at autonomy and utter self-mastery, sexual desire will not always act as we would will it to. It remains irreducibly a mystery, and like all mysteries it demands respect and due caution.

The modern response to the mystery and uncontrollability of sex is to strive harder for total mastery through technology and commodified ingenuity. Surprised by pregnancy? Abortion may be a "contraceptive" of last resort. Visited by impotence? Take Viagra. Worried about the inadequate sexual appeal of your teeth, torso muscles, baldness, flat chest, body odor, clothes, car, apartment, and so on? Buy this or that product. But we can never come up with an effective chemical or commodity for every sexually related dilemma or failure. In fact, the workings of advanced consumer capitalism often manufacture new possibilities for sexual insecurity along with the creation of new products. Consider: For teeth-whitening strips or pastes to sell, a market as well as a product must be fabricated. People must be persuaded to regard the ordinary whiteness of their teeth as inadequate. On their own terms, then, we cannot expect commodification and technology to eliminate sexual frustration or anxiety.

And in any event, many of us suspect a life without consequences would be a life of no consequence. We hope existence has more significance, more weight, than a pill or a perfume bottle. The Christian tradition helps us see and admit that sex is a mystery, and that in a fallen world it is a potentially dangerous and painful mystery. As such it is something we should not try to all handle all by ourselves, as unrelated individuals. Classical Christian spirituality pushes us to ask how our sexual desire and behavior will affect others, whether or not they will build up or tear down the community. Consequently Christian marriages are public, not private, affairs. Christian marriage liturgies, like that of my own Episcopal communion, include calls to all those witnessing wedding vows to "do all in your power to uphold these two people in their marriage." Christian spirituality would equip us to live out our sexuality and face any challenges it may bring communally and corporately, not always or only privately and technologically.

The Case of the Sick Lover

The tradition shows us that unchecked sexual desire can hurt and disintegrate our lives in other ways. Sexual desire and its satisfaction are among our most intense and attractive pleasures. With it as with other strong desires, I may succumb to its pull and consider only myself and my pleasure. Then I am not using sex to enjoy my lover and our shared love but using my lover to indulge my pleasure. This is what Luther was talking about when he said that in a fractured and disordered world, lovemaking can mean "each seeks to satisfy his desire with the other, and it is this desire which corrupts this kind of love."

Sexual desire is indeed an attraction to beauty, the beauty of another's God-created body. But in our fallen state it is precisely the fact that the body is that of *another* that is easily eclipsed and neglected. Lust can turn us in on ourselves. Even as we are drawn to another, captivated by the beauty of another's body and self, concupiscence turns that beauty which is beyond and other than us to our own ends, and at its darkest only to our own ends. Then the other is no longer another, a creature of God, but simply the means for the satisfaction of our desire. That eroticism is not always innocent, unqualifiedly beautiful and true, comes home to me when I reflect on a day or a season when my wife was sick. I suspect you can recall similar occasions.

My lover lay in bed pale, weeping, maybe feverish, consumed by her flu or another malady. I lay down beside her and held her in my arms, really wanting the best for her: that she be well for her own sake. Her forehead on my shoulder, the smooth small of her back under my stroking fingers, her silken hair in my nose and eyes—these were all beautiful and good, as true as dawn after a desperate night. And holding and caressing her was an act of pure, grateful love, that her beauty is freely shared with and offered to me and that it, with her health, should be restored to its fullness. After a few minutes, I gradually realized I was aroused. This in itself was not wrong. Her beauty was beauty, true beauty. Rightly ordered desires are aroused by true beauty. A lack of arousal, of recognition and response, in the presence of true beauty would be inappropriate. The lack itself would betray wrongly ordered desires.

But then I linger not so much on *her* beauty as on *my* arousal. My passion grows, and like a sycophantic servant I eagerly feed and nurture it. In minutes, even moments, her weeping recedes into the dim background of my consciousness. What rushes to the fore is my increasing desire, the desire that to some real degree has now overtaken me and become me. I no longer feel the sick fever under the skin of her forehead and back. I forget, or at least want to forget, that she in her body is ill: that is who she is right now, and who she will be as long as illness remains. In my increasing passion, I push aside who she is and want her in my arms, writhing not in spasms of pain but of ecstasy. I fleetingly wonder if I might kiss her neck, pull the sheet off her belly and thighs, and coax her into my enjoyment right now.

Then I return to my (other) senses. I cannot so forget or ignore her and her plight that I actually now try to draw her into an activity I know she is not ready or suited for. So I kiss her cheek gently, not ravenously, and keep my stroking hand in check. I displace my desires and passion enough to see her as she is: beautiful, yes, but sick and hurting no less. The ability to displace my desires demonstrates that I have not been consumed, or swallowed and defined, by them. To an important degree at least, I remain their master. But still I have caught a glimpse of what St. Augustine called concupiscence, the darkness of disordered desire which would make of the self a god and of all other creatures (and even of God Almighty) means or tools of the self's satisfaction and aggrandizement. I have seen that lurking near the heart of all concupiscence is the potential for rape. It is the potential for taking what the self wants when it wants it, with no regard for the desire or welfare of others.

There is of course a very real and significant difference between rape and the potential for rape. And authentic love between men and women, especially married love, is about learning sexual desire and expression that really can see and attend to the other. It is about learning, in the acts of bodily love, to come into a true union—a union of two free selves, not the domination of one self over the other. So I am not eager to follow the church fathers in what often does indeed appear an overstated suspicion of sexual desire. The church, as we have seen, has often thought that even the married couple copulating for procreation should try to stifle and deny their pleasure. Relying on the tradition to critique the tradition, I have suggested this denial of sexual desire is a species of realized eschatology and of mistaking angelic for human spirituality. But if demurring from the earlier masters and ascetics to this degree makes sense, it would not be sensible to dismiss their wisdom on sexual passion altogether. The reflection on the sick lover—within the purview of every man's and woman's experience, modern as well as ancient—shows the enduring insight of Augustine's suspicion of concupiscence. This concupiscence, thank God, will not sweep most of us into acts of rape, but an inclination to rape is ineradicably at its dark center. Sex, in a broken and disordered world, is not entirely or simply innocent. This desire, like other desires, demands disciplining and direction. To think that it should only and "naturally" be indulged is romantic nonsense, not Christian spirituality.

Desire Rightly Ordered

What, then, is the rich and rightful place of bodily, sexual pleasure in Christian spirituality? There is no better or more important framework for answering that question than the three key features of the Christian story and logic explored in the previous chapter. Creation, incarnation, and resurrection all crucially include and involve the body. The body (along with the rest of human being and nature) is created good. The body's goodness is affirmed and enhanced when, with the incarnation, it is drawn or "assumed" into the divine nature. Finally, the resurrection underscores the body as an eternal and not simply a perishable good. The body is good enough not only for this earth but (in a transformed state) for the new heavens and the new earth.

It is characteristic of the good to elicit admiration, delight, and felicity, a sense of rightness and fittingness. Pursuit of a good may not always bring immediate gratification. Practicing the piano over months and years can be dull and even painful. But there are moments of gratification along the way, and eventually the ability to passably play Mozart or Scott Joplin repays with a great deal of satisfaction and delight. When we play Mozart or Joplin well, as they ought to be performed, we should know pleasure. We should admire, delight in, and find felicitous this beautiful music, as well as the thorough participation in it that our long-disciplined piano abilities enable. Otherwise the music is not really beautiful and good, or our response to it is inappropriate.

So far as Christian spirituality is concerned, it is at the point of our response to the good that difficulty can enter. God has created all things good. But we are fallen and, though still good, confused in our sinfulness. In our disordered condition, we may value certain goods inordinately and disproportionately. Accordingly, says St. Augustine, "greed . . . is not something wrong with gold; the fault is in a man who perversely loves gold and for its sake abandons justice, which ought to be put above comparison above gold." Gold is a good creation of God. Evil is not the gold itself made bad but instead occurs in a human response to gold, a response that esteems gold inordinately and puts the possession of gold above respect for justice. Likewise, and more to the point of our consideration of bodily pleasure, Augustine declares, "Lust is not something wrong in a beautiful and attractive body; the fault is in a soul which perversely delights in sensual pleasures, to the neglect of that self-control by which we are made fit for spiritual realities far more beautiful, with a loveliness that cannot fade." Evil, then, lies not in the "beautiful and attractive body" itself, or in a recognition of that beauty and attractiveness, but in overvaluing the desired body, or valuing it out of order. We know how to rightly value and order the many goods of creation, including the body, by looking to the end, the goal and crowning purpose, of creation as revealed in Christ. Our true and ultimate human end, says, Augustine, is "to reach the kingdom [of God] which has no end."

Clearly, then, if we esteem and desire sexual pleasure more than God, our love of sexual pleasure is out of order. We are called to love and serve God through our neighbors, including our sexual partners. As Luther recognized, another human being is a greater good than sexual pleasure. So to use another person for my sexual enjoyment is a distortion and perversion of the good of sexual pleasure; it is in exactly that way and for exactly that reason an evil. Such exploitation makes another person instrumental to my pleasure. When I am sexually exploitative, I make love if and as my lovemaking will allow and enhance my pleasure. I put myself and my enjoyment ahead of God's call and authentic love of my neighbor, a practice that obviously does not fit and prepare me for the kingdom of God which has no end. And if I pursue sexual pleasure compulsively, I am enslaved by it. To use contemporary parlance, I am a sex addict, pitiably ordering my entire life around sex rather than the kingdom of God. This is sex out of order.

So sexual pleasure may be mishandled. But in this it is like any other important good, including the love of a parent or a child, service in a powerful office, and the enjoyment of food and drink. We may follow and benefit from the Christian tradition's warning against sexual pleasure that is exploitative or compulsive, while challenging—on the deeper and more primal grounds of the tradition itself—a traditional tendency to denigrate sexual pleasure altogether.

Sex, like a contested election, is one of those things about which there is always more that can be said. I will say more about it in a later chapter. But to adequately say more about sex, and much else regarding Christian spirituality, I need now to turn to other aspects of the body: the social body and the eucharistic celebration at the center of the social body we Christians call the church.

3

PUTTING ADAM
BACK TOGETHER
AGAIN

*Christian Spirituality
and the Social Body*

When a friend of mine returned to her apartment near the recently fallen World Trade Center, she discovered a human finger on the balcony. It is almost too horrible to contemplate, but she reported that her neighbors found similar grim evidence of the carnage of September 11, 2001. We know that paramedics and physicians encounter this kind of horror all too often, on battlefields or at the sites of car and plane crashes, and few of us envy them their dreadful duties. The carnage of dismemberment shocks us, of course, because it all too graphically represents death and bodily disintegration. A limb or finger or eye violently separated from the rest of the body is patently and terribly incongruous.

We are not repelled by fingers or legs or heads in and of themselves. For instance, we are at ease with photographs that picture people from the waist or neck up. But a head or other part actually severed from its entire body is immediately awful. In a sense the severed part is human—it belonged to the whole body of a member of the species *Homo sapiens*. Yet it is not quite human; it is only a part, and removed from the body it is frightfully, repulsively out of place.

Revulsion at dismembered physical bodies is not unique to us moderns. In history's bloody chronicles there have been few if any cultures that did not share this revulsion. Yet we moderns (or postmoderns) are unique as regards our response to another sort of dismemberment. Unlike any known culture before it, the modern West has seen individual physical bodies as the basis of the social body. The individual is real and primary, the social body a derivative fiction. The modern West has, in essence and contrary to the apostle Paul, said that individuals as "hands" or "feet" are most themselves in isolation from any social body of which they may be members. Premoderns saw matters differently. The individual, inasmuch as such a creature could be conceived, was preceded by and dependent on the social body. The whole person existed only in community. Anyone apparently beyond all community was at best quasi-human, to be greeted with an alarm similar to that evoked in our day by a severed hand or foot.

Traditional Christian spirituality cares about many things. One of them is shaping people so that they can see and prevent the horror not only of physical dismemberment but of social dismemberment as well.

Will the Real Mother Please Stand Up?

Among the preeminent modern shapers of what "religion" and "spirituality" are, and are about, the nineteenth-century psychologist and philosopher William James stands tall. Though he rejected orthodox Christianity, James maintained an intense interest in religion and mysticism. This passion culminated in his still famous book *The Varieties of Religious Experience*. Like other moderns, James insisted that spirituality is an asocial, essentially individual concern. He wrote in a letter, "I believe myself to be (probably) permanently incapable of believing the Christian scheme of vicarious salvation. . . . The ground I am taking is this: the mother-sea and fountain-head of all religions lies in the mystical experiences of the individual. . . . All theologies and all ecclesiasticisms are secondary growths superimposed."

So James saw spirituality and spiritual experience beginning with the individual. Individuals had mystical religious experiences. Then they might—or might not—seek to associate with others who have had similar experiences. So churches (what James called "ecclesiasticisms") and theologies were secondary. They resulted when individuals with their separate experiences subsequently responded to one another.

James rightly intuited that such an approach put him at odds with traditional Christianity. The "Christian scheme of vicarious salvation" means that there is no such thing as atomized or isolated individuals. Human beings are social creatures, linked in solidarity. As the Christian poet John Donne insisted, "No man is an island." In one, Adam the proto-human, many are created and can fall into sin and destruction. In one, Christ the second Adam, many can be restored or recreated. Christianity sinks its roots into the reality and priority of the social or corporate body. In such a vision, the identity and welfare of each member are embedded in and intertwined with the identity and welfare of the whole, the many united. Without an appreciation of the social body, orthodox Christianity can simply make no sense. Immured in an individualism James exemplified, we moderns and postmoderns may easily find ourselves, like him, constitutionally incapable of believing (or even understanding) the classical confession that the world has been saved through the death and resurrection of Jesus Christ.

In short, modern individualism makes it hard for us to see the forest for the trees, the whole for the parts. When we look at a single physical body, we easily tend to think of it as freestanding or autonomous, unrelated to other bodies. Our medicine, for example, concentrates on individual habits and diet. Worrying about a possible cancer, the physician asks the individual if she smokes—not if she lives in a community near a toxic waste dump. Even as patient after patient reports severe stress (one doctor told a friend of mine that he attributed over 80 percent of the patient complaints he heard to the effects of stress), modern medicine concentrates on helping the individual "adjust to" and "cope with" stress. That is our gross individualism speaking and defining the conversation, blocking other possible and important questions. For instance, noting chronically high rates of stress, we might ask if the community, the social body, is sick. And we might wonder how it could be changed so that members of the social body might adjust to a standard of health rather than illness.

Of course, modern hyper-individualism has in recent decades come in for its knocks. One such challenge comes from historians, who remind us that the notion of the autonomous, unconnected individual is—in the span of history—an idea so anomalous as to be bizarre. Former cultures have seen the individual rooted in and identified by communal ties. The individual physical body was real. But no less real, and in fact preceding and living on after every individual body, was the social body. Premoderns saw the two bodies related, corresponding, each affecting the other. The use of the human body as symbolic of human society dates at least as far back as 900 B.C.E. and has been noted in India, Iran, Russia, and across the Mediterranean. The microcosm of the physical body seemed most handily to illustrate and explain the macrocosm of society—how unity can exist with an interdependent diversity of parts, or members. The language I use here is telling to our point: *microcosm* means "a little cosmos." In the view of many peoples throughout history, the human body is the world writ small. The single physical body reflects and imitates the configuration, workings, or mechanics of the universe. Moreover, it is influenced by and participates in the designs of the universe. The part constantly relates to the whole, and vice versa.

Roman architects scrutinized the human body and saw it structured in geometrical, symmetrical relationships. The bodily parts are proportioned one to another, and limbs, eyes, and ears match across the two sides of the body. Accordingly, as in Rome's Pantheon, the architects constructed buildings with equal and opposite parts to their matching sides—bilateral niches, bilateral placement of statues, and so forth. Likewise, when Europeans in the seventeenth century discovered that blood, pumped by the heart, circulated throughout the human body, the design of urban infrastructures was affected. Officials banned the dumping of chamber pots on street surfaces. City planners built sewage systems beneath the streets and wanted the dirt and filth of the city, like the impurities of the physical body, to circulate under the surface, toward their elimination. In cases like these, the interplay of physical and social bodies determined the concrete shape and substance of the world in which people lived and moved. There are many other possible examples, of hardly less importance or influence. For instance, medieval Europe regarded the bodies of kings as symbolic of the social bodies these kings ruled. An attack on the king was equivalent to an attack on the society as a whole.

However much modern individualism obscures perception of the social body, it has not entirely blocked it. We moderns can, for instance, readily relate to the notion of an individual figure representing a community or society. Mayors are spokespersons for cities, ambassadors act on behalf of entire countries. And a state would perceive another nation's assault on the person of its president or prime minister as an assault on the society as a whole. The interaction and interdependence of the physical body's limbs and organs remain extraordinarily suggestive and readily apparent. The diverse parts of the physical body work together to serve the whole, and only in relation to the whole can the parts remain healthy. The apostle Paul was not the first or last to notice this and to compare the physical to the social body. Paul said the individual body consists of many members, but what good would it do for any one member to try to go off on its own? "If the foot would say, 'Because I am not a hand, I do not belong to the body,' that would not make it any less a part of the body. And if the ear would say, 'Because I am not an eye, I do not belong to the body,' that would not make it any less a part of the body. . . . If all were a single member, where would the body be? As it is, there are many members, yet one body" (1 Cor. 12:15–20).

Here the apostle spoke of the social body we call the church. The parts (the individuals) of that social body, he said, do not look out for their own interests or gain. Each has gifts of the Spirit, but not for personal enrichment or enjoyment. Instead, the gifts are given "for the common good," for the edification or building up of the social body as a whole (1 Cor. 12:7). In fact, as the *Oxford English*

Dictionary indicates, earlier uses of the word *spirituality* simply indicated "the [corporate] body of spiritual or ecclesiastical persons." In one example cited by the *OED*, we find a speaker in 1441 preparing to address "the spirituality," which consists of a convocation of two cardinals and five bishops. Here Christian spirituality just is participation and formation in the church, the social body created and sustained by the Holy Spirit.

We can see how orthodox Christian spirituality differs from William James's modern spirituality. For James, individual experience is the "mother-sea" of all spirituality. For Christians, the church is the mother of spirituality. Standing on the shoulders of many church leaders before him, John Calvin declared, "The church is the common mother of all the godly. . . . There is no other way to enter into [spiritual] life unless this mother conceive us in her womb, give us birth, nourish us at her breast."

Consumer Capitalism and Dismemberment

These profound differences between Christian and modern spirituality do not mean Christian spirituality has no appreciation whatsoever of the individual. Christian spirituality does not want to abolish all differences between persons. It is not echoed, for instance, in Communist schemes to dress everyone alike, in the same gray, drab uniforms. Recall the apostle Paul's use of the body metaphor. The foot should not want to be the hand or the ear to be the eye. Each is different and has its own function. The body cannot run effectively on its hands or tie knots with its feet. If the body wants to hear, it had best use its ears. And if it wants to see, it turns to its eyes. Likewise, says Paul, the church as a body needs different, and differently gifted, members. In this regard Paul, and Christian spirituality following him, respects and upholds individuality. Diversity within the body is not only tolerable, it is necessary and good.

What classical Christian spirituality does deny is diversity, or difference and individuality, separated and removed from the whole. Paul wants the members to be different, but different as members of one body. When modern individualism speaks of the "self-made" man or woman, it imagines that the foot can be most gloriously itself if it is cut off from the body as a whole. Paul would say otherwise: the foot really is most wonderfully and felicitously a foot when it operates as an organic member of the whole body. The person likewise realizes and enjoys his or her humanity at the fullest as a member of the social body. To be an "individual" in the sense of being primarily unrelated and separate is not to be fulfilled but to be amputated.

Hence the early church saw individualization (in the negative, alienating sense of the word) as a result of the fall into sin. Maximus the Confessor said that by original sin "the one nature [of humanity] was shattered into a thousand pieces." Humanity was to have been a harmonious unity in which "mine" and "yours" presented no cause for conflict, but with sin humanity exploded into an uncoordinated horde of suspicious and frightened individuals. "And now we rend each other like wild beasts." Using similar imagery, St. Augustine wrote, "Adam himself is now spread out over the whole face of the earth. Originally one, he has fallen, and, breaking up as it were, he has filled the whole earth with pieces."

To the degree that a modern spirituality, then, exhorts a person to focus only on self (as in "self-esteem," "self-realization," "self-fulfillment," and the like), it is in the terms of Christian spirituality perversely making the fall its ideal. It puts forth the alienated and amputated individual as the highest and healthiest human condition. And—seen with Christian eyes—that is an illusion. The amputated limb is a dying limb. It is not more but less effectively itself for its severance from the body.

If you are looking for the premier modern spirituality that shapes persons as unattached and alienated individuals, consider consumer capitalism. It may seem odd to think of consumerism as a "spirituality." But if spiritualities are ways of life that form persons, giving them something to live for and by, consumer capitalism certainly qualifies. After all, captains of industry and advertising executives in the early twentieth century saw that they needed to change the attitudes, hopes, and habits of the populace if consumer capitalism were to succeed. Machinery and assembly techniques were at hand that enabled the manufacture of goods far exceeding any existing markets—especially in a land of thrift. Eventually, habits of saving needed to be replaced by habits of free spending. Attitudes favoring the old and familiar needed to be replaced by lust after the new and novel. People who might question and discipline their desires needed to be taught to honor and indulge them as "felt needs." Today, we are formed and encouraged as consumers in countless actions: by presidents who urge shopping as a patriotic duty, by credit cards (and the "check cards" enculturating youngsters in the use of credit cards), by the multimedia flood of advertising and marketing, by the retooling of nearly all fields and professions along a market model, by the giving over of "public" spaces such as parks and sports venues to corporate sponsors, and so on and on.

Perhaps traditional Christian spirituality and consumer capitalist spirituality are most clearly contrasted if we consider their opposed understandings of desire. For Christian spirituality, desire can never be considered apart from its object. A desire is known as "good" or "evil" only when we take account of what is desired—the object of desire. As St. Augustine simply put it, desire is wrong or distorted "if the love [the object of desire] is bad, and good if the love is good." So for Augustine, as for orthodox Christian spirituality in general, desire must be specified and directed. To be healed and rightly aimed, desire must serve a proper end or goal. For Christian spirituality, that end is the God of Israel, met in Jesus Christ. "For you [God] have made us for yourself," Augustine famously exclaimed, "and our heart is restless until it rests in you." All desires are judged by how well they do or do not serve the Creator and Redeemer God.

Consumer capitalist spirituality, on the other hand, cultivates a starkly different sort of desire. Capitalism, and the liberalism out of which is arises, wants to focus on desire that does not specify its object. It interprets desire in a formal, blank, unintentional manner. Its desire is a matter of open-ended choice, and the more choice the better. The market demands that questions of the common or ultimate good be set aside and marginalized. The individual must pursue whatever she privately desires, with indifference to the good of the social body. Consequently choice (at least apparent choice) must multiply. Capitalism deifies dissatisfaction and exercises what might be called a preferential option for the options. The kaleidoscope of choice spins freely and wildly, ever changing and expanding. It can be directed, if *direction* is the word, only by the mysterious workings of the market and its "invisible hand." The market is considered amoral and is supposed to carry no judgments about good or bad choices and the desires behind them. Thus the neighborhood drugstore sells cigarettes right beside stop-smoking aids, without any sense of irony or contradiction. Whether smoking or not smoking is intrinsically better escapes notice. So long as there is a demand to smoke and a demand to quit smoking, the market will meet either desire (or both). This is what I mean by calling capitalistic desire formal or blank. It is empty of substance. It does not specify desires according to the substantive, actual objects of those desires. It promotes desire for desire's sake.

Confronting Capitalism with Augustine

Though he knew no such economic animal as our present-day capitalism, St. Augustine did address unspecified or merely formal desire. He said such desire was not neutral but "can only be understood in the bad sense." That is the case because unspecified desire is no longer related to and ordered by reference to God and God's love of all creation, but only by reference to the one who desires. Lust or evil desire is "in love with being in love," desire for desire's sake. The lustful, concupiscent lover alienates and severs herself from the social body and God's harmonious arrangement of it. She no longer considers the welfare of the object of her desire so much as the pleasure and satisfaction of her own desiring. So even when unspecified desire's objects are good in themselves, the desire itself is no longer subordinated to serving the Creator. It is instead desire subordinated to serving the (alienated) creature, the human desire-er.

Augustine protests, "What does it matter in what direction or by what way the unhappy state of man sets out on the pursuit of felicity, if it is not guided by divine authority?" Such desire and striving in a shiftless, aimless yearning can only be enmeshed in sin, as the human being or society gropes in the confusion and ignorance of its fallen state. More exactly, it encourages the sin of idolatry, since the desire-er focuses on pleasing self rather than God. In these terms,

wildly manufacturing and pursuing "felt needs" for an unending
gusher of new products and experiences can hardly be considered
spiritually wise or healthy. It breaks up the social body and scatters
it in as many directions as there are self-interests. It corrupts the
individual by making him a slave to his desires. As Paul puts it in
Philippians 3:19, the slave to his own desires has made his belly, his
appetites, his god. Where is the human dignity in that? Inasmuch,
then, as the consumer capitalistic ethos is about cultivating desire for
the sake of desire (shopping as a way of life), Augustine could only
regard it with repugnance.

By Augustine's lights, God originally meant to impress upon the
human that "healthy obedience" and true freedom (the freedom to
be what the human is intended to be) are found in "free service" to
God. This "free service was in that creature's own interest." But the
human acted originally and prototypically, in the Garden, against
God and so against its own genuinely human interest. Consequently,
the creature making his own desire his god is severed not only from
the true God and from the social body but from himself. He "who
in his pride had pleased himself was by God's justice handed over
to himself." As creature trying to act as his own Creator, he was
divided and pitted against himself. The result was "not that he was
in every way under his own control, but that he was at odds with
himself, and lived a life of harsh and pitiable slavery, instead of the
freedom he so ardently desired." The "punishment of that [original,
and in ensuing generations habitual] sin" was and is "nothing but
his own disobedience to himself, so that because he would not do
what he could, he now wills to do what he cannot." Human desire is
now disordered and as such often desires what, for its own good, it
should not. It is also frequently thwarted by pain and bodily limitations, and ultimately always by death. So in our defiance of God "we
have only succeeded in becoming a nuisance to ourselves, and not
to God." Boring to the heart of the matter, Augustine sees that the
worst slavery of all is the slavery to a self given over to disordered
desire. In his view, it would in fact be better to be slave to another
human being, especially a virtuous and wise one, than to fall under
the tyranny of one's own corrupted and confused desire.

As I noted in this book's introduction, within the consumer capitalistic ethos we have resisted naming this bondage to self as itself a kind of slavery and subjection to tyranny. But we have not been able to entirely hide or disguise it, and so the language of addiction has spread pervasively. Addiction goes well beyond strictly physical or substance addictions, as to heroin, alcohol, and prescription drugs. Twelve-step groups have proliferated to confront "addictions" to shopping, food, and sex, as well as what are deemed unhealthy dependencies on other persons or relationships. In its exaltation of formal or blank desire, its yearning for ever novel experiences and material goods, the consumer capitalistic ethos cultivates addiction to the new and the untried. Though this ethos rarely identifies itself as addicted to addiction, it forms addictive personalities and commodifies addiction itself. The consumer capitalistic economy feeds on the addictiveness of consumers. The tourist seeks ever new and different destinations and experiences. The smoker who tries unsuccessfully to quit will buy more stop-smoking aids. It becomes "cool" to belong to a twelve-step group, even as we struggle against victimization by one or another addiction.

Augustine sought to unveil and remove the disguise not merely of particular addictions but of addiction and slavery to self in general. He confessed to God, "I was sure that it was better to give myself up to your love than to give in to my own [disordered] desires. However, although the one way appealed to me and was gaining mastery, the other still afforded me pleasure and kept me victim." A better dissection of addiction, I submit, will not be found in any modern literature of dysfunctionality. Addicted to unspecified desire, we can submit neither to God nor to others. The social body is rent into millions of pieces, each anxiously looking out for number one.

Augustine Cross-Examined

Now, as inhabitants and beneficiaries of the consumer capitalistic West, at least we affluent Christians might push back at Augustine in some defense of our ethos, our way of life. We have rehearsed such defenses well. We might point to how life spans have doubled and even tripled from Augustine's day. We might call attention to our comparatively low rates of infant death and the eradication or control of several diseases that formerly spelled premature death. We can bring into the dock the advantages, joys, and comparative safety of modern transportation and mobility; we can point to the much greater proportion of the population that never knows hunger or want of basic shelter and even enjoys such comforts as air condition-ing and media amusement, undreamt of by the wealthiest monarchs in Augustine's day. We might present on modern capitalism's behalf the abundance of simple joys such as fresh wine and leisured week-ends for the great masses of our citizenry, or the availability of basic and even higher education (without the brutal floggings the young student Augustine routinely endured!) to a majority of citizens. We could submit the granting of a voice and nearer equity to women (highly developed capitalistic technology has neutralized the brute upper-body strength of males over females, rendering incredible any assumptions of comprehensive male superiority). Likewise, we could note the virtual disappearance of chattel slavery, replaced by machinery.

We could argue that these and others are genuine and profound goods and that the capitalistic economy must in considerable part be credited with their attainment. In his remarkable wisdom and compassion, Augustine would not, I think, be likely to gainsay or deny all this. He could, after all, be quite eloquent and exhilarated in his delight in earthly, material, and physical goods. And he never expected the City of God, in its pilgrimage in this age, to deny or refuse the temperate use of temporal goods. So maybe he could come alongside us and approve certain aspects of our way of life.

But he would hardly back off his critique altogether. Stumbling out of a time machine into our world, perhaps he would echo the 1922 assessment of G. K. Chesterton, which carries shades of Au-gustinianism:

> A wise man's attitude toward industrial capitalism will be very like Lincoln's attitude towards slavery. That is, he will manage to endure capitalism; but he will not endure a defence of capitalism. He will recognise the value, not only of knowing what he is doing, but of

knowing what he would like to do. He will recognise the importance
of having a thing clearly labelled in his own mind as bad, long before
the opportunity comes to abolish it. He may recognise the risk of even
worse things in immediate abolition, as Lincoln did in abolitionism.
He will not call business men brutes, any more than Lincoln would
call all planters demons; because he knows they are not. He will regard
alternatives to capitalism as crude and inhuman, as Lincoln regarded
John Brown's raid; because they are. But he will clear his *mind* from
cant about capitalism; he will have no doubt of what is the truth about
Trusts and Trade Combines and the concentration of capital; and it is
the truth that they endure under one of the ironic silences of heaven,
over the pageants and the passing triumphs of hell.

Whether or not Augustine would want Chesterton's words put in
his mouth, we can, judging from the fourth-century bishop's evaluation of the powerful and wealthy in his own world, suggest with
some plausibility how he might respond to our defense of twenty-
first-century consumer capitalist spirituality. He would surely protest
that our list of temporal goods (lengthened life spans, technological
advancements, and so forth) are only fully and really goods so long as
they are rightly used. Certainly they are only disastrously made ends
in themselves, rather than subordinated to the end of serving God.
He would sternly warn against the dangers of an uncritical embrace
of earthly prosperity. In his own day, he recognized that the earthly
citizen was concerned for "peace and general prosperity" and tended
to desire these "without moderation" instead of "with restraint,
with self-control, with reverence." He would assert that a longing
for earthly, temporal goods apart from, or in denial or ignorance of,
humanity's Final and Supreme Good, is the worst folly of all. Luxury,
Augustine said, "is more deadly than any human enemy." The various
spectacles and amusements of the gladiatorial games represented a
"moral corruption far worse than all the fury of an enemy." Better to
suffer bodily injury or disease than the corruption and deterioration
of the soul (or character). Moral and spiritual evils are the worst of
all evils because they attack "not the body but the character." He
railed against the Romans, "You seek security not for the peace of
your country but for your own impunity in debauchery." This was
desire like consumer capitalistic desire: focusing the individual on

himself and on pursuit of immediate satisfaction, without reference to the social or common good.

Ever mindful of the lust for domination at the heart of the earthly city thinking only of itself, Augustine averred that discord, greed, and ambition are the evils "which generally spring up in times of prosperity." He worried about the real health of a polity whose concern for its poor was only that they remain docile, whose attempted "justice" aimed mainly to protect the personal property of the wealthy and powerful. He lamented that anyone questioning the affluent Roman's libertarian hierarchy of values would be scorned and "hustled out of hearing by the freedom-loving majority."

Others may of course disagree, but I see similar attitudes in our own day, with the bread and circuses of mass media and other amusements serving in part to distract attention from injustice and poverty. Guarding personal peace and security, we among the affluent are a "freedom-loving majority" that will brook few critiques of class or other injustices so long as our blank, unspecified "freedom" to indulge consumer choices and comforts is protected.

Abhorring regulation or restriction of consumer choice, our culture proliferates crude and titillating amusements. What would Augustine say to exhibitionistic talk shows and degrading "reality" TV and radio shock jocks, or a general propensity for equating any innocence with naïveté? Perhaps something like this: "Full publicity is given where shame would be appropriate; close secrecy is imposed where praise would be in order. Decency is veiled from sight; indecency is exposed to view. Scenes of evil attract packed audiences; good words scarcely find any listeners. It is as if purity should provoke a blush, and corruption give ground for pride." What might he say to plutocratic politics, blatantly serving the interests of the rich? Maybe something like this: "We have self-indulgence and greed, public poverty and private opulence. . . . No distinction is made between good men and bad; the intrigues of ambition win the prizes due to merit. No wonder, when each of you thinks only of his own private interest; at home you are slaves to your appetites, and to money and influence in your public life."

We may debate the degree to which our current ethos of consumer capitalism agrees or comports with these characterizations. But that it does to some real degree is a judgment now widely shared. To the degree that in consumeristic spirituality "sensual pleasure is put above virtue, it is sought for its own sake, and it is believed that virtue should be brought into its service—that is, that the only purpose of virtue should be the achievement or maintenance of sensual pleasure," then we know Augustine's verdict: "Now this is certainly an ugly way of life."

Keeping the Feast

I began this chapter by recognizing the importance of the social body throughout history until modernity. Next I reviewed how orthodox Christian spirituality accounts for the division and conflict of our world: the harmonious social whole God created and intended has been ripped into pieces. Then, using Augustine as a touchstone, I explored how Christian spirituality might evaluate the current dominant ethos of consumer capitalism. In my judgment, the tradition would see alarming and strongly destructive tendencies in our ethos. It is, at least in significant degree, a way of life that rends each and every social body and encourages alienated individuals to guard their own interests quite apart from any common good. Where does this leave us?

In the Christian account, we are not left simply to flounder and flail at one another. God in Christ has come to restore us to true humanness, and that humanness includes restoration of the social body. After all, human beings are creatures and as such are contingent on their Creator. That Creator also made us so that we are members of one another: we were created as social and interdependent creatures. So any full restoration to true humanity must include the mending of the social body. The church is the anticipatory sign and foretaste of the restoration of humanity to full harmony and wholeness. Christ demonstrated in his own life what it means to live toward that restoration. He gave himself up for others and loved even his enemies. He prayed that his disciples might be brought to unity, made one as the Persons of the Trinity are one (John 17). He called his disciples to make for him friends and followers out of every nation, "baptiz-

ing them in the name of the Father and of the Son and of the Holy
Spirit, and teaching them to obey everything that I have commanded
you" (Matt. 28:19–20).

Baptism and induction into this body makes one in Christ of those
formerly divided—by ethnicity, by gender, by class or political sub-
ordination (Gal. 3:27–28). Many categories divide people. We may
find ourselves separated by race or sexual orientation or nationality
or income. We draw lines that cannot be crossed by others whom
we will still consider "one of us." For the writers and readers of the
New Testament, the starkest dividing line was that between Jews and
Gentiles. And in Christ even that iron curtain of social partitition and
enmity was knocked down. In Christ, Jew and Gentile were made
"one new humanity" (Eph. 2:15). When anyone is baptized, "there is
a new creation"—the restored and reconciled humanity, the mended
world, is glimpsed and foreshadowed (2 Cor. 5:17).

Given all this, it is clear why the church's great tragedy is its own
division. We are, exactly as Christians, seriously crippled by our frac-
tion into Eastern Orthodoxy, Roman Catholicism, and hundreds of
Protestantisms. The church's lack of unity, its own internal conflict,
obscures the oneness of Christ's body, the very oneness meant to show
the world the healing, reconciling power of God. Still, it is only in
and through the church that we glimpse or fleetingly touch and know
the unity of creation. For Christ "is before all things, and in him all
things hold together. He is the head of the body, the church; he is
the beginning, the firstborn from the dead, so that he might come to
have first place in everything. For in him all the fullness of God was
pleased to dwell, and through him God was pleased to reconcile to
himself all things, whether on earth or in heaven, by making peace
through the blood of his cross" (Col. 1:17–20). As the modern martyr
Dietrich Bonhoeffer saw it, it is by baptism and participation in the
church that "we live in full community with the bodily presence of
the glorified Lord. Our faith must become fully aware of this gift.
The body of Christ is the ground of our faith and the source of its
certainty; the body of Jesus Christ is the one and perfect gift through
which we receive our salvation; the body of Jesus Christ is our new
life." Despite its shortcomings, Bonhoeffer said, the church "is a living
witness to the bodily humanity of the Son of God. The bodily pres-

ence of the Son of God demands bodily commitment to him and with him through one's daily life. With all our bodily living, existence, we belong to him who took on a human body for our sake. In following him, the disciple is inseparably linked to the body of Jesus."

Bonhoeffer makes apparent how Christian spirituality is participation and formation in the church, the social body created and sustained by the Holy Spirit. We can no more become and grow as Christians apart from the church than we can become accomplished painters and sculptors apart from the guild and ongoing history of painters and sculptors. Those who fish for a livelihood learn from those who fished before and now alongside them. There can be no Americans apart from the formative social body America, no Germans apart from the country Germany. So, too, those who would follow after and become like Christ give up their physical bodies to his social, corporate body, the church (Rom. 12:1–2).

Thus in classical Christian spirituality the physical (individual) body cannot be separated from the social body. The physical body and the social body are constantly involved in an interplay, constituting and enabling one another. Christian spirituality interlinks the individual and the social in ways foreign to modern consumer capitalist spirituality. Modern spirituality divides between "social" and "personal" ethics. Sexual attitudes and behavior are then a matter of personal, private, or individual morality. So long as the sex is mutually desired, it is a private affair between the individuals involved. But traditional Christian spirituality cannot so easily compartmentalize and segregate the private and the social. Christian spirituality must not only consider the individual bodies involved but also ask how their actions serve (or fail to serve) the church as a social body. Accordingly, as we will see more fully in chapter 10, St. Thomas Aquinas saw fornication and adultery as issues not simply of sex but of justice. Thomas's censure of sexual sin centers on the consequences of lust as they weigh on women, children, and wronged spouses. He worries that sex outside marriage "rules out proper provision for bringing up any offspring of the act." Children need parents for their survival and nurture. Such an "exercise of the sex-act outside marriage is promiscuous and disadvantageous to the care of children, and for this reason a fatal sin." Adultery is "not merely a sin of lust but also itself a sin of injustice, a type of greed; and a man's wife is dearer to him than his possessions." Marriage and sexual intercourse are matters of justice because they are meant to "serve the general good of mankind."

Sexuality is but one example. Christian spirituality, as participation and formation in the body of Christ, is constantly concerned for the edification or building up of that body. Only in its thriving can the individual members of the body thrive. But again, and especially in a hyper-individualistic age, it is not easy to learn to "discern the [social] body" and look to its health. How are we cultivated to do so, to remove the cataracts of isolation and atomization from our eyes?

For orthodox Christian spirituality, the premier and most dramatic constitution and appearance of the body of Christ is at gathered or corporate worship. There the church hears the Word proclaimed, rehearses the story of the world's creation and salvation, offers up its praises and petitions, and circles in unity around the sacrament of the Lord's body and blood. There, then, is the epitome of our remembering (bringing back to mind and active imagination) and re-membering (putting back together) the body.

Misled by modern spirituality, contemporary Christians some-times assume their most important spiritual practices occur in their solitude, with private daily prayer, Bible readings, and so forth. As a high school football player, I often spent fall afternoons in the yard alone, throwing the football up and catching it, passing it through a tire swing, and running to stay in shape. It was worthwhile to practice alone, but I never imagined that my solitary exercises overshadowed or were more important than team practices, let alone actual games. I knew my individual work and play derived from a pastime that was first of all social and corporate and always knew its fullness as a social and not a solitary endeavor. Christian spirituality is similar. Our individual and daily exercises are important and worthwhile, but they do not precede corporate worship. They are derived from corporate worship and circle back to find their fulfillment in corpo-rate worship. Ultimately, if others had not played football with me, I think I would have quickly left off the solitary practice as a silly waste of time. Ultimately, if others do not pray with me, Christian faith and spirituality will become small and trivial, beaten down by a world so much bigger and more interesting than my individual obsessions and desires.

So Christian spirituality, bodily both physically and socially, is born from, nurtured by, and always destined to corporate worship. "Therefore," as the classical liturgy has it, "let us keep the feast."

4

LEARNING HOW TO BE SPIRITUAL WITH YOUR BODY

Christian Spirituality and the Sacraments

I know what it's like to be born and reared in rural America, then grow up and move away to the big city. These are two different worlds. And one of the major differences is the separate ways I, in and as my body, occupy these worlds. Physically speaking, there's not much I took with me from the world of my youth, except the small collection of childhood scars I had from mishaps with heavy machinery and spooked cattle. On my father's farm and ranch I worked in dirty jeans and T-shirts. Now I live in a world where "work clothes" include a coat and tie. (The Clint Eastwood-style wide-brimmed hat I wore as a teenager would not accessorize too well with my current office attire.)

I do have a cabinet of objects that, upon examination or handling, remind me of where I came from. In that cabinet stand thick old 78-rpm records from Granddad Adams's stock—some Hank Williams and Bob Wills. Another shelf is backed with a piece of the screen from the movie theater of my childhood, a white stucco building that three years ago collapsed to the ground; it was the site of my first kiss and the place where my love affair with film began. Beside the cabinet sits the last pair of my Granddad Clapp's cowboy boots.

These objects remain more or less mute to others. But they speak, richly and volubly, to me. I can remember Granddad Clapp without the prompting of the boots. But to pick them up and glance at the worn soles reminds me of how hard he worked all his life, building an Oklahoma farm at the tail end of the Dust Bowl era. The smell of the leather can set off a long chain of associations: other smells, like his Camel cigarettes and Old Spice aftershave; and a whole series of sights and sounds, like the time he stopped while crossing a ditch and, cussing eloquently, stomped on a snake (I like to recall it as a rattle-snake). The piece of fabric from the movie screen, likewise, unfolds "new" or temporarily forgotten memories. Right now, fingering its satiny surface, I first recall big, looming Mrs. Hawes, the old widow who ran the theater during my childhood, and how I talked her into a late showing of one of my favorite movies after eighth-grade graduation. That in turn makes me think about the thousands of images projected onto the screen over seven or eight decades. Then I recall that Granddad Adams, as a young man working a second job to support a new family, was one of the theater's earliest projectionists. Remembering how much Granddad loved movies, I next recollect the many weekends of my childhood when I stayed overnight at Grandma and Granddad Adams's house. Grandma was always off to bed early (Granddad said she used to fall asleep beside him in the theater projection booth), but Granddad and I sat up watching the late movie, bantering between pruney swigs of Dr Pepper straight from the 10-2-4 bottle.

As I say, I can recall my childhood without boots or a rag from a movie screen, but it's remarkable how many more memories flow, and how much more vividly they return to life, with the aid of such objects. Apparently my body—with its senses of sight, smell, touch, hearing, taste—has a memory, or at least is profoundly connected to and part of my memory. So the more I can involve my body in reminiscence, the more copiously and vigorously I remember. Several years ago, a bit lost between the dreams of my childhood and the searchings of my early adulthood, I returned home one June week to help with wheat harvest. I drove the combine and reexperienced dimensions of skin-feeling I'd forgotten, dimensions you can know only when you're hot and dusty and thirsty enough for cold water from a jug to taste like fine wine, when wheat chaff scratches your back and sweat runs in a muddy rivulet across the wrinkles on the inside of your elbow. Ahead of me, the wheat fell in neatly collapsing rows before the combine's blades. Behind, when I glanced, I saw grain pouring into the bin and piling like golden sand in the bottom of an hourglass. I not only heard the big machine's churning rhythm but felt it in the pulsing vibrations through my butt and thighs.

There was plenty of time to think, and any given sight or touch or smell, from minute to minute, could set off a cascade of memories and dreams and plans. I spent only four or five days on the combine, but in that time my whole body recovered a sense of itself. I knew who I was and what I wanted to be about, and had now a stock of spiritual energy to get back on and stay the course.

My past and memories are unique to me, but the phenomenon of recalling and reliving them with the aid of objects and bodily participation is not. Who among us doesn't keep treasured objects and rehearse periodically the formative events of our lives? Families are reconstituted at Thanksgiving and Christmas dinners. Deceased relatives and friends again come alive when we put our bodies through the motions (knitting, fishing, carpentry) they taught and shared with us. Souvenirs are collected on vacations; children's finger paintings are hoarded like great art; precious cards and letters that arrived at just the right time are tucked into books or drawers. As embodied, timely, and social beings, we take seriously what is done in and through our body and in the events of our personal history. Whether we have consciously reflected on it or not, we never let go of objects and rituals that aid us in whole memory—not just the abstracted memory of the mind but the tactile and concrete memory of the body.

It strikes me as rather odd, then, that many Christians casually propose to drop the memory aids and enablements of objects and bodily involvement when they turn to the practice of their faith. Of course, there are historical reasons that some churches stripped statuary and even crosses from their walls. And I suppose there is some continuum between revered sacramental bread and the tawdry healing hankies hawked by television evangelists. But what of profound human value can't be misused or distorted?

As I have been at pains to emphasize, we aren't angels. Angels don't have bodies and they gaze directly on God. They look and they see God's power, just as I can look and see the gasoline that ignites to fuel my car's motion. Remarkably, St. Augustine speculates that there will be a day, in a renewed world and with resurrected, transformed bodies, when we will see God and God's animating power wherever we look. Then we may be able to

> observe God in utter clarity and distinctness, seeing him present everywhere and governing the whole material scheme of things by means of the bodies we shall then inhabit. . . . It will not be as it is now, when the invisible realities of God are apprehended and observed through the material things of his creation, and are partially apprehended by means of a puzzling reflection in a mirror. Rather in that new age the faith, by which we believe, will have a greater reality for us than the appearance of material things which we see with our bodily eyes. . . . Similarly, in the future life, wherever we turn the spiritual eyes of our bodies we shall discern, by means of our bodies, the incorporeal God directing the whole universe.

But we are not yet living in that day and in that way. Before time's end and culmination, we apprehend God and the ways of God "through the material things of his creation," yet only "partially" and somewhat blurrily, as if through the "puzzling reflection in a mirror." Because of this inescapable reality, Jesus Christ bequeathed two sacraments to his church. These are the bodily, visible signs and participatory rites of baptism and the Eucharist. Martin Luther spoke very much in the train of classical Christian spirituality when he referred to the Eucharist as a bridge or ford or door or stretcher, by which and in which we embodied and historically embedded creatures "pass from this world into eternal life." It is a fact that a wide and raging river can be crossed without use of a bridge and a wall can be passed through without a door's being opened. We can cross the river in a canoe, rupture the wall with a sledgehammer. But then we would still be using aids or tools (a canoe and a hammer), and what is the sense of the extra time and trouble and increased possibility of failure (we might, after all, flip the canoe and drown, or encounter steel girders with our hammer)? Likewise, we can seek avenues to God that minimize physical aids, but in so doing we heighten the possibility of failure and needlessly try, as it were, to reinvent the wheel. Christian spirituality is for people, not angels. When we undertake it while ignoring or downplaying the sacraments, we are like the canoeist stubbornly struggling against almost impossible currents, trying and resting and trying again, all the while in the shadow of a great and trustworthy bridge long ago provided by someone wiser and surer than he.

The Church's Sacramental Spirituality

In truth, spiritual journey via the bridge of the sacraments is hard enough. The bridge will not break; but we can, through our sinful perversity and confusion, easily fall off it (or, worse yet, rip up its timbers and try to build a better bridge by our own dim lights). Still, the sacramental bridge is a wondrous gift, and it has been provided by Christ. The Gospels depict Jesus going down into the baptismal waters of death and new life himself, then calling us to follow his example.

"Now when all the people were baptized, and when Jesus also had been baptized and was praying, the heaven was opened . . ." (Luke 3:21)

"Go therefore and make disciples of all nations, baptizing them in the name of the Father and of the Son and of the Holy Spirit . . ." (Matt. 28:18)

Similarly, the Gospels portray Jesus' enacting the first Lord's Supper with the disciples and inviting them to ever afterward "do this in remembrance of me" (Luke 22:19).

The newborn church follows this lead. Following Jesus' death and resurrection and the descent of the Holy Spirit on the church, the apostles baptize those who embrace the gospel and together devote themselves to "the breaking of bread and the prayers" (Acts 2:41–42). The apostle Paul's letters, among the earliest documents constituting the New Testament, are peppered with references to the practice of baptism and Eucharist and exhortations about their powers and benefits.

For Paul, baptism is incorporation into Christ's body. In that body we know and live new life and even a new creation (Rom. 6:4; 2 Cor. 5:17). Baptism, as I mentioned earlier, is induction into a body-community that breaks down thick, old, and killing partitions between people who formerly were most radically different or opposed and even saw one another as enemies. So now united and one are Jews and Greeks, slave and free, male and female (Gal. 3:28). In the same vein, the Eucharist acts vitally as a practice that regularly edifies or "builds up" this community. The apostle reminds the young church that Jesus called his followers to drink the wine and eat the bread "in remembrance of me," that partaking of the Lord's body and blood is itself a proclamation of "the Lord's death until he comes" (1 Cor. 11:23–26). Paul sees the Eucharist as pregnant with spiritual ramifications, formative of the people who participate in it. Accordingly, it is crucial when eucharistically eating and drinking not to fail in correctly "discerning the body," rehearsing the Eucharist in a manner true to the way of Christ, building up the whole (1 Cor. 11:27–34). Among other things, this means Eucharist must be kept congruent with baptism—just as there is "no slave or free" through baptism, the eucharistic ritual must not divide rich and poor (see also James 2:1–7).

So the sacraments of baptism (undertaken once by each believer) and Eucharist (partaken of regularly) are at the root of Christian spirituality in the New Testament. And this root is not neglected or torn from the soil of Christian life in the post–New Testament church. A second-century church manual called *The Didache* includes careful instructions on baptism and the Eucharist. Baptism follows study of the apostolic teachings and admits the baptized into the full, eucharistically sustained life of the social, spiritual body of Christ. Thus Eucharist is followed by a prayer acknowledging, "Almighty Master, 'you have created everything' for the sake of your name, and given men food and drink to enjoy that they may thank you. But to us [the church] you have given spiritual food and drink and eternal life through Jesus, your child." Other second-century sources echo the importance of baptism and Eucharist in Christian spirituality. Ignatius exhorts, "Let baptism be your arms" in the fight of faith, and he celebrates the eucharistic bread and wine—"an immortal love feast indeed!" Justin calls baptism the "bath of repentance and knowledge of God" and observes that the sacramental bread and wine are not just common food but the "flesh and blood of the incarnate Christ." Reliance on baptism and Eucharist for undertaking and sustaining the Christian spiritual life is abundantly clear in later luminaries: baptismal and eucharistic appreciations from Origen, Irenaeus, Augustine, and others can (and do) fill books. No wonder one eminent historian concludes that, for the fathers of the church's first five centuries, the Eucharist was "the chief instrument" of the Christian's spiritual sustenance and growth.

Famously, Christian spirituality centered on the sacraments continued through the Middle Ages. What is not so well known or appreciated is the fact that the Protestant Reformers, in the main, continued to regard the sacraments as central to Christian spiritual health. Luther and Calvin indisputably held "high" views of the sacraments. They saw the Spirit distinctively at work in baptism, a rite of incorporation into the church, which Calvin called the "mother" of Christian faith and life. He and Luther, like Justin, saw the Eucharist as no ordinary meal but one at which the resurrected Christ was really and uniquely present. We will hear much from Luther on this count in the pages that follow. For now, I only cite the Heidelberg Catechism, the sixteenth-century Calvinist affirmation of faith that stood and stands as one of the most authoritative and widely accepted Reformed confessions. The catechism declares that to partake of the Eucharist is not only to embrace with a believing heart all the sufferings and death of Christ, and thereby to obtain pardon of sin and life eternal; but also, besides that, to become more and more united to his sacred body, by the Holy [Spirit], who dwells both in Christ and in us; so that we, though Christ is in heaven and we on earth, are, notwithstanding, flesh of his flesh, and bone of his bone; and that we live and are governed forever by one Spirit, as members of the same body are by one soul.

The early church's and magisterial Reformers' deep respect of the Eucharist for the spiritual life was continued by later Protestants. Methodist founder John Wesley, for instance, called for frequent celebration of Holy Communion and admonished those who would neglect it: "Whoever therefore does not receive . . . either does not understand his duty or does not care for the dying command of his Saviour, the forgiveness of his sins, the strengthening of his soul, and the refreshing of it with the hope of glory."

Bucket-Faith: Worshiping with the Head Alone

All this more than suggests why I think it is a mistake—and a departure from traditioned, orthodox Christianity—to downplay or neglect the sacraments. This neglect occurs when churches celebrate Communion only two or three times a year. It occurs when some Christians insist the sacraments are "just" or "only" symbolic. And it occurs whenever the emphasis about what happens in baptism or Eucharist falls on our own human recollection and meditation. A burden of my next chapter will be to insist that the first and most important thing happening in and through the sacraments is the real, objective presence of Jesus Christ. Of course, the examples I used at the beginning of this chapter don't allow for such a real, objective presence. I don't believe the actual spirits of my dead grandfathers visit when I handle boots or theater screen fabric. But I do believe that the living Holy Spirit visits and Christ's real presence occurs through the sacraments. Then, as with my grandfathers' character-istic objects, my memory and imagination are ignited and involved. My subjective thinking and feeling response to the sacraments is important, but it is not the most significant and certainly not the only thing happening when I receive the eucharistic bread and drink the eucharistic wine.

Before turning to the objectivity and efficacy of the sacraments, though, I need to honor and take account of the reservations or blocks to sacramental realism shared by many modern (especially some Protestant) Christians and inquirers.

At the outset, I admit that sacramental realism does not comport easily with modern rationality. I am inescapably a modern person myself. And we moderns have effectively, largely if not entirely, banished spirits from rocks and trees and animals. We have disenchanted the world. This is not all to the bad. Like you, when I complain of a lingering flu, I don't want a doctor who will search for evil spirits. I want a modern physician who will take a throat culture, identify the bacterium plaguing my body, and prescribe an antibiotic that will eradicate it. When I climb on an airplane, I don't hope for a spiritual adept in the cockpit, praying to keep her aircraft aloft. I want a trained pilot who knows her machinery. These are, I think, indisputably rational expectations.

But perhaps, as many reflective people have noticed in the past century, we take our modern rationalism too far. As modern medicine, transportation, media technology, and other instances indicate, we humans can accomplish a great deal when we put our minds to it. Yet we find the world is still not at all entirely under our control. In fact, even our inventions escape our control and eventuate in unexpected new problems and complexities. Especially since World War II, for example, we affluent Westerners have embraced one after another electronic gadget or digital technology that was supposed to "save time" and grant us more control over our lives. Yet cell phones and heaping e-mail leave us even more frenetic, harried, and feeling out of control than our ancestors. We seem not so much to have "saved" time as to have sped it up. The best-laid plans of our admittedly spectacular intelligence again and again unfurl down unpredictable paths and into new perplexities.

Furthermore, despite pervasive predictions about the secular assassination of "religion," most of humanity has persisted in believing that we are surrounded by forces bigger than us. Not only have traditional faiths such as Judaism, Christianity, and Buddhism failed to die out, but New Age beliefs and practices have birthed and proliferated, and even outright paganism has risen from its ashes. I agree with the hardened secularist that much in both the old and new spiritualities is wishful thinking and delusion—but all of it? Perhaps there is more to life and existence than eye can see or hand can touch.

There is a widespread and deep sense that modern rationality has been reductionistic. It has so concentrated on the powers of the intellect that persons have been reduced to little more than minds, and bodies to cumbersome carriers of the brain. (Even physicians, resisting this reductionism, now declare that the spirit, however exactly it is defined, may have something to do with physical health.)

Near the end of my seminary studies, I suffered a dream with an all-too-transparent interpretation. I saw myself in a bucket, with only my huge, swollen head looming over its rim. The rest of my body—trunk and limbs—had so attenuated and shrunk that it entirely fit inside the bucket. The bucket rested beside a swimming pool. As I uneasily peered about in that slightly off-kilter "this-seems-real-but-something-is-not-quite-right" way we do in dreams, a passing normal-bodied person bumped my bucket into the swimming pool. My great head-self disengaged from the bucket and sank with alarming rapidity. I screamed but no one above water heard my gurgling. My dwindled licorice legs dangled uselessly beneath me; my little noodle arms flailed to no effect.

Then I woke up, and confirmed the continuing possession of proportionately sized arms and legs with the sweetest relief. (Although I must say, I would have kept the reduced belly.) I'm sure this dream says much about seminary education (and me). But mainly I take it as a parable of concentrating nearly exclusively, educationally or otherwise, on the mind, the head. In seminary I had struggled mightily to absorb as much church history, theology, and ethical studies as I could in the span of a few years. I read shelves of books, wrote reams of papers, honed arguing skills in the classroom and countless bull sessions. But I had not learned much more about actually, bodily practicing prayer, or ministering to the sick, or serving the needy. In these regards my training was excessively modern. It was all about pinning down and dissecting objects supposedly amenable to my intellectual mastery—and neglectful of much of my person (not to mention actual, lived Christian spirituality).

Part of my response to this gaping neglect was to reclaim and reappreciate treasures of the Christian tradition and practice that allow me to worship, to pray, not just with my mind, but with hands and feet and eyes and tongue. A church's sanctuary is much more than a lecture hall. And Christian spirituality is much more than mental recall (though it certainly includes that). As the nineteenth-century Reformed theologian John Williamson Nevin commented, modern rationalism in relation to Christian worship, including the Eucharist, "is *too* spiritual." It takes little account of the outward forms of prayer and of the worshipers' entire bodies. "All must be resolved into the exercises of the worshiper's mind."

Or, to put that entire last paragraph into a single sentence, don't squeeze your body into a bucket and worship only with your head.

Spirituality for Non-Desert-Island Dwellers

Modern, rationalistic reductionism has affected our attitude to the sacraments in another way. Just as it neglects the physical body, it neglects the social body. In this mode, discussions about the sacraments are often shrunk to minimal requirements. Absolutely must the individual be baptized to be saved? Can the individual not grow in grace without regularly partaking of the Eucharist? Usually in these speculations desert islands soon lurch into sight. All other horizons are blocked from view. "What if someone is on a desert island and finds a Bible? There is no church, there are no ministers to baptize him or present him with the Eucharist. Can he not confess Christ in his heart and be a Christian?"

In point of fact, the orthodox, classical Christian sacramental tradition has always recognized exceptions. It has, as we will see in the next chapter, steadfastly insisted on the importance of the lively and real faith of the participant for the sacraments to be full and effective. It has made numerous provisions for such cases as the deathbed confession of faith, at which no ordained clergy are present or available. But the tradition has sanely kept these exceptions in

view exactly as exceptions. It has not, like some minimalistic modern
Christian movements, slipped into making the exception the rule.
Actually, such minimalizing tendencies precede modernism, or at
least cling to its roots.

At the dawning of the Reformation, Luther met the objection that
the sacraments are not "necessary" to full and genuine Christian life.
He responded with characteristic impatience and bluntness, observ-
ing that the sacraments were provided by God in Christ for all of us
(at least those of us not stranded on desert islands). "Do you wish
to instruct God as to what is necessary and unnecessary, and have
him according to your notions?" he roared back. "It is better for us
to reverse this and say: God wishes it thus, therefore your notions
are false." In his inimitable fashion, Luther cut to the marrow of
this reductionism, insisting on the fullness of life and salvation as it
has been provided in Christ. Christian spirituality in its riches and
depths is communal, not solitary. It is a matter of the heart or mind
but also very much of the entire person and her bodily, social, and
historical context.

A tendency to debunk or downplay the sacraments aroused Luther's suspicions. Probing and pushing for bare minimums to meet
suggested to him a hidden evasiveness, ingratitude, and stinginess.
Like the high school student pressing the teacher to disclose the
absolute minimum amount of completed homework required for a
passing grade, this form of Christian spirituality may be looking for
what is just enough to believe and be to get by. Construing the faith
along the lines of minimum requirements and passing grades is a
travesty of the faith, sure to warp our spirituality. In addition, though
supposedly focused on the individual's faith and sincerity, it suggests
an ironic halfheartedness, a yen to do or believe as little as possible
and hold back all that can be held back. Would we not question the
sincerity of the mother who professed to love her children in her heart
but refused as "mere outward forms" the actual feeding of them? Or,
more aptly as regards the Eucharist, wouldn't we wonder about the
sincerity of the child who protests he trusts his mother completely
but rejects the food on her lovingly prepared table?

Faced with such attitudes and arguments, the great champion of
justification by grace through faith could only thunder, "You might

as well tell me that because faith alone justifies, Christ is not necessary." When a banquet is laid out, why quibble about whether or not one might survive just on the celery stalks? Such narrow focus, such austere (and evasive?) minimalism and necessitarianism, might be crucial to your faith and spirituality if you wash up on a desert island. Until then and unless that, Luther said with a kick in the pants, get with the program and join the party.

A Baked God?

As you have surely gathered, I am not patient with the extremes of modern reductionistic rationality. Armed for bear (and bull) as I am on this count, however, I still admit it. The Eucharist and eucharistic real presence can appear, well, flat-out weird and possibly revolting. Baptism itself seems relatively understandable and, in sheer formal terms, inoffensive. After all, what could be offensive about a bath? (Of course we Christians are willing to offend on this count as on others: we can talk about baptism as a kind of washing and dying in the blood of Jesus. But stave off talk of bloody baths and drownings, and baptism can on its face appear fairly palatable.) The Eucharist, on the other hand, is both literally and figuratively hard to swallow. Eating the body and drinking the blood does sound an awful lot like cannibalism, and Roman detractors of the early church were not slow to denounce Christians for just that. By Luther's day, the stakes had lowered a bit and some humor was injected into denunciations of eucharistic real presence. Some wags looked on the sacramental bread and suggested Christians prayed to "a baked God."

A doughboy deity is not what the Eucharist is about, and Christians do not aspire to cannibalism. At this juncture, I can only remind us that many cultural practices, encountered for the first time or from a distance, appear strange and sometimes repulsive. Chinese chopsticks, for example, may intuitively appear to Westerners as more primitive than our civilized, polished forks and knives. But to the Chinese, dismembering hunks of meat at the table, rather than discreetly cutting them up and leaving the knives in the kitchen, can intuitively seem less civilized. For that matter, cannibalism does not necessarily manifest itself in a clear and indisputable fashion. Hindus convinced of the transmigration of souls, after all, avoid eating cattle so as not to consume a once and possibly future human soul. Happily, nearly all cultures now reject anything they understand as cannibalism. The church will, with St. Athanasius, stand *contra mundum*, against the world, on certain issues. But the church and Christian tradition are with most of the rest of humanity on cannibalism.

As with any (initially or distantly) odd cultural practice, understanding what happens in and through the Eucharist takes some patience and willingness to consider the practice on its own terms. So we turn to what the objectivity and efficacy of the Eucharist entails in considered orthodox Christian spirituality. To put it otherwise, how, more or less exactly, is Christ really present in and through the Eucharist? And what are the expected benefits for Christian spirituality in regularly partaking of the sacrament?

5

HOW TO SEE
AND LAY HOLD
OF CHRIST

*Christian Spirituality
and the Eucharist*

S omehow, over a lifetime and sometimes in spite of myself, I have
been befriended by dozens of people. Hands down, I know no
greater, surer, more inexhaustible joy and sustenance than friendship. Because it is so deep and wide and so varied in its manifestations,
there are many definitions of friendship. Furthermore, friendship gets
complicated because friends are the most dangerous people we know.
We keep our guard up and armor on around strangers, but to our
friends we bare our soft spots. So friends can always hurt us more
than our most vengeful enemies. A friend knows exactly where to
plunge the knife. And only a friend can become a traitor—we never
expected the enemy to take care for us or our cause.

Given all this, survival and any happiness in life depend on our learning how to distinguish true friendship from false friendship, or enduring friendship from a friendship of mere convenience or, worse, exploitation. At this point, pressing toward a recognition of true friendship, we could wax philosophical and haul into the dock Aristotle or Aquinas. But instead I propose a simple test, one, as they used to say, you might try in the comfort of your own home. This test comes in two parts.

1. Think of some of the happiest events and discoveries you can recall. Maybe it was a graduation party. Maybe it was stumbling across a book or some music that opened new worlds to you. Maybe it was walking a trail in a state park, winding up and to cliffs above the treetops, overlooking a wide river and a stunning vista. The possibilities are endless. It must only be an event or discovery when you thought or felt, "This is it. It can't get any better than this." But then you realized it could. It could be even more if a certain person were there to share it with you. That certain person is your friend, or at least someone you want to be your friend.

2. Step one reliably determines someone you want as a friend. This second step determines whether or not someone reciprocates and actually is your friend. It's obvious enough: if that certain person would want to be with you at the party or delving into a new book or at the top of the trail—and in fact often is so with you—he or she is your friend.

Like all good tests (and, truth be told, not unlike Aristotle's and Aquinas's philosophy of friendship), this one has some corollaries. There are degrees of friendship, even real or true friendships. One way to identify the deepest, most endurable friendships is to turn part one over and play its flip side. Think of times of trial, of humiliation or anxiety or despair, when you knew you hurt desperately and were going to hurt for some time, and nothing and no one could take away the pain. But you also knew that the presence of a certain person would somehow help you through it. And that certain person would willingly be (or perhaps was) there with you through such times.

That certain person is not only a true friend but among the most important friends in your life.

The upshot of all this is clear. A friend is someone whose presence can only sustain and enhance our life. A friend is someone we make ourselves available to and who makes himself or herself available in turn. The richest, most important friendships cannot persist on a diet of only phone calls or e-mail messages. At least on occasions our friends must be there with us, beside us, to share our joys and help us bear our trials. We need to be able to look directly into their eyes, hear their voice, squeeze their shoulders. We need to be able to lay hold of them.

Groping for the Word

For Martin Luther, this kind of presence and availability is at the heart of the Eucharist. Luther called the sacrament the *objectum fidei*, the object of faith. As the last word in that phrase indicates, he understood internal, not directly visible faith as crucial in effectively apprehending the sacrament. But it is essential, Luther said, to recognize that the bread and wine are public and visible. The sacrament "*first* lies outside the heart and is presented to our eyes externally." It is objectively provided. The Eucharist does not begin or end in the individual heart or as a subjective invention of Jesus' followers. Christ visibly, publicly instituted the sacrament, saying, "Take, eat, this is my body," and "Do this in remembrance of me."

As a catholic and evangelical Christian, Luther interpreted the Eucharist in light of the Trinity. That is, he saw God as Father, Son, and Holy Spirit active in the eucharistic celebration. He was well aware that this God was present and active in all of creation. After all, this is the God who made the heavens and the earth and all their creatures, the God in whom "all things hold together" (Col. 1:17). So Christ is "present in all creatures," said Luther. He might be found "in stone, in fire, in water, or even in a rope, for he certainly is there." Yet without an interpretive clue, a key, a clear sign, we might miss or mistake his presence in creation. (We might, as many German Christians did, think we discern Christ and his way in Hitler's Third Reich;

we might see Jesus only in our affluence and never in our neighbor's poverty; we might delude ourselves that he calls us to "take up your cross and relax.") Thus Christ provided for the bread and wine as special, unique signs of his body and blood. So, said Luther, Christ does not wish that we seek him in creation "apart from the Word, and cast [ourselves] into the fire or the water, or hang [ourselves] on the rope. He is present everywhere, but he does not wish that you grope for him everywhere. Grope rather where the Word is, and there you will lay hold of him in the right way."

The sacraments dramatically demonstrate to us and remind us that the first, last, and always most important factor in our lived spirituality is God's action, God's Word in Christ. We as God's creatures can commune with God not because we seek but because God first sought us. The primacy of God's Word is made especially clear in one of Luther's discussions of infant baptism.

> The unchanging Word of God, once spoken in the first baptism, ever remains standing, so that afterwards they [children baptized as infants] can come to faith in it, if they will, and the water with which they were baptized they can afterwards receive in faith, if they will. . . . [Yet] even if they contradict the Word a hundred times, it still remains the Word spoken in the first baptism [the baptism of Jesus by John the Baptist]. Its power does not derive from the fact that it is repeated many times or is spoken anew, but from the fact that it was commanded [by Christ] once to be spoken.

The prior and always precedent action of God is what makes baptism "a strong and sure foundation." Certainly one should "add faith to baptism." But we are not to base baptism on a ground as slippery, brittle, and often confused as our own faith. Luther is clear. "If I am baptized on [God's] bidding I know for certain that I am baptized. Were I to be baptized [merely] on my own faith, I might tomorrow find myself unbaptized, if faith failed me, or I became worried that I might not yesterday have had the faith rightly." He can put the matter even more emphatically: "We can and must constantly maintain that God will not deal with us except through his external Word and sacrament. Whatever is attributed to the Spirit apart from the Word and sacrament is of the devil." It is God's decisive action in Christ, once for all in ancient Palestine and now rehearsed and made present in the sacraments of baptism and Eucharist, that grounds Christian spirituality. The always precedent working of God supports Luther's faith, his confidence that even if he were somehow to find himself thrown "into the depths of hell" and "in the midst of devils, I would believe that I would be saved because I have been baptized, I have been absolved, I have received the pledge of my salvation, the body and blood of the Lord in the Supper."

Thus the Eucharist, celebrated in light of and as part of the biblical story, and enlivened by the Holy Spirit, is how we regularly grasp or lay hold of Christ. It is the key for reading our lives and world rightly. It is the provided, objective way Christ makes himself present and available to us. By it, not fire, we are taken into the life of Christ's body. By it, not the hanging rope, we take hold of (and are taken hold by) God in Christ. "This does not mean that [Christ] is not present in other places also with his body and blood," said Luther, "for in believing hearts he is completely present with his body and blood. But it means that he wishes to make us certain as to where and how we are to lay hold of him."

Like any real, living friend, then, Christ gifts us with his presence and allows himself to be laid hold of. But he wants to ensure that it really is him we lay hold of, and not some misguided notion we may sometimes hold of what and who he should be. Friends objectively exist. They are bodily and spiritually external to us. They are their own people, not our clones or products of our imagination. It is often pleasing, indeed, to have friends be like me, but ultimately they cannot really be friends or enrich my life without being other than me. I can try to please myself anytime. I can talk to myself incessantly and always say exactly what I want to hear. But one acute form of loneliness is growing sick and tired of my own company. Without others who are genuinely other, I can only remain a stagnant and puny self. Without others, I in my self-destructive sinfulness surely will consume myself. So—and especially because for Christians he is the Friend above all friends—Jesus Christ in the sacrament stands apart from us and comes to us.

The Real Presence of Christ

And how does Christ come to us in the Eucharist? Obviously Jesus of Nazareth does not present himself in his preresurrection, ordinary human body. The church has never claimed or expected that an olive-skinned, five-feet-two-inch first-century Jew will appear at the altar in the middle of its eucharistic celebrations. Instead, it has taken seriously the resurrection convictions I sketched in earlier chapters. The resurrected body is not an ordinary human body. It is not *less* than physical, in our typical usage of that term, but it is *more* than physical. We might, borrowing from a contemporary scholar, profitably think of it as "transphysical," a marvelously transformed physical body. Moreover, it is the transphysical body of no ordinary man but that of Christ, the Savior of the world and Second Person of the Trinity. Christ has died and been resurrected to a new body: this is the conviction and hope of orthodox Christian spirituality. But Christ has also been "highly exalted" and given "the name that is above every name" (Phil 2:9): a status and being that are not and never will be possessed by any other. It is the risen and exalted Christ who is really present at the Eucharist.

Biblically understood, the power of life is in the blood. By modern scientific means, we know that circulating blood carries oxygen and nutrients (that is, life) to all parts of the body. But even the ancients could observe that when the blood is poured out, the body weakens and dies. They saw that blood enables us to live as earthly creatures. And they recognized that we are able to be seen and known by others in our body. Contemporary films about the spirits of the dead, such as *Ghost* or *The Sixth Sense*, glance at this point interestingly. Ghosts stranded on everyday earth are isolated and lonely exactly because they are without a body; they typically cannot be seen or touched or heard. Bodiless, they cannot communicate with the living.

So in the Last Supper Jesus identifies his internal energy and life (his blood) with the red wine and his external, observable, social and relational self (his body) with the bread. In so many words—and actions—he is saying to the disciples, "Even when I have left you and ascended into heaven, you will through this ceremony continue to draw on my life-giving power and really know me as fully as you have known me in my ordinary bodily presence."

Again, and of course, we do not in the Eucharist see and touch Jesus as Peter or Andrew saw and touched him on a Galilean shore. But we do see and touch Christ as he is now is—risen and exalted, human and divine. We see and touch him in the bread and wine, his (transphysical) body and life. As John Willliamson Nevin wrote,

> [The Eucharist] is not simply an occasion, by which the soul of the believer may be excited to pious feelings and desires; but it embodies the actual presence of the grace it represents in its own constitution; and this grace is not simply the promise of God on which we are encouraged to rely, but the very life of the Lord Jesus Christ himself. We communicate, in the Lord's Supper, . . . with the living Saviour himself, in the fulness of his glorified person, made present to us for the purpose of the power of the Holy [Spirit].

There is more. We see and touch Christ in the bread and wine, but, no less important, we also see and touch him in those gathered with us around his table. The baptized who now partake of the Eucharist are grafted into Christ, made members of his body. Christ in an essential, nonnegotiable sense remains a distinct person, standing apart from his church. This important recognition is at work in the logic of the Christian tradition when it insists that Christ is always the "head" of the church. He is not just another member of the body, but as the head he is the master and source of the entire body and its (subordinate) parts. Still, the tradition is not bashful about asserting that the church really is Christ's body. Baptized, Christians are inducted into the community of God and reborn as new creations who now live and will die in Christ. At the Eucharist, Christians find their sustenance in the very life force of the risen and exalted Christ.

Consider this analogy. The acorn, a single "individual," is planted and grows into a great oak, living for a hundred years or more. Over this time it produces many more acorns, which in turn produce more trees—all, originally, from the single acorn. Similarly, humanity originates and springs from the single life of Adam. But Adam fell into sin and—like a harmful genetic strain introduced into an acorn—brought destruction into the life of all humanity. Just as all subsequent oaks will be mutant and misshapen until the harmful genetic strain is removed or transformed, humanity demands a radical cure. It remains mutant and cancerous until it is changed at its root or seed. As we have seen in Irenaeus and others, the Christian confession is that the human acorn or genetic strain was restored and transformed to true humanity in Christ. Baptism brings rebirth and incorporation into a new (social or corporate) body, that of Christ. In the Eucharist, it is that root or acorn, that animating principle, that living energy of Christ—springing from the individual (Jesus Christ) but, in the individual, made available and now spread to billions of people across centuries and continents—that we partake of and are nourished by.

This is, as the acorn and oak metaphor suggests, an organic process. It takes time and the overcoming of many obstacles for an acorn to grow into a mature oak. Likewise, as Nevin has it,

> we are not set over into this new order of existence [in Christ, as Christ's body] all at once. This would be magic. We are apprehended by it, in the first place, only as it were at a single point. But this point is central. The new life lodges itself, as an efflux from Christ, in the inmost core of our personality. Here it becomes the principle or seed of our sanctification which is simply the gradual transfusion of the same exalted spiritual quality or potence through our whole persons. The process terminates with our resurrection.

The Body Not Dismembered but Re-membered

The organic language I have been using is biblical language for the Eucharist and Christian spirituality. The apostle Paul, as in 1 Corinthians 12, talks about Christians as members of the body of Christ. John's Gospel, while it doesn't refer to acorns and oaks, uses an organic, horticultural trope to suggest Jesus is the "true vine" onto which we, the branches, are grafted and nurtured in order that we might "bear fruit" (John 15). But there is another sort of biblical language that can complement and deepen our understanding of Christ's real presence in and through the Eucharist. It is the language I used in the last chapter, the language of memory and remembrance.

In what the church calls the institution narrative, Jesus introduced his holy meal with the words "Take, eat: This is my body, which is given for you. Do this for the remembrance of me." As we have noted, in some Protestant traditions, and especially in the train of the modern emphasis on individualistic subjectivity, this "remembrance" can be understood in a rather pale and diluted fashion. That is, it becomes simply the individual communicant's memory of and meditation on Christ's Last Supper and sacrifice on the cross. Such an approach weakens recognition of God's precedent, initiating action in the sacrament and disallows Christ's real presence. Yet it seems to comport accurately and naturally with our typical usage of the language of remembrance. We think of remembering as a mental, cogitative process and believe whatever memory produces exists only inside our head. (I recollect my deceased grandfather and can "see" and "hear" him, but only in my imagination or head.) Does the biblical language of remembrance mean anything more than this?

The biblical Greek term we translate as "remembrance" is *anamnesis*, and it does indeed mean much more than a psychological recall of past occurrences. It has been famously remarked that God is in the details; now I will suggest that sometimes God is in the hyphens. Biblical and liturgical scholars tell us that in the Bible, *anamnesis* and its cognates carry the sense of "re-calling" or "re-presenting" before God a past event, so that the past event becomes operative and alive in the here and now. The hyphens make a difference. To "re-call," as when a mother beckons her children a second or third time, is to expect the called one to arrive. To "re-present" is to make present again.

Plumbing the depths of *anamnesis* requires noting that this re-calling and re-presenting is done "before God." That is, it is not only we human participants in the sacrament who are reminded to bring out of memory Jesus Christ's sacrifice and victory. God too—or, really, first and foremost—is "reminded." So has it always been in the history of Israel and the church. In the third chapter of Exodus, for example, God hears the groaning and straining of God's enslaved people and then remembers the covenant with Abraham, Isaac, and Jacob. It is then that God acts to resume the initiative of the covenant made with Israel's forefathers. Or consider the common Israelite prayer form, as instanced in Psalm 25:7: "According to your steadfast love remember me, for your goodness' sake, O LORD!" In the Old Testament God's remembering is not merely or even primarily an isolated or insulated event within God's "psyche" (if we could so speak). Instead, God's remembering occurs as God hears and answers Israel's cries and laments—their prayers. When God remembers, God's answer creates what it declares, just as God creates the heavens and the earth by fiat, by speaking them into existence.

God's words are accordingly the preeminent instance of performative speech. Performative speech is that talk that accomplishes what it says by the very act of its utterance, as the bride and groom who say "I do" thereby accomplish their marriage. In this vein, Christ is also fittingly designated as God's utterance or Word, God's performative and salvific address of broken creation. The performative power of divine speech was rightly discerned by the centurion petitioning the Lord on his sick servant's behalf: "Only speak the word, and my servant will be healed" (Matt. 8:8). Following this pattern, at the Eucharist we remember the Son to the Father, and by the Spirit the past event of salvation is re-presented, made a present event, alive and effective in our gathering.

This objective, formative, effective sacramental presence is evidenced repeatedly in New Testament eucharistic accounts. Given that all the New Testament texts were written after sacramental practices were instituted and were ongoing, it is illuminating to revisit eucharistic incidents and observe their objective effects. In John's Gospel, Jesus at the Last Supper declares that the one to whom he hands a piece of bread will betray him. Then he dips bread and hands it to Judas. When Judas takes the bread, Satan enters "into him" (John 13:27). That is, whatever Judas's subjective state at the moment, Jesus' words and ritualistic act occasion Judas's overwhelming by evil. More famously, two disciples meet the resurrected Lord on the road to Emmaus but do not recognize him. He walks some distance with them, doing a bit of peripatetic Bible study, yet they remain ignorant of his identity. It is only at dinner, when the risen Christ takes, blesses, breaks, and gives bread to them, that their eyes are "opened" and they recognize their host as the beloved Jesus (Luke 24:30–31). Here, despite subjective states of (we might suppose) weariness and wariness, a graceful eucharistic performance enables the disciples to recognize Jesus' presence. Finally, consider Paul's assertion that hasty, inconsiderate, and careless conduct of the Eucharist in the Corinthian community has brought on some all too objective conditions of weakness, illness, and even death (1 Cor. 11:27–33). A fearful thing: God may answer our prayers even when we really don't want that.

When We Are Not Really Present

So, as I have said, the first, last, and most important thing to recognize about the Eucharist is that in and through it God objectively acts. Something of the above, rooted in biblical language of living organisms and remembrance, is what the Christian tradition means when it insists on Christ's real presence in and through the Eucharist. The Eucharist is not simply commemorative, an aid and spur to our memory and meditation. At the same time, our response (or lack of response) to God's preceding presence and action matters. The Eucharist is not magic or mechanical. Its power and efficacy can be blocked or rendered ineffective to any particular participant in the Eucharist. Christ objectively offers his body and blood in the Eucharist, but to receive it we must respond with faith. As some in the tradition have put it, faith is the stomach of the sacrament. Imagine the most nutritious, energizing meal possible—perhaps vegetable and fruit, some source of protein, an excellent juice for drink. The food is really there and really nutritious. But if someone approaches it with no stomach—or with a damaged or off-kilter stomach that cannot receive and digest food—he will not be able to avail himself of the life-giving sustenance and benefits of the meal. Just so, Christ is really present in and through the Eucharist, but without faith his presence and grace may not be received. To sustain biological life, physical food must be ingested, received into the stomach, and from it absorbed into the body. To sustain spiritual life, the body and blood of the Lord must also be ingested, received into the stomach of faith.

As Nevin puts it, "The force of the sacrament is the sacrament itself. Our faith is needed, only as the condition that is required to make room for it in our souls."

Thus faith, the heartfelt trust of Christ as the Son of God and Savior of humanity, is significant and even necessary. But it is secondary. How much more secondary and less important, then, is the moment-by-moment consciousness, mental awareness, or mood of the faithful as they gather and participate in the celebration of the Eucharist. Obviously it is best to come to the Eucharist concentrated on the celebration, confident of God's love, with staunch resolve to live every day in grateful obedience to the gospel. (As one eucharistic prayer puts it, "Deliver us from the presumption of coming to this Table for solace only, and not for strength; for pardon only, and not for renewal.") But it is a reality that at times I approach the Eucharist tired or distracted or bored. And at times I approach it with less than vigorous resolve to turn away from a known sin. Often (thank God) my spirit is moved at Eucharist, and another step of healing is taken or new energy is given for resolve to be changed more and more into a Christ-bearer. But not always and not immediately, by any means. On those occasions has God not acted, or has Christ failed to be present—at least to me? Classical Christian spirituality respects individual intentionality in worship: there certainly is good cause and advantage for me (for each and all of us) to approach the Eucharist alertly and resolutely. But, thank God, grace prevails over my weakness: God is fully present even when I am not. When I participate in the Eucharist, I participate as part of a *community* that God has constituted and resolved to meet. So when at Eucharist my attention wanders or I nurse resentment and my mind is elsewhere, it is better to say that I have failed to be (completely) present than to say God was absent from the entire gathering.

The Various Bodies at the Eucharist

It seems worthwhile, in closing this chapter, to remark on how the classical understanding and practice of the Eucharist comprehends and comports with the Christian spirituality I have tried to describe earlier in this book. Engaged by the tradition, I have insisted that orthodox Christian spirituality is animated by the work of the Holy Spirit in history, particularly the history of Israel, Jesus Christ, and the church. The Eucharist flows out of and rehearses exactly this history, filled as it is with biblical words and gestures. Again engaged by the tradition, I have insisted that Christian spirituality vitally includes our physical bodies. The Eucharist engages our physical body as we listen, speak in response, stand, kneel, cup our hands in reception of the bread, and taste the eucharistic wine in our mouth. Also engaged by the tradition, I have said Christian spirituality is fundamentally social—it begins and ends in community. The Eucharist is a communal celebration: a minister alone cannot celebrate a proper Eucharist. She or he must be joined by others, since Christ's body is not simply present in the bread and wine but in its gathered members.

The Eucharist, then, is a sensuous ritual, a celebration of the community (and individuals in community) at which the risen and exalted Christ is really, truly present. It is fair enough to say that Christ is *spiritually* present, especially when we want to avoid any erroneous notions of cannibalism or magic. But the spiritual, understood Christianly, does not stand at odds with the physical and the historical and social. What it does is comprehend and transpose all of these, casting them into a new octave or key: the key of life, the key of hope for the entire cosmos. Humble in some respects, the Eucharist is actually the grandest and most ambitious dining ritual we can undertake. It is meant to change us, but first to change the world.

6

THE SACRIFICE
OF COMPASSION

Christian Spirituality
and the Benefits
of the Eucharist

Because I could not read, I almost failed first grade.

A country rearing, coupled with an acutely bashful disposition, made mine a withdrawn and largely solitary early childhood. I became most comfortable with the companions of my imagination, the company of my thoughts. This inner life became rich and capacious. Today when I return to the farmhouse of my origins and its surrounding flat, treeless pastures, I see the dullness and monotony of the terrain. But with only a little work I can summon up tinges of the magic I found while hiking those same pastures as a boy, making of the occasional rattlesnake, jackrabbit, and prairie dog a zoo all the better for being uncaged and unpredictable. The sagebrush and yucca plants became my forest, harboring their own verdant secrets—at dusk they cast long, haunting shadows. For a lone, imaginative boy, the occasional pond teemed with exotica and potential for adventure. There were frogs and turtles and water bugs to be pursued and captured, and I might as well have been stalking big game on an African safari. The muddy water concealed its two- or three-foot shallowness and so for me could be as fathomless as an ocean and nearly as full of mysteries.

The limitations of remoteness and shyness, then, pushed me further into the depths of the dusty little world I inhabited and honed senses of wonder and curiosity that could magnify the spare grain of my surroundings. But they were real limitations, such that starting school was a terrible trial. I feared strangers. I was afraid of being humiliated by my clumsiness and of even mere notice in the eyes of child or adult. The school bus driver wore the first mustache I had ever laid eyes on, so that I could describe it to my parents only as "an eyebrow over his lip." Though he was a kind man, the displaced eyebrow made the driver assume sinister shades for me. Some mornings my father carried me crying and squirming down the sidewalk and onto the bus.

The new surroundings at school disoriented me. I was terrified of being called on to perform in any small way. The prospect of reading aloud in front of teachers and other students, or doing arithmetic at the blackboard, seemed hardly preferable to facing a firing squad. I think the overload of alien stimuli and constant dread of failure froze my mind for the entire school year. At the end of it, the teacher called in my mother for a visit and suggested that I repeat first grade. The teacher was particularly concerned with my meager progress in learning to read and did not see how further schooling could be effective without a shoring up of that foundation.

The threat of her son's being flunked, as it was then so resoundingly put, galvanized my mother. She certainly agreed that I must learn how to read, and she committed herself to my sufficient preparation for second grade over the three months of summer vacation. She drilled me daily with flashcards and phonics. She subscribed to a children's book club and sat with me for hours as I struggled with those stubborn, unyielding marks on the page. Out from under the gaze of teacher and other unfamiliars, I found courage to grapple with letters and pronunciations and syntax. I gradually learned to look for and purchase footholds in the cliff's face of language which, weeks earlier, I could only slide down in mute terror. I relaxed, my mind thawed, and books opened up to me as bountifully as the dusky ponds in the pastures behind the house. Before summer's end, trips to the mailbox were breathtaking pilgrimages, with hopes on the way that the box would open to a new book from the club.

I entered, then, into second grade, and midway through the year I announced that I wanted someday to be a writer. In third grade, staying in from recess with another young author named Sharon Barkley, I wrote my first book. And so it went, on through junior high, high school, college, and graduate school, to what is by now a twenty-five-year career in magazine and book publishing.

In some salient ways the Eucharist bears comparison to reading. To learn how to read, I had to accept a discipline much bigger than me. Reading was not invented for my pleasure. So long as I could focus only on myself and my fears, reading yielded no benefits for me. There was no escaping the demands and hard work of learning how to read. But once my mother successfully inducted me into the discipline, it—though still much bigger and not existing just for me—gifted me with unending wonders and discoveries. In crucial ways, it became nothing less than the basis of my life and work. Likewise, the Eucharist was not invented just for me (or you). To participate well in the Eucharist as a mature Christian requires long learning in the biblical story and practice of the customs of the church. And just as reading was not (and still is not) always fun, participation at the Eucharist can be hard, at times drudgery. Yet once I have learned participation in the Eucharist and learned to appreciate it as a discipline not simply centered on me or my pleasure, it benefits me and my spiritual life immeasurably.

Especially in our consumer-oriented society, talk of benefits can turn any practice or even person into solipsistic instruments of private pleasure. Nevertheless, the Christian tradition has spoken boldly and often of the benefits of the Eucharist to the spiritual life. I will employ the traditional language but, particularly in our consumerized world, want to emphasize that the Eucharist—like all of our worship or prayer—is not our instrument or tool. Worship is first and foremost the service of God and needs no other justification. If I (or you) come

to the Eucharist primarily to be benefited, then we will hardly be
benefited, because then we will be back to concentrating on ourselves
rather than God. That said, and without further qualification, I now
turn to the benefits of Holy Communion. What does the Eucharist
do in the world, to our lives?

Eucharistic Citizenship

Perhaps the most basic effect or aspect of the Eucharist is that
its celebration constitutes the body of Christ in the world. Classical
Christians have noted that many grains of wheat gathered make
one loaf of bread. So too, they have said, the many individuals who
come to Eucharist and encircle Christ's table, partaking of a single
loaf, are made a body.

As I remarked in chapter 3, we human beings cannot become full
persons outside membership in a communal body (or bodies). Our
individual lives can mean little or nothing outside incorporation
into a tradition and community that is bigger than any individual,
that precedes the individual's birth and will go on after her death.
Without traditions and communities to ground and guide us, we are
simply lost. Of course, there are such things as bad (and even evil)
traditions and communities. Racism is sustained through institutions
such as the Ku Klux Klan and Nazi skinhead gangs, for example.
Stalin's communism gave millions of Russians a project bigger and
apparently grander than themselves yet proved horrifically destructive. So it is possible to find social groundings and remain lost—or
perhaps become even more desperately lost. The letter to the Ephesians suggests such is the case for all Gentiles. We who are Gentiles
were lost before Christ. We were "aliens from the commonwealth
of Israel, and strangers to the covenants of promise, having no hope
and without God in the world" (Eph. 2:12). We may have had communities with which we sought survival, purpose, and even some
kind of immortality, but they were not true communities. They were
not communities built on the truth, on the peace and justice of the
God of Israel, the King and Maker of heaven and earth. "But now
in Christ Jesus you who once were far off have been brought near

by the blood of Christ. . . . So then you are no longer strangers and aliens, but you are citizens with the saints and also members of the household of God" (Eph. 2:13, 19).

Surely Martin Luther had this passage in mind when he wrote of the Eucharist, "To receive this sacrament in bread and wine, then, is nothing else than to receive a sure sign of this fellowship and incorporation with Christ and all saints. It is as if a citizen were given a sign, a document, or some other token to assure him that he is a citizen of a city, a member of that particular community." Even today, an immigrant ceases being an "alien" and is "naturalized" as a full citizen once she undergoes a ceremony and receives papers documenting her official belonging. For Luther, the Christian's documentation of naturalization, of full humanity and citizenship in the body of Christ, is participation in the Eucharist. Just as citizenship papers make national belonging real and final, participation in the Eucharist constitutes and reconstitutes the church and makes all its partakers members of a single body. And just as a resident of a city shares with "all the others the city's name, honor, freedom, trade, customs, usage, help, support, protection, and the like," Christians at the Eucharist enact and practice a like sharing of name, honor, freedom, customs, support, and so forth.

"In times past," Luther observes, "this sacrament was so properly used, and the people were taught to understand this fellowship so well, that they even gathered food and material goods in the church, and there—as St. Paul writes in 1 Corinthians 11:23—distributed them those who were in need." The rituals and customs of a nation shape its citizens: Americans learn and practice what it means to be Americans through Thanksgiving dinners and Independence Day festivities. Likewise, Luther expects that, properly formed by the Eucharist, Christians will "help the poor, put up with sinners, care for the sorrowing, suffer with the suffering, intercede for others, defend the truth, and at the risk of [their own] life, property, and honor seek the betterment of the church and of all Christians."

So the Eucharist gives, renews, and shapes life in a community of truth, justice, and peace. With this comes reason to live, hope for our children and grandchildren and those of our neighbors, courage in the face of difficulty and enmity, and a sense of proportion about our suffering. Yet the church, when true to itself and its Lord, is not turned in on itself. It is not one more sect in a divided world, granting its members identity and excitement by eagerly delineating our "us" versus a series of hated and feared "thems." Instead of the all-too-easy and popular way of the world, which is to secure a communal future by sacrificing enemies, the Eucharist teaches and forms the church to sacrifice itself for the sake of the world. And in that sacrifice, of course, to gain its own life.

The True Meaning of Sacrifice

The language of sacrifice is unpopular in our contemporary world, and not without good reason. Too many times sacrifice has been demanded of others, usually those possessing less power than those eager to demand sacrifice. Any language can be misused, and we do well to remain suspicious of such use of the language of sacrifice. Yet sacrifice still makes a certain sense to most of us. To learn to read, I had to repeatedly sacrifice my immediate comfort. Was the sacrifice worth it? Many times over. So, too, parents willingly sacrifice for their children. They forgo acquisitions and extended vacations to clothe and educate their offspring. But anyone who has been a parent knows how much a child's success and own contribution can more than repay sacrifice. A parent's love, joy, and sense of accomplishment can increase through and with her child.

"Sacrifice" is hateful and abhorrent when it means I will take what is yours and leave you with nothing. But in classical Christian spirituality, sacrifice is a language of abundance rather than scarcity. That abundance flows from the life of God. The trinitarian God creates the world not out of any lack or need but out of surplus, out of overflowing grace. Ancient Mesopotamian creation myths, rife in the world surrounding Israel, repeatedly have the gods making human beings so that humans will slave at planting and irrigating crops, thus providing food for the gods. The biblical God, however, needs nothing from human beings. God does not "eat the flesh of bulls, or drink the blood of goats" (Ps. 50:13). As the source and sustainer of all life, how could God need what we offer back from God's own provision? As St. Augustine puts it, "No one is going to say that he does any service to a spring by drinking from it, or to the light by beholding it." Accordingly, sacrifice is not for God's sake but for the good of the sacrificer and human community, "the intention of which is that we may cleave to God and seek the good of our neighbour for the same end." The sacrifice God expects is the "sacrifice of thanksgiving" (Ps. 50:14). God is not pleased with a sacrifice of calves, rams, and other treasures—even to "tens of thousands of rivers of oil." Instead, sacrifice true to Christian spirituality is a life dedicated to doing justice, loving kindness, and "walking humbly with God" (Micah 6:6–8). In the New Testament, the "sacrifice of praise" and thanksgiving includes doing good and "shar[ing] what you have" (Heb. 13:15–16).

The Eucharist, of course, is exactly this kind of sacrifice. *Eucharist* literally means "Great Thanksgiving." At the Eucharist we offer up our treasure (money as well as bread and wine, all fruits and symbols of our labor). We share bread and wine with those who come to the table, regardless of their class, race, gender, or any other characteristics that might be made marks of merit. In these ways we rehearse, with body and spirit alike, a life born of abundance and sustained by generosity. This is what the apostle Paul means what he exhorts us "to present your bodies as a living sacrifice, holy and acceptable to God" (Rom. 12:1). To offer our bodies "as a living sacrifice" is not a matter of laying out throat-slit corpses on an altar. It is a matter of devoting our living souls and bodies to the good of all.

So the ritual and celebration of the Eucharist is a rehearsal of compassion. An act of compassion done for the sake of God is a sacrifice, in the best, most deeply Christian sense of the word. The Eucharist reveals to us the true shape and pattern of the world. It shows us the world as God means the world to be done. This is a world in which sharing only multiplies abundance and increases the fullness of life for all, much as a second child in a family does not thin out the parental love formerly focused on a single child but creates more love to go around. And the Eucharist does not only show us the pattern of God's generosity. Even more important, it inducts or incorporates us into the world as it was "wonderfully created, and yet more wonderfully restored" in Jesus Christ. By no means, then, is the Eucharist an insulated or self-contained ceremony. Just as the drills of a basketball coach are meant to be carried out of practice and into the game, the skills learned in eucharistic "drills" are meant to be carried out of gathered worship and into the surrounding world. In Augustine's words,

> The true sacrifices are acts of compassion, whether towards ourselves or towards our neighbours, when they are directed toward God; and acts of compassion are intended to free us from misery and thus bring us to happiness. . . . This being so, it immediately follows that the whole redeemed community, that is to say, the congregation and the fellowship of the saints, is offered to God as a universal sacrifice, through the great Priest who offered himself in his suffering for us—so that we might be the body of so great a head—under the "form of a servant" (Phil. 2:7). . . . This is the reality, and [Christ] intended [the Eucharist] of the church to be a sacramental symbol of this; the church, being the body of which he is the head, learns to offer itself through him.

When the Trees and Animals Come to Church

The sacrifice I have been discussing, certainly crucial to the Eucharist, is a sacrifice of compassion by and for humanity. But it would narrow the Eucharist's scope if we do not see this sacrifice encompassing all of earthly creation—rocks, trees, skies, seas, and animals as well as people. After all, it is not only the human creation that was created by and can serve God. The eucharistic celebration includes creation by taking up the natural elements of grain, grapes, and water. Bread and wine are products of human culture, but not merely of human culture. There can be no bread without grain sprung from the earth, then ground and mixed into bread. There can be no wine without grapes, a fruit of the earth, harvested and then fermented into wine. Much as bread and wine stand in for the body and blood of Christ, they also stand in for or represent all the beauty, bounty, and potential of earthly creation.

The flora and fauna of creation are good in and of themselves. They exist first and foremost not for human use or enjoyment but for God's pleasure. At the same time, it is romantic foolishness to imagine that human presence and industry will not affect wider ecology. Even the humblest agriculture alters the landscape. And from some point in the nineteenth century onward, the largest share of energy controlled or shepherded by the human race switched from agriculture to the construction and maintenance of urban (and later suburban) habitats. Geologists now calculate that humanity, especially in its great numbers and urbanized concentrations, arguably "sculpts" the landscape more profoundly than such gargantuan natural phenomena as earthquakes, sea-floor spreading, and mountain erosion. Add to this the massive atmospheric effects of the burning of fossil fuels, and it is clear that humanity bears an awesome responsibility for the good or ill of natural ecology.

In classical Christian spirituality this responsibility is a priestly responsibility. The stuff of creation cannot realize its full potential apart from its human cultivation and development. In this sense human beings are the priests of creation. Put simply, priests are mediators between God and creation. Priests mediate God's will and ways to creation, and they mediate the needs, concerns, and praise of creation back to God. So Israel is called out as "priestly kingdom" (Exod. 19:6), and the church is declared a "royal priesthood" (1 Peter 2:9). When they are true to their biblical roles, Israel and the church call all humanity to its rightful priesthood—to live humanly is to live in the light of God, on behalf of all creation.

Accordingly, in Genesis 1 woman and man are made in God's image and set in "dominion over the fish of the sea, and over the birds of the air, and over the cattle, and over all the wild animals of the earth." They are called to "fill the earth and subdue it" (Gen. 1:26, 28). The language of "dominion" and "subduing" can carry a harsh accent and in fact has been used to justify wasteful exploitation of the earth and its creatures. But in biblical context, it is not meant as permission or command to pillage and rape creation. Instead, men and women are meant to be priestly stewards of creation, cultivating and nurturing it so it might achieve its true potential. To "fill the earth" is partly to see flora and fauna prosper and spread in their great diversity and richness. The earth at creation is new, young, and raw. To reach its intended, splendid maturity, it needs the priestly stewardship of gardening and husbanding. Through the splendor of its maturity, it will offer its own sacrifice of praise.

And all creation does want to offer up thanksgiving and praise to God. The psalmist features creation poised to praise God in all its variety, exhorting the praise of sun, moon, stars, fire, hail, snow, mounts, fruit trees and cedars, "wild animals and all cattle" (Ps. 148). Isaiah imagines mountains and hills ready to burst into song, the trees set to clap their hands (Isa. 55:12). Paul recognizes (with prophets before him) that nonhuman creation is oppressed by sin and groans in "futility" but "waits with eager longing" to be "set free from its bondage to decay" (Rom. 8:18–24). Such texts suggest creation may be capable of praising God exactly along the lines so beautifully expressed by the Christian poet Gerard Manley Hopkins.

> As kingfishers catch fire, dragonflies draw flame;
> As tumbled over rim in roundy wells
> Stones ring; like each tucked string tells, each hung bell's
> Bow sung finds tongue to fling out broad its name;
> Each mortal thing does one thing and the same:
> Deals out that being indoors each one dwells;
> Selves—goes itself; *myself* it speaks and spells,
> Crying *What I do is me: for that I came.*

As Hopkins intimates, "each mortal thing" praises God by being itself. The clean river, teeming with life (such as flaming dragonflies), is the river that most richly and fully praises and thanks God. The priestly stewarded prairie (not the polluted one) is the one that may ascend to the ideal of "prairieness" intended by God and so realize its praise by achieving its potential. So may humanity either loosen and free the tongue of creation for its own Eucharist or fill and stop creation's throat with death. We can give creation voice for praise by helping it to be itself, in its "wildness" but also in its cultivation and intentional development. Noticing that Revelation 5:8 pictures angels in heaven taking up harps made by the hands of men and women, Karl Barth remarks, "Surely the playing of musical instruments is a . . . human attempt to articulate before God this sound of a cosmos which is otherwise dumb. Surely the perfect musician is one who, particularly stirred by the angels, is best able to hear not merely the voice of his own heart but what all creation is trying to say, and can then in great humility and with great objectivity cause it to be heard by God and other men."

So instrument builders and musicians are, at their best, premier exemplars of priestly stewardship. Taking up wood and steel, they can fashion them into a guitar or violin, releasing from wood and steel a song with which they were already pregnant but could not otherwise have sung. Human ingenuity and craft can unlock the gifts of natural elements. They can free them to more completely be themselves and in that gracious being contribute to the inexhaustibly rich and beautiful praise of God. Properly tending creation, then, we allow and add instruments to the swelling, magnificent orchestra and chorus that is all of creation's prayer. To prepare for the Eucharist, we as priestly stewards make grain into bread and grapes into wine, thereby releasing otherwise unrealized possibilities of grain and grapes. At the Eucharist we carry these representative, culturally developed elements of nature into our celebration—a celebration that, by the inclusion of the elements, is that celebration not just by or of humanity but of all creation. The benefit, if that is not too puny a word, should be apparent to anyone who has ever gasped at a lakeside sunset, savored a fine wine, or wept in joy at the strains of a song.

The Eucharist and Encouragement

Taking account of the social and even cosmic, ecological dimensions of the Eucharist, we are in position to properly appreciate its other, derivative benefits for each of us as individual worshipers. The Eucharist is a communal rehearsal and re-presentation of cosmic redemption. Included in it, I (or you) am given strength and confidence in the gift of the forgiveness of my sins. I see and know that I am not alone, that I have not and will not be abandoned. Think of the soldier poised against an advancing army. When she sees her own army gathered, standing tall, her hope and confidence soar. Left alone, she is overwhelmed and beaten before the first bullet is fired.

Quite apart from such a dramatic, explicitly life-and-death situation, I know that my convictions and hope can waver, can falter. Facing opposition and difficulty in a project at work, for instance, I can fret long and hard in the solitude of my office. I begin to wonder if I have it wrong—maybe the project should be undertaken differently or is a (my) bad idea altogether. I mull over previous discussions and arguments. I think about what I should have said or done otherwise. I rehearse some stinging rejoinders from colleagues and begin to think I really may be incompetent. Worse, perhaps I am too demanding or am pushing only for my own way. Perhaps I have acted rudely or manipulatively. In other words, I think as my spirits sink, it may be that I am not just a bad worker but a horrible person.

Not discounting my possible need of correction, let's assume this particular project really is a worthy one. In that case, what will help me carry on is a sense that others also see it as worthy, that we will work together on it. And I can also use some tangible sign or token not only that the project under duress is of some worth but that I as a worker and person am of real worth. That sign may come in the form of an encouraging e-mail from my boss or a handwritten note from the president of the company. Then I am apt to savor and even save the e-mail or note, at least for a while, returning to it and rereading when my spirits again sag.

The Eucharist is just such a communal encouragement of my Christian convictions and practices. Besides seeing the gathered faces of those who share my convictions, in the Eucharist I see and grasp the body and blood of Jesus Christ. The bread and wine are palpable signs of my salvation, "tokens" that I am a worker and person of genuine worth. And in a hard world they are happily signs that I can return to again and again, much as I revisit the encouraging note at the office.

More than this, the sacraments are signs that participate in the reality that they symbolize. A stop sign is merely indicative—it could be any number of different colors or shapes, and it possesses no inherent quality of actual "stopness." (If stop signs were carved on granite boulders and put in the middle of roads, then they might intrinsically "participate" in stopness. But as we know them, stop signs communicate by social convention and nothing more.) My boss's encouraging note, however, and my wife's kiss are signs that participate in the realities they embody. The note participates in the reality of my boss's encouragement; my wife's kiss is a sign of love largely by itself being an act of love. Similarly, the sacraments are signs that participate in the reality of Christ's presence and the communion of the Trinity. To eat and drink of these signs is to enter into Christ's presence, to enjoy the personal communion of the Father, Son, and Holy Spirit.

Of course we can and must cling to internal and "invisible" faith. But we are people, not angels. Unlike angels, we do not gaze directly on the majesty of God. And unlike angels, we are bodily creatures in need of bodily sustenance and encouragement. Faith and confidence themselves, internal or psychological and "spiritual" as they are, demand embodiment. Luther, tormented as he was by an accusing conscience, recognized that the heart is "much more tenuous and elusive than [the] bread" of the sacrament. When in doubt, when discouraged, when continued introspection offers me nothing more than a spiral of confusion and anxiety, I can bite down on the bread and taste the wine. Then, even when I cannot "see" it or feel it in my heart, I can rest assured that the Spirit has not fled me, that Christ still comes into my presence.

In and through the sacrament God comes alongside to help me bear my worry and fear. But in the sacrament Christ also surrounds me with other members of his body. The Christian haunted by sin or death, Luther said, should

> go joyfully to the sacrament of the altar and lay down his woe in the midst of the community and seek help from the entire company of the spiritual body—just as a citizen whose property has suffered damage or misfortune at the hands of his enemies makes complaint to his town council and fellow citizens and asks them for help. The immeasurable grace and mercy of God are given us in this sacrament to the end that we might put from us all misery and tribulation and lay it upon the community, especially on Christ. Then we may with joy find strength and comfort.

Particular churches may ensure that the burdens are laid upon the community in a variety of ways. At my own parish, prayers and anointing for healing are available during the Eucharist. Partakers of the sacrament may rise from receiving the bread and wine and proceed to an alcove where their specific concerns will be heard and met in further ministry. Small groups and "prayer chains" are other avenues for allowing members to share their specific trials (and joys). However it is done, it is important that the Eucharist be particularized, that individuals can bring to and from it their daily struggles and hopes. Then we will realize a priceless benefit of the Eucharist, being vitally assured that "the immeasurable grace and mercy of God are given us in this sacrament."

Resurrection Food

It is in and as a body, obviously, that you or I partake of the Eucharist. And in a truly final sense, our bodies participate in the grace and mercy mediated by the sacrament. The Eucharist not only is a present meal, strength for the journey today, but is a preparatory meal. It prepares us for the expected resurrection of our bodies. The Christian tradition has explicitly recognized this benefit of the Eucharist. Ignatius, for instance, famously called the sacrament "the medicine of immortality, the antidote of death."

We may be tempted to dismiss such language as hopelessly primitive, magical in the crudest sense. Are we to expect the sacramental bread and wine to be absorbed like marvelous antibiotics into our bloodstream, somehow killing death as if it were a bacterium? I doubt Ignatius had quite so literal a view. In any event, we will do better to return to an earlier metaphor of this book. I have suggested that in the new heaven and earth our resurrected bodies will be so transformed that they will be sustained by the very love and power of God. Sustenance as we now know it will be, comparatively, junk food: not really all that tasty and relatively empty of nutrition. Just as the eucharistic celebration foreshadows the eschatological wedding banquet of the Lamb, then, the eucharistic elements foreshadow the fare on that banquet table. The sacramental bread and wine are the grace and life of Christ. Consuming them, we partake of inexhaustible food and living drink—a repast that will leave us never hungry or thirsty and that nourishes eternal life (John 4:7–15). So, said Irenaeus, our bodies, "when they partake of the Eucharist, are no longer mortal, having hope of resurrection to the life everlasting."

The sick woman spites and staves off death so long as she can eat and hold down her food. At the Eucharist we consume a food that does not just stave off death but vanquishes it. This is one last benefit of the Eucharist, one more reason our forebears in Christian spirituality rushed again and again to the feast of the Great Thanksgiving.

PART TWO

CLASSICAL CHRISTIAN SPIRITUALITY IN THE LIGHT (AND DARKNESS) OF THE 21ST CENTURY

7

SIN AND SALVATION
AT GRACELAND

*The Difficulties
of Christian Spirituality
in Elvis World*

In the first part of this book I have striven to lay out the rudiments of classical, orthodox, or traditional Christian spirituality. The Christian tradition is not a dead museum piece, so I have never pretended to offer anything other than an account from the perspective, and in light of the interests, of a Western twenty-first-century believer. But I have kept my eyes mainly on the classical sources of Scripture, the church fathers, and later exemplars who clearly stood in this line of Christian orthodoxy. In the second part of this book, I will shift focus somewhat. While seeking to depart not at all from classical Christian spirituality, I will look more intently than before on our contemporary time and place and on how classical Christian spirituality may be most faithfully and effectively lived in this setting.

One thing is clear: the present is a time of profound, even epochal change. Commentators from various angles speak of a shift from Christendom to post-Christendom; from industrialism to post-industrialism (or the information economy); from colonial hegemony to multicultural pluralism (and more recently the new American imperialism); and from modernity to postmodernity. On global and national scales alike, the day in which we now live is not a settled period but one of monumental flux and ferment.

Arguments about how to best characterize this period in history are many, varied, and often hot as badgers dropped into a snake pit. It would require a truly angelic, nearly omniscient intellect to adjudicate these debates, drive to their heart, and settle on a single label that most adequately designates where the world is and where it is going. Anyone who has read this far will be abundantly satisfied that I possess no such angelic intellect. Fortunately, I am not trying to describe and recommend Christian spirituality for angels but for people. It behooves me, then, to stay as down to earth and concrete as I can. So I will resist temptations to rush off into technical, academic jargon and grandiosely insist which "post" is the most basic or determinative in the fence now thrown up around us. Instead, more humbly and manageably, I propose to designate our current time and place as Elvis World.

Why Elvis? Because the story of Elvis Presley is the story of one man, which will help keep us down to earth. But of course Presley was not just any man. He was without doubt one of the most well-known figures of the twentieth century and nearly three decades after his death remains one of the most famous persons into the twenty-first century. More specifically, Elvis was key to the formation of an eventually global culture of mass-mediated celebrity. If we now live in the age of the image, when surface personalities are painstakingly "invented," "reinvented," and promoted not just by movie stars but by politicians and business executives and pastors, the story of what this means and how it came about cannot be told without attention to Elvis Presley. If we now live in a world of virtual reality in which we cannot separate myth from fact and life itself becomes a form of entertainment, Elvis lived there first.

But Presley can also help us focus on the earlier, more central concerns of this book. His story suggests much about an ambivalent regard for the body. When he burst into fame in the mid-1950s,

Elvis attracted attention not least because of his physically antic, remarkably sensual stage performances. Yet the man whose earliest nickname—Elvis the Pelvis—associated him with a body part by no means had a comfortable or simple grasp of his own body and sexuality. Relatedly, the King of Rock and Roll was no stranger to Christian spirituality. Presley grew up in the Pentecostal Church and was forever marked by it. His struggles to remain true to his Christian tradition (and the musical traditions associated with it and other cultures) mirror and reveal some of our own.

Obviously, then, I come to Elvis with my intents and purposes. I am far from the first, and certainly will not be the last, to try to make Elvis serve my ends. So I can't and don't at all claim to know and tell *the* story, the single and definitive account, of Elvis Presley. In a sense there are now as many Elvises as there are accounts of him, and in books, films, academic conferences, and other media these already number in the hundreds. Yet there really was a single, unique, palpable human being named Elvis Presley, born in Tupelo, Mississippi, in 1935, died slumped on the floor of his Graceland bathroom in 1977. How can we respect the man and not merely exploit the myth? I answer unabashedly as a fan: we do have his music. Whatever anyone may say about this or that aspect of his life and myth, a direct encounter with his art is as near as the closest stereo.*

---

*It's true, Elvis put a lot of dreck on record. But by way of respect, and for those who want to consider or reconsider his musical and performative greatness, I make the following recommendations: The early, fresh, and still exciting Elvis is wonderfully captured on recordings made in 1954 and 1955 at Memphis's Sun Records (*Sunrise*, RCA 67675–2). Elvis became world famous explosively, in the span of a single year; the remarkable music he made in that year is found on *Elvis '56* (RCA 6513512). Through most of the 1960s Presley stagnated musically, departing the stage to make second- or third-rate movies (filled, for the most part, with equally uninspiring songs) at the mediocrity-guaranteed clip of up to three a year. But in 1968 he returned to the stage and, with great vigor, regained his vocal and emotive powers. The passel of blues, country, gospel, and rock recordings he made in 1969 with Memphis producer Chips Moman are, by many accounts, among the most outstanding popular music of the twentieth century. This glorious material is

Elvis, TV, and Vegas: The Rise of the Age of the Electronic Spectacle

The kind of fame enjoyed (and suffered) by Elvis Presley could not have happened at an earlier time in history. He talked his way into Sam Phillips's Sun Recording Studio in 1954. (Phillips, one of most storied figures in popular music, would eventually introduce to the world not only Elvis but also Carl Perkins, Charlie Rich, Jerry Lee Lewis, and Johnny Cash.) Nineteen years old at the time, Presley came of age when post–World War II consumerism was ripening. More Americans than ever before had more disposable income and leisure time than ever before. The credit card was introduced in 1950; the first McDonald's restaurant opened the same year Elvis met Sam Phillips. The first postwar baby boomers were entering adolescence in the mid-1950s. This generation (thirteen million strong) burgeoned not only in its population but in its wallets. In 1956 the average teenager had a disposable income of $10.55 a week, matching the disposable weekly income of an entire family just fifteen years before.

Presley was a member of this generation, the initial teenaged cohort to grow up with phonographs, jukeboxes, and radios as ordinary, everyday items. Another electronic gadget was coming into its own just as the Memphis teenager did. That would be television, which was invented in the 1920s but through the 1940s remained a novelty for the wealthy. In 1939, the National Broadcasting Company televised the opening of the World's Fair to fewer than one thousand TV sets. Only six stations were broadcasting in 1946. But seven million sets were sold in 1951, and by 1956, 442 stations were operating.

---

compiled on *Suspicious Minds* (RCA 67677). From the early 1970s until his death, Presley, stultified in drugs and the lonely echo-house of his unrivaled celebrity, managed typically only to posture and feint at his former brilliance. But 1970's *That's the Way It Is* (RCA 54114–2) encapsulates the best of the mature Presley, performing balladry and other fully orchestrated music with striking confidence and effect. Finally, it shouldn't be forgotten that Elvis's first and last love was gospel music, and he made gospel records with respectfulness and passion in the late 1960s and early 1970s. The best of this music is found on *Amazing Grace* (RCA 66421).

Elvis was an acutely bashful truck driver still living at home with his parents when Phillips set him up with a guitarist and bassist and, after much experimentation, recorded "That's All Right." Phillips persuaded a prominent Memphis disc jockey to play the record one summer night. The song was a hopped-up, giddy blues that Memphis teenagers—already comfortable with musical if not other kinds of miscegenation—took to immediately. The DJ, flooded with phone calls, played the song seven times straight. Over the next year, Presley and Phillips released more than a dozen other songs. Elvis's music leapt arrestingly out of the radio. It was not entirely unfamiliar—he appropriated blues, country, and bluegrass songs already recorded. Yet the songs and the music were different, sung and played with an intense energy that sounded spontaneous and was altogether infectious. Their infectiousness was proved when Presley took the stage. Initially he only shook a leg in rhythm to the music. An intuitive performer of considerable talent, he took note of the audience approval and tried a series of other gestures and movements. He kept those that excited his listeners and dropped those that didn't. Here was a singer you might not only listen to intensely but also never wanted to take your eyes off. He shimmied and shook. He prostrated himself and writhed on the stage. He directed his band with shakes of his shoulders and, yes, hips. He gave his whole body, not just his vocal cords, to the music.

His young fans, especially girls, could respond with similar abandon. Early in 1955, Florida devotees pursued Elvis into a locker room and ripped off his coat and shirt before he was rescued. Later that year, in Cleveland, a string broke on his guitar and he smashed it on the floor. Overcome, fans rushed the stage and tore a sleeve off his jacket. The next year, in Kansas City, a concert crowd rioted and overran the band; the upright bass was trashed, the drummer cascaded into the orchestra pit. By then Presley was a master at enthralling audiences. At one show, he shouted off-microphone to the band, "I'll bet I could burp and make them squeal." Returning to the microphone, he burped and they did.

Television propelled Elvis to national and later worldwide fame. Musicians had been televised before him, but their performances were stationary, immobile, as if they were in radio studios that just happened to have a camera in front. For instance, watch footage of proto-rocker Bo Diddley performing his eponymous tune on the *Ed Sullivan Show* in 1956. The song rides a bouncy Latin beat, but Bo's feet are nailed to the floor. Television needed performers who could exploit its visual potential, and Elvis's kinetic act and sly, fluid facial expressions fit the bill. His June 5, 1956, rendition of "Hound Dog" on the *Milton Berle Show* ignited a national firestorm of excitement and controversy. His tamer, but still decidedly physical, September 9, 1956, performance on *Ed Sullivan* was watched by an incredible 83 percent of the U.S. television audience. By the end of the year Presley was a millionaire. He was now recording with RCA, and his singles constituted two-thirds of that giant's entire singles sales for the year. His popularity, measured in accounting or most any other terms, rivaled anything in the history of show business. The vast remunerative possibilities of merchandising a star were also realized with Presley. By the end of the next year there were at least fifty Elvis products—belts, skirts, jeans, scarves, lipstick, Western ties, and so on—totaling more than $40 million in retail sales. At the time, Presley tie-ins constituted the largest merchandising campaign ever targeted especially at teenagers.

The unparalleled scale of Presley's celebrity can be gauged by the reaction of another star. Actress Natalie Wood spent several days with Elvis at his (and his parents') Memphis home in late 1956. Wood was no stranger to fame. She was originally a child star who had played in fourteen movies by age twelve. Just a year before visiting Elvis, she was nominated for an Academy Award for her role opposite James Dean in *Rebel without a Cause*. *Life* magazine crowned her the nation's most beautiful teenager. Yet she was bowled over by the adoring masses outside Presley's home day and night, with ice cream and hot dog vendors working the sidewalks. "When we went out on Elvis's motorcycle, we had an instant motorcade behind us," she said. "I felt like I was leading the Rose Bowl parade."

By this time the mythification of Elvis was well under way. But the apotheosis came in the early 1970s, after Presley rose to top of the image and celebrity machinery a second time. He was drafted into the army in 1958, and he and many around him thought his career was finished. By the time he returned from the service, his ardent teenage fans would be grown up. Rock and roll was considered a passing fad by Presley himself. What he and others didn't count on was the staying power of rock music or the shrewdness of Elvis's manager, Colonel Tom Parker. Parker kept Presley's image in the public eye and arranged a series of movies that would occupy Elvis for most of the 1960s. The singer's career was not over then, but it still went into eclipse. The movies, though extremely profitable, were hack jobs and everyone knew it, including Elvis. By 1967 the record sales and movie profits—though still impressive by most standards—had slumped well below Presley's peak and showed every sign of sinking further. It was in 1968 that Elvis returned to the stage, with an NBC television special that showed a reinvigorated star, a hot, leather-suited rocker who could still put everything into a song and claim it from the inside out.

Shortly after this he took his show to Las Vegas. Reborn as a performer, he commanded the stage in front of a basic rock band, a small choir of backup singers, and an orchestra. Presley was all over the stage, even cartwheeling and somersaulting. He captivated Vegas showgoers, shattering all attendance records, drawing crowds two and three times larger than those attending other top-tier acts. Stars rushed to Las Vegas to see him and were themselves entranced. Cary Grant said Elvis was the greatest performer since Al Jolson. Comedian Totie Fields was so taken at one show that she mounted a tabletop and windmilled a scarf over her head. Presley songs returned to the top of the charts, and album sales surged.

The King's first coronation was on and through the medium of television. His second was in that exotic city in the Mojave Desert, the prototypical postmodern metropolis. Las Vegas is a glittering facade, built almost entirely on surface imagery and devoid of substance. It is a town in the middle of nowhere that has become one of world's leading tourist destinations (closing fast on Orlando's thirty-five million annual visitors). It is a gusher of wealth that produces nothing in terms of tangible goods and subsists on illusions of quick and easy riches. It is a resort mecca built by mobsters, now catering to family values. Even Vegas's physical infrastructure is a mirage, a virtual reality not locally based or maintained in any proportion to the physical environment it actually occupies. The copious electricity demands of the Strip are filled by coal-burning plants on the Moapa Indian Reservation and along the Colorado River. Located in a desert basin receiving only seven or eight inches of rain annually, Vegas pipes water from distant places, irrigating lawns and golf courses and filling fountains, artificial lakes, and lagoons at the rate of 360 gallons daily per capita. (By comparison, Los Angeles's rate is 211, Tucson's 160, and Oakland's 110.)

The Vegas paradigm—brilliant on the surface but hollow at the core—perfectly encapsulates the bitter ironies of Presley's celebrity. Elvis, who grew up in a shotgun shack in Tupelo and a housing project in Memphis, felt he owed everything to his fans. Still, it was not long before the fame became a cage. The inevitable public commotion made it impossible for him to go out for a hamburger or attend church. He was tortured by realizations that as much as the masses apparently loved him, none among them really knew him. He was a screen onto which the most obsessive fans projected their own needs and dreams: Elvis as lover, as best friend, as proof that anybody could become wealthy and famous, even as savior. Relatives and friends wanted jobs, cars, clothes, or just cold hard cash. (Years later, at Presley's funeral, an opportunistic cousin snapped a picture of the corpse in repose for a check from the *National Enquirer*.) In 1976 he lamented, "I think I became a dollar sign. . . . In the process [those who wanted to profit] lost sight of Elvis. That can easily happen. It happened, man. I've become an object, not a person. I'm not that sign, I'm not that image, I'm myself." But by then Elvis was mostly impersonating and almost parodying his own image, stumbling on stage in a fog of prescription drugs, probably weighing close to 350 pounds, striking poses in jumpsuits and capes like a superhero or demigod. As rock critic Greil Marcus wrote before his death, "Elvis is a man whose task it is to dramatize the fact of his existence."

Obviously, few of us live in Elvis World in terms of adulation from the faceless masses. But we do live in Elvis World as we enjoy and confront the power of imagery, especially commercial imagery. Television remains a, if not the central, medium of this imagery. Las Vegas symbolizes a pervasive tendency to dwell on and manipulate surfaces, creating spectacle that may only be an inch deep but lures interest (and money) by virtue of novelty and titillation. Las Vegas, in a sense, is everywhere. We visit faux tropical seafood shacks in shopping malls or plastic-and-plaster Mexican cantinas in Minneapolis. We are appealed to unrelentingly as crowds of consumers, drawn by quickly absorbed impressions that tap into basic human drives and emotions: sexual arousal, fear, anger, aversion to boredom, greed, even bloodlust.

Traditional Christian spirituality has long recognized the innate power of crowds and mass emotion. Luke's Gospel, for instance, records Jesus' triumphal entry into Jerusalem. He is greeted by cheering crowds, waving palm fronds and laying their cloaks in his path. But Luke notes that a mere three days later, when an arrested and mute Jesus is led before the same crowds, they scream repeatedly for his crucifixion (Luke 23:4–22). Crowds, in other words, are both fickle and vehement. Their potent and even violent emotions may, on the basis of a few broad impressions, shift and reverse themselves within days or even hours. St. Augustine, the ever astute psychologist, attests to the power of mass fervor. He remembers a friend who tries to wean himself from the bloody spectacle of the gladiatorial games. Thinking he has mastered his emotions and wanting to remain sociable, the friend returns to the games with some companions. He promises himself he will close his eyes, but soon he hears the roar of the crowd and his eyes are pried open. Then, says Augustine, "he was no longer the man who entered there, but only one of the crowd that he had joined, and a true comrade of those who brought him there. What more shall I say? He looked, he shouted, he took fire, he bore away with himself a madness . . ."

As my earlier chapters would suggest, the response of classical Christian spirituality to a culture of celebrity and spectacle is not attempted retreat into individual isolation. The tradition affirms that we are social creatures, one in the common humanity symbolized in Adam, and, as Christians, organic members of the body of Christ. Thus, while we are wise to remain wary of the brute and gross psychology of crowds (crowds can be neither smart nor subtle), we will entertain no illusions that we are not formed and influenced by social bodies. Christian spirituality, while not averse to participation in all other communities (or even crowds), is anchored in the church, the mother and nurturer of faith.

The church is possessed and lives by its own imagery, especially the stories of Scripture and the living symbols of the sacraments. This is the imagery that saturates and builds truly Christian imaginations. Turning and returning to the Scripture and the sacraments, we are saved from the solipsism that would have us believe the world exists (and will be redeemed) only for our entertainment or distraction. Of course we can and too often do misread or abuse Scripture and sacrament, but orthodox Christian spirituality at least sets up real resistance to our destructive fantasies.

For instance, one of our darkest temptations in Elvis World is to turn Jesus into a celebrity. By a celebrity I here mean a figure who is more a reflection of our own (often misguided) fears and dreams than an external, objective other. The objective other, unlike the celebrity, is someone who to a degree stands outside our fears and hopes and cannot be simply molded in their image. The cult of celebrity encourages an infantile psychology. The infant can imagine mother and father only as extensions of herself and her needs. Mother and father mean food or dry diaper when I cry. As the infant matures into a toddler and beyond, she learns more and more that mother and father have an existence apart from her and are not there simply for her bidding. The celebrity mentality, transferred into and distorting Christian spirituality, makes Christ (and the Trinity as a whole) a mere extension of my needs and wants. Clearly, the providential objectivity of the sacraments and Scripture (discussed in chapter 5) signifies the real presence of Jesus as an objective other, not a malleable celebrity.

Thus a classical Christian spirituality, recognizing the importance of social and sacramental embodiment, fits us with resources to engage and, where appropriate, resist the cult of celebrity and spectacle that now affects all fields of communal human endeavor. Put otherwise, Luke and St. Augustine have plenty to say to those of us living in Elvis World.

Presley, Tradition, and the Movement of the Spirit

Elvis's fascinating story also repays study in terms of a constant theme of this book: the actual power and constitution of tradition, and particularly Christian tradition. Elvis World typically ignores or denies tradition. It depends on the dubious myth that we can invent and reinvent ourselves and our personalities, just as Elvis supposedly invented and (in Las Vegas) reinvented himself. By this account, Elvis was a poor country boy who one day wandered into a studio, did spontaneously what came natural to him, and achieved stupendous success. (In accounts flattering to him, Elvis was an innate genius; in those derogatory, he was an idiot savant.) Manifested as Christian spirituality, this narrative emphasizes an individual relationship with God. It also tends, romantically, to play down the body and its inherent limitations (such as mortality and the hindrances of advancing age) and focus on the putatively limitless strengths of the spirit. In secular guise, this mentality simply boasts, "You can be whatever you want to be." In Christianized guise, it adds a modest qualification: "*With God's help*, you can be whatever you want to be."

While I think Elvis's life story, finally to his detriment, reinforces a consumer culture of celebrity and spectacle, the score is different on the count of tradition. Here only a moment's attention to Elvis's history contradicts and repudiates the myth of self-invention, the man made utterly and uniquely from the whole cloth of his own fabrication. Elvis himself never used the language of inventing rock and roll (let alone himself). He repeatedly acknowledged the roots of his music in gospel, rhythm and blues, and country music.

Though Presley's rise to fame and accomplishment as a performer was unusually rapid, it was not literally sudden. He sang first in the Assembly of God churches of his childhood. In 1957 he told the press, "I lose myself in my singing. Maybe it's my early training singing gospel hymns." And he added, " I know practically every religious song that's ever been written." A minister, and later a minister's son, taught him how to play guitar. As a young teenager, he regularly attended the All-Night Gospel Singing at Memphis's Ellis Auditorium. (He first witnessed the mannerism of shaking a leg in rhythm at these "singings," where the flamboyant bass singer of a gospel quartet called the Statesmen did exactly that.)

Presley grew up in a day when popular radio was not, as it is now, homogenized and dominated by a handful of styles and broadcasting conglomerates. On his radio he heard a vast array of blues, country, pop, and black gospel music. His earliest nationally famous songs appeared on country and western charts. His national debut, in 1954, was on the Grand Ole Opry. Enterprising publicists first labeled him the "Hillbilly Cat" and the "King of Western Bop." One country music magazine designated him the "Folk Music Fireball." A Louisiana radio executive said he "sings hillbilly in r&b time," while a Memphis journalist called his music a "curious blending" of "the r&b idiom and negro field jazz." The point of all this is not that Elvis failed to do something fresh but that his music—like any human cultural creation—was only relatively original. Presley drew on various preexisting musical traditions, themselves usually not absolutely distinct from one another. For example, we can differentiate "white" from "black" gospel music—the "extremes" of each do sound distinct. Yet the Pentecostal tradition of Elvis's youth was, from its beginning, built from black no less than white musical and worship influences. This is how traditions work and change, and how "new" traditions form. They, or, more precisely, their practitioners, jostle up against one another, borrowing and adapting directions, ideas, stylings, and the like. To those unfamiliar with all or most of the precedent traditions, Elvis's music may have sounded completely new, as if he snatched it out of thin air. But to Elvis and other southerners in wonderful musical mixing pots such as Memphis and New Orleans, the precedents were obvious enough.

Nor were Presley's recordings strictly spontaneous, made up on the spot. The first Sun records developed slowly, over weeks of rehearsal and experimentation. When Presley and Sam Phillips arrived at a sound they liked, those and the later Sun records were

> laboriously constructed out of a series of hits and misses, riffs and bits of phrasing held through dozens of bad takes. The songs grew slowly, over hours and hours, into a music that paradoxically sounded much fresher than all the poor tries that had come before; until Presley, [his bassist, and his guitarist] had the attack in their blood, and yes, didn't have to think about it. That's not exactly my idea of "spontaneity" or "unself-consciousness."

None of this will surprise working musicians or performers, who know the performance that sounds or looks most "natural" and "off the cuff" is the result of much hard work and repeated, intentional effort. Elvis carried such a work ethic into his recording with RCA. In its studios, he could spend two hours wrestling with a song and finally decide to throw it away. Before he was satisfied, he pushed through thirty-one takes of "Hound Dog" and twenty-eight takes of "Don't Be Cruel"; he toiled three hours to arrive at the master for "Money Honey."

Elvis's engagement of musical traditions, respecting their objectivity and demands but keeping them alive and organic, exemplifies other appropriations of tradition, including the tradition of Christian spirituality. His story suggests that we best approach tradition with the language of improvisation rather than that of invention. Improvisation acknowledges precedent, deliberately building on and from tradition. But in the current culture of romantic individualism, our ears can hear "improvisation" as a kind of creation ex nihilo. I remember, as a boy, sitting down to my mother's piano and attempting improvisation, or at least what I thought was improvisation. Yet I had no piano knowledge or practice and within minutes grew bored of pointless banging on the keys. Real improvisation, as in that of skilled jazz musicians, comes only after years of practice and mastery of the panoply of chords. The improvising jazz musician searches and probes the harmonic possibilities of given chords and "quotes" bits of melodies from a range of precedent sources. He stands on a ground there before him, explores the niches and borders of a territory he did not invent but received as an inheritance.

Likewise, orthodox Christian spirituality extends into new times and places by improvisation. It proceeds from a past, builds on a legacy. It makes changes but knows not just any changes can be true to tradition. The jazz musician may discover fresh harmonic possibilities, appropriately lengthening the possibilities of a song, but if she stumbles outside the chords of that song she has departed it as a "tradition." So too Christian spirituality lives and meets new challenges. It is a symphony (or jazz suite) of vast possibilities, flexibilities, and latent dynamisms, saturated with harmonic potentials which have not been exhausted over millennia. Extending the Christian tradition is often, even usually, a messy, extended, and laborious process. It is not always immediately apparent just what is an authentic appropriation of the tradition and what is an appropriation that, so to speak, stretches chords to the point of breaking them. But as practitioners of Christian spirituality live (and fight) on over decades or centuries, the genuine extensions of the tradition become clearer.

Presley's experience offers an analogy of the vital struggle in and with a tradition. His second Sun record was a startling adaptation of a beloved bluegrass composition, "Blue Moon of Kentucky." Bill Monroe, the progenitor of bluegrass and writer of the song, waxed it on vinyl in a stately waltz meter. Elvis, driving for music that would "mooo-ve me," as he said about another venerable piece, set "Blue Moon" to a slapped bass beat in 4/4 time. Many in the bluegrass community were shocked. The performance struck them as a desecration of, and certainly an abrupt departure from, the tradition. Monroe was a large, passionate, and opinionated man. Phillips heard rumors that he was "going to break my jaw." Not so. Monroe, a master practitioner of the bluegrass tradition, sensed new possibilities in Presley's appropriation of his song. A week after he first heard Elvis's record, he went into the studio and recorded his own revised version of "Blue Moon" in 4/4 time.

Classical Christian spirituality, similarly, is best respected and lived when it is not treated as an untouchable, frozen, and unchangeable deposit. It is better inhabited from the inside out, constantly pushed and probed, presented with unprecedented questions and objections, and sometimes daringly taken in a direction not previously considered. We live by faithful improvisation. Only then will the Spirit "mooo-ve" us from the past, into the future.

Elvis and Sex: "Have a Laugh on Me"

Of course, as I have noted in earlier chapters and will again in a later chapter, a key area where any daring in Christian spirituality has been regarded with acute sensitivity is bodily sexuality. Once more, Elvis's story illuminates tensions and possibilities.

I have already remarked that Presley was reared in the Christian tradition and was controversial especially because of his patent sexuality. These remarks deserve elaboration. Not only was Presley marked early by Christian spirituality, but he carried its stamp to his dying day. Remember that this was a genuine southern mama's boy. Mother Gladys walked her sheltered only child to class into his early high school years. He lived with his parents through the earliest years of his fame. When he was drafted into the army in 1958, military rules allowed soldiers who had completed basic training to live off base with any dependents. By that time the wealthy Elvis's parents were his legal dependents, and he moved his mother, father, and grandmother to a house near his Texas station. Gladys died later in 1958, but when Elvis was transferred to Germany he took Dad and Grandma along.

Friends and new acquaintances meeting Presley into the early 1960s remark again and again on his "innocence." This was a boy who didn't dance at his senior prom because he hadn't learned how. He did not drink or smoke. He forbade profane language in his home. Natalie Wood reported, "I hadn't been around anyone who was [that] religious. He felt he had been given this gift, this talent, by God. . . . He thought it was something that he had to protect. He had to be nice to people. Otherwise, God might take it all back." Elvis's main squeeze in 1956–1957, Dottie Harmony, spoke of dates not atypical of those reported by other young suitors: "We used to read the Bible every night, if you can believe that—he used to read aloud to me and then talk about it."

Presley was at times quite public about his faith. Pushed in 1955 by a reporter worried about the rawness of his physicality on stage, he responded:

> I read my Bible, sir, and this is not story just made up for now. My Bible tells me that what he sows he will also reap, and if I'm sowing evil and wickedness it will catch up with me. I'm right sure of that, sir, and I don't think I'm bad for people. If I did think I was bad for people, I would go back to driving a truck, and I really mean this.

And after all, he would often protest, "I know my mother approves of what I'm doing."

In late 1960, asked about his greatest dislikes, Elvis responded that he hated not being able to attend church regularly. He daydreamed, not least as his life began to come apart in the 1970s (some might say he was reaping what he had sowed), about quitting the superstar gig and becoming a revivalist or gospel singer. In late 1976, months before his death, televangelist Rex Humbard visited him backstage following a concert. Elvis desperately petitioned Humbard: should he quit singing and devote himself to the Lord? He was briefly appeased when Humbard told him he should use his God-given talent to continue giving pleasure to so many people. But then Presley launched into harried chatter about Armageddon and the second coming of Christ. Humbard later reported, "I took both his hands in mine [and] said, 'Elvis, right now I want to pray for you.' He said, 'Please do,' and started weeping."

I am not trying to build a brief for Elvis's elevation to sainthood. Eventually there were the drugs—mostly prescription, but those abusively, and he dabbled with marijuana and LSD and may have more than dabbled with cocaine. He would grow selfish, sometimes mean and violent, toting pistols and shooting out chandeliers and TV sets, at least twice nearly (if unintentionally) plugging people. By the 1970s he habitually cursed, even on stage, rambling into vulgar soliloquies and X-rated renditions of "Love Me Tender." And the first behavioral mark of his strict Christian upbringing to go was chastity. From the late 1950s on, there was a string of women (and teenage girls), many taken into bedrooms not merely for private Bible readings. Further, though he clearly never discarded his Christian convictions, he would, as in the mid-1960s, rather sloppily imbibe bits of other spiritualities, including numerology, astrology, and westernized scraps of yoga.

In short, Presley was no pure paragon of Christian comportment. He was a profoundly conflicted man, faced with temptations of wealth, power, and free sex on a magnitude the rest of us don't encounter in dreams—or nightmares. (The conflict manifested itself not only in straightforward guilt over his promiscuity but in some odd attitudes. For instance, after daughter Lisa Marie was born, Presley refused sex with his wife, saying he couldn't have intercourse with a woman who was a mother.) Consequently, to focus particularly on the body, we don't need to posit Elvis as an exemplar of Christian sexuality. But his own conflicted sexuality, and the culture's reaction to it, may still speak edifyingly to us—especially from a perspective some decades removed.

Granted, I (and my readers generally) may be jaded by the much cruder and more sensationalistic sex that has filled concert stages, and movie and television screens, since Elvis's debut. But I would still argue that much of the outraged response to the early Elvis was itself over the top and born of conflicted sexuality. America in the 1950s was repressed, unduly afraid of the energies of its youth, ready to sound alarms about juvenile delinquency if kids chewed gum in the classroom. Frankly, some of the histrionic reaction to Elvis was motivated by class bias and racial prejudice. Recall that jazz was still not respected as an art form. The guardians of "higher culture" could imagine no vernacular American musics to be worthy of respect. As for racism, it not infrequently slid prominently into Elvis attacks. In early 1957, a New York congressman patronized that "rock 'n' roll has its place . . . particularly among the colored people." Elvis's rhythms evoked for some echoes of "jungle beats," as for the New York journalist who characterized his music as "a terrible twist on darkest Africa's fertility tom-tom displays."

Furthermore, sex was (of course) already in the picture, even if this was not carefully noticed. Before Elvis swung his pelvis, Milton Berle was doing boob jokes and crossdressing on national television. The June Taylor Dancers, appearing on two Jackie Gleason-produced shows, shook their fannies—perhaps not as vigorously as Elvis, but in scantier clothing. In retrospect, it appears that Presley provoked controversy because of his youth, because of the enthusiastic youthful response to him, and because the sexual element of his performances was (and is) undeniable. In an important sense: so what? Human beings are, among other things, sexual animals, and thus our sexuality is always somewhere in the equation, even if we try to keep that part of the equation written in invisible ink. As the father of a now teenaged daughter, I can appreciate how much simpler life might be if she and her peers were asexual. But no amount of wishing will banish adolescent hormones. Perhaps a healthy sexuality, a worthily

Christian spirituality of sexuality, doesn't focus on trying to ignore or deny all sensuality and physicality.

I am not suggesting that a classical Christian spirituality can dispose of some real control of bodily, sexual expression (and if some want to call that repression, so be it). But there is more than one way to contain and channel our sexuality. Too often we approach sexuality—especially the sexuality of youth—only with gravity. Then we fixate on the sometimes tragic ramifications of sexual behavior: broken families, abortion, teenage pregnancy, lethal venereal diseases, and the like. These are real and serious possibilities. But sex and sexuality also have a comic dimension. Some of Mozart's operas and Shakespeare's plays are historical exhibits of the recognition that sexuality can be contained and defused by approaching it comedically. Men and women are those odd creatures a "little lower than the angels," capable of rationality and spiritual nobility—and at the same time "naked apes," susceptible to hormonal impulses, ready to go to great (and sometimes ridiculous) lengths to mate. Mozart, Shakespeare, and others play on the abundant comic possibilities of this incongruity, exploiting mistaken identities, cross-gender confusions, and the absurd situations a lover can get into. Sex is potent, but sometimes we can tame it by laughing (not just derisively but affectionately) about it. We are reminded that sex and sexuality are, among other things, funny. And the humor allows some distance and perspective. It helps us keep sex in its place.

Indulging that possibility, let us turn to the Elvis act that released the torrents of shock and criticism, his 1956 performance of "Hound Dog" on the *Milton Berle Show*. There certainly is a sexual element to Elvis's performance. But to these eyes at least, viewing it today, the performance hardly seems dirty or shocking. Elvis is clad in a white sport jacket. The jacket is long, extending twelve inches below his waist, squarely shrouding and rendering his pelvic region nondescript. He wears dark pants and shoes, with white socks. The shapeless midsection, and the contrast between white socks and dark pants and shoes, draws the eye to his jack-knifing knees and quick-stepping feet. This is especially the case because the white socks flash conspicuously as the hems of his trousers bounce up and down. He moves his knees primarily to the percussive blows on the drums, almost as if they were marionette-attached to the drummer's wrists. In other words, if the performance evokes for some Gypsy Rose Lee, it also evokes Pinocchio.

Elvis begins the song explosively, blasting immediately into full tempo. He does three machine-gunning choruses of the song and apparently ends it. Only momentarily, though. Then he slides gradually back into the song. It's here, languidly teasing the audience and dancing less antically, that his performance most resembles a bump-and-grind, Pinocchioesque parody of a burlesque dancer.

How does the auditorium react to this, the most controversial portion of the performance? It catches the comic elements and responds accordingly. There is some hysterical screaming but also noticeable laughter—laughter that sounds more that of surprised delight than of embarrassed shock. (Among other things, consider the lyrics of the song—Presley originally understood and presented it as a novelty piece.) When Elvis finishes, Berle darts on stage, shouting, "How 'bout my boy," grabbing him at the wrist, then going into his own mock routine of Presley's "Hound Dog." While Elvis smiles somewhat timidly beside him, Berle stomp-dances right out of his shoes.

The atmosphere is not the grim, lustful drama of a strippers' lounge but relaxed amusement. This and other early TV and newsreel performances generally neglect shots of the audience; when audience shots are included, they are so brief and grainy it's difficult to make out facial expressions. But early still photographs sometimes do capture the crowds, more or less sharply in focus, and I'm struck by the wholesomely wide smiles and open-mouthed laughter in them. One of the best is a famous shot from New Orleans in 1955. The photographer is positioned stage right, behind Elvis. We have a full view of the first several rows of the audience because Presley has gone face down on the stage. The audience is clearly having a carefree good time. The few boys present smile broadly enough to show teeth but remain straight in their seats. The girls are more involved. Many lean forward. Two raise both arms in the air. A couple cradle their faces in surprise. And to a person they are laughing. If they are also screaming, and I assume some are, their screams must be like those on an amusement park roller coaster: it is an occasion to let go, but no one is taking the emotion too seriously.

Elvis was a strongly intuitive performer and didn't explicitly articulate the levity inherent to his act. (If he could have so articulated it, he might have been a critic instead of a performer.) He did insist that kids at his shows were just enjoying themselves. And the filmed early performances show him indisputably having a good time, not altogether taking himself seriously. He fools with lyrics, at times clowningly rolls and crosses his eyes. He plays with the audience and expects it to play back. It's call and response as a vigorous bodily game of tag, the "Marco!" of his shoulders, hips, and legs alternating with the "Polo!" of the audience's shouts and handclaps. He saw himself as an entertainer. There were, in his estimation, more important occupations, and one of them was that of the evangelist. Of course some fans were obsessive (death threats and lawsuits from would-be lovers or friends were down the road of fame). And I have already recounted occasions of riots and near riots. But another response was possible, was in fact made, and was certainly more dominant than stage-crashing hysteria. That response was laughter, amusement, and enjoyment at—and with—a masterful performer who, at least on stage, put sexuality in perspective. In a 1975 recording of Billy Swan's "I Can Help," Elvis ad libbed, "Have a laugh on me. I can help." And so he could.

8

THE PROBLEM
WITH BAMBI

Death and the Beginning
of Christian Spirituality

A while back, a midwestern friend let a seven-year-old daughter and her neighbor playmate watch a controversial video. Here's the thing: my friend is a conscientious and painstakingly caring mother. Every day she goes out of her way to maintain a world, or a space within the world, that is protective and nurturing for children. She is not the type of parent to abandon kids to their own devices in front of a television and VCR. She didn't, and wouldn't, allow them to view a slasher or a teen sexploitation flick. She really had no inkling that it might be considered irresponsible to have the girls watch Walt Disney's *Bambi*.

But in the story Bambi's mother is killed. The playmate went home with a disturbing new realization: parents aren't immortal. They can die, and a child may be left alone in the world, or at least without a mother or father. And the neighbors had no religious convictions.

To them, death simply is the end. There's nothing more to be said about it than that, and how can you reassure a child if this is all you can know or say in the face of death? So my friend was upbraided by the mother of the playmate. The girl simply shouldn't have been exposed to an image of death. She should have continued to be shielded entirely from it, even at the comparatively safe, theoretical distance of a fairytale or children's fable.

The neighbor's attitude, as my friend realized after talking to her, wasn't irrational or—on her terms—anything but prudent parenting. All modern parents of any sensitivity, including Christians, are careful to shelter their children from certain realities. We recognize that children are vulnerable. We want them to be and to feel safe. War, crime, the extent of adult mendacity, the vistas of sexuality a child can hardly even conceive—these are all undeniable realities that we don't foist on young children. To one degree or another, we minimize their appearances in our children's world. We expect that exposure to difficult truths should come gradually, as a child matures and gains the capacity to confront them.

And of course many moderns, whether they style themselves "secular" or something else, hold no hope for a life or a world beyond death. Thus they may quite reasonably, as caring parents, determine that a young child will ideally catch no hints of the brutal, final reality of self-extinction. Socrates, that paragon of reason, himself concluded that the human being either was devised for some kind of eternity or was a frightened monstrosity: an animal, unlike others, that *knows* it will one day cease existing. Socrates opted for an immortal soul and eternity. Those who are convinced death simply is the end probably should hide it from their children as completely as they can for as long as they can.

Children, Death, and Christian Hope

The attitude of classical Christian spirituality has been different. The church does see death as something terrible. Death is tragic: it separates loved ones from one another and is enough of an unknown in any specifics that some fear of it is inevitable. Death is, in the apostle Paul's reckoning, "the last enemy" (1 Cor. 15:26). But it is not the end—there is reality and hope beyond all tragedy and enmity. Death is an enemy that has been destroyed and overcome in Christ. So it is fearsome, but it can be faced. The soldier sent into battle with weaponry, armor, and fighting companions is afraid, but not afraid so utterly (and realistically) as the soldier charging enemy lines alone, with no weaponry or armor. Christians are like the equipped and well-accompanied soldier. We are, honestly, frightened. But we have some resources that help us countenance the thought and reality of death. In the light of the resurrection, death has lost its ultimate "sting" (1 Cor. 15: 55).

So we find in the history of Christian spirituality specimens such as Jacobus Koelman's *The Duties of Parents*. Koelman was a seventeenth-century Dutch Reformed pastor. He wrote a handbook to help Christians raise their children responsibly and faithfully. He lived in a world in which children often died. And he believed in the gospel. So he counseled parents "from time to time" to take children "eight or ten or twelve years old" aside and ask them questions such as: "Do you not know, my child, that before long you will have to die?" and "Could you not very well die tonight, or this week, or this month, like other children who die so young?" Pastor Koelman also advised parents to "make good use of a time of illness. . . . If you, father or mother, are sick, call the children to your bedside and tell them that perhaps you are now going to die and how dreadful your death would be for them." Then speak to them, he urged, of fear and comfort of God, out of the conviction that death is not simply the end. On these and other occasions, help them understand that this physical or "natural" death is not to be feared so much as a "spiritual or second death" that would eternally separate them from God.

> Make known to them that they must daily prepare themselves for their death and consider their mortality. After all, they know *that* they must die but not *when*. Speak with them about the fragility of human life; how it is like a flower of the field, a vapor, a shadow; how swiftly life passes; how few people live to old age; how many die in their youth. Tell them that they do not know whether they will see the next day so

that they may learn to number their days and become wise and seek
to be assured of their salvation.

Of course, the situation has changed for today's Christians, at least
those of us who live in the wealthy West. Now most people do live
into old age. It is comparatively rare to die as a youth. In addition,
many of us have imbibed enough developmental psychology that we
are careful not to assume children are basically adults in miniature.
I myself would not counsel a young child to contemplate his or her
death on a daily basis. So our world is not identical to Koelman's.
But I share Koelman's rock-bottom faith that death will not have the
last word. I might, in fact I have, let young children watch *Bambi*. I
shelter children in my care from death to a degree Pastor Koelman
could not. Yet I don't try to hide it entirely from them. It is a reality
that Christian spirituality enables me—and with me even my child—to
admit and to contemplate.

The Imprudent Denial of Death

In the span of world history and cultures, we affluent moderns
really are curious people. Premoderns, with shorter and nastier life
spans, could not cloister death. It was an intimate reality on almost a
daily basis. In Elvis World we (and this "we" includes many or most
orthodox Christians) are prone to deny death.

Elvis himself was haunted by death. He was born a twin, but his
brother died at birth. He was taught that the strength and talents of
his stillborn twin were somehow added to those innately belonging
to him, the surviving child. Throughout his youth, he and his parents
regularly visited his brother's grave. He believed that his dead brother
sometimes "spoke" to him and counseled him. But most of us were
not reared under the constant (if strangely comforting) shadow of
a sibling's mortality. We would rather ignore death as much as we
can. We can even be reluctant to admit Elvis's own demise. Some so
want to deny death that they insist Elvis is still alive and occasionally to be sighted, outside an apartment above a diner in Kalamazoo,
Michigan, for instance.

Whether or not you or I think it possible to run across the living Elvis, we are apt to keep death away from our daily lives. With
modern scientific and medical breakthroughs, we have seen life spans
increased, on average, by 60 percent over those in 1900. Our medicine, our safety devices ranging from seatbelts to smoke detectors,
our purified water and food delivery systems, our regulated and less
hazardous workplaces—all these make our societies comparatively
quite safe. After September 11, 2001, the lethal possibilities of terror-
ism are no longer practically ignorable. Yet by any objective standard,
contemporary North Americans still live more safely—more sheltered
from the intrusion of death—than any other people in history.

At the same time, and ironically, we seem to live in more conscious
or imagined fear than many other cultures before us. We segregate
reminders of mortality from our everyday lives, dying in hospitals
rather than our bedrooms, holding wakes in funeral homes rather
than our houses. We obsess on healthy foods and lifestyles, seeking
to extend our individual life spans as far as we can with subscriptions
to health and diet magazines, close scrutiny of nutritional labels on
supermarket packages, regular visits to the physician, and so forth. We
buy all sorts of insurance. We insure against catastrophic collisions,
though most of us will never suffer a major car accident. We insure
against fire, though very few of us will ever see our house burn.

Much of this is simple prudence, and we can unreservedly thank
God for human ingenuities that have made our lives and those of our
children remarkably safer and longer. But the fact remains that we do
not feel so safe and that we put much more energy into ignoring or
denying and fearing death than did our ancestors. The ancients would
have seen us as a race myopically focused on the short run, building
sandcastles on a stormy shore. For even if we have added decades to
our life spans, it remains that we will, each one of us, die. No matter
how much treasure and energy we spend on the sandcastles of our
mortal existence and physical possessions, it is certain that every
such castle, viewed in history's span of centuries (let alone geology's
span of millennia), is made of sand and will soon enough crumble
and wash away in a gale.

Of course, our very safety has in a way made us more afraid. It
is one thing to be poor when most around you are poor. My grand-

parents spoke with some nostalgia about the years of the Great Depression, because most people around them had shared their circumstances and pulled together. Comparatively speaking, they weren't deprived. But it is another thing to be poor when many around you appear rich and comfortable, when reminders of the uniqueness of your grim deprivation are as near as the television screen. Similarly, we moderns can reasonably expect to live to age seventy or eighty. If we die young, we've lost forty or fifty expected years, not the ten or fifteen years of premoderns who died young. We sense that we have more to lose than our premodern ancestors and that, with some entirely practical prudence, we have less reason to lose it than they. In this regard, our tendency to push death and mortality back is sensible. And it is not unchristian, since the church sees death as a real enemy, an enemy to be denied its spoils in all ways prudent and reasonably possible.

Yet there remain many ways and manners in which we imprudently and unreasonably deny death, especially as Christians. To state the obvious, death remains inevitable. It is also, according to Christian convictions and practice, not ultimate. We will die, but we also anticipate the resurrection of the body. Given that these convictions and hopes of Christian spirituality were laid out and emphasized in earlier chapters, it remains now to suggest what this Christian spirituality may entail for facing bodily death in our own day and situation.

As I argued earlier, we are at bottom most ambivalent about our bodies not first of all because of their sexuality but because of their mortality and susceptibility to change, especially the changes of death and disintegration. So as I move to commenting on Christian spiritual exercises for facing death, it seems worthwhile to note that Christian, bodily spirituality *begins* by grappling with death, not sex. By most any account, Christian or otherwise "religious" or not, it is little short of bizarre that we moderns can focus so much on sex and so little on death. After all, whatever is made of death and any possible life after it, sex in comparison to death is mundane and trivial. Sex we can come by and experience daily, by masturbation if no other means. Death, however, is a singular, monumental event of (as *Time* magazine tepidly puts it) "transition." One sexual act, no matter how ecstatic, can rarely define an entire life. But death is onetime and defining by, well, definition. In any accounting, then, death has to be one of the most significant events of our lives, and it is one event we are certain will happen to us, even if we don't know exactly how or when. As the great country-and-western philosopher Hank Williams said, we'll never get out of this world alive. How can we live anything like prudent or profound lives and not take account of that reality?

There is another reason it seems to make no sense to concentrate on sex (however wonderful and important) and resolutely ignore our own deaths. Sexual intercourse is something most anyone can figure out how to do. Bodies are attracted to bodies, and particular orifices and organs, to put it bluntly, will be reliably stimulated to the rewards of great and immediate pleasure. Sex is other and more things, but it is a kind of organic plumbing. Given time and opportunity, people figure it out, with or without expert direction. On the other hand, death is equally "natural" and inevitable, but learning how to die is not. First-time sexual experiences are usually awkward and often frightening, but there will be many subsequent opportunities to practice and get better at it. Not so with death. It is a onetime engagement. We do our dying right and well the first and only time or not at all. So what sense does it make to put little or no forethought, imagination, and preparation into dying? By our modern reckoning, former generations (like that of Pastor Koelman) may seem morbidly fixated on death. But on reflection, their attitudes look less odd or foolish than do our modern attempts to blithely deny and ignore the huge, looming, inescapable reality of death.

How, then, might classical Christian spirituality fit us twenty-first-century believers for facing death?

Overcoming Death Phobia

A first and basic Christian spiritual exercise is to acknowledge death. It seems clear enough, as I have suggested, that a great deal of energy goes into our attempted denial of death. I have over years suffered anxiety from obsessive thoughts. The more I worry that I may think about something that bothers or frightens me, the harder it is not to think about it. One psychologist told me of a simple experiment. Command "Don't think about a white elephant," and what happens? You have likely already imagined a white elephant. If someone stands beside you and repeatedly commands you not to think about a white elephant, you will have to devote considerable energy to diverting your thoughts elsewhere. It's certainly been so with my anxiety. When time and counseling have tamed the obsessiveness—when I am not repeatedly shouting "White elephant!" in my head—I have freed-up energy for other thoughts, emotions, and actions.

I suspect that we moderns and postmoderns devote a lot of energy—call it phobic energy—to suppressing our realization of death. If we are like the secular mother with whom I began this chapter, we clearly must expend effort and emotional vigor to protect and guard our children even against the likes of *Bambi*. Our children aside, hints of death are simply impossible to screen out entirely. We may see a death depicted in a play or film, sung about in a song, described in the newspaper. We may, on any given day or week, receive a phone call letting us know a relative or friend has died. Death can't be entirely ignored. So if we encounter reminders of death and do not want to admit to ourselves that we too will die, we must devote energy to containing thoughts or intimations of death. We might work rapidly to distract ourselves, to shift our attention away from death. We might be averse to silence and solitude, states in which it is difficult to find distractions from our fears. We might do the best we can not to spend any more time than necessary with someone sick or dying—and if that is someone close to us, effort and ingenuity also go into excuses and avoidance. We might spend time and money pursuing plastic surgery and other technical means intended to erase any sign of our aging and eventual death.

One therapy for clinical obsessiveness may seem initially counterintuitive. The therapist leads her patient in facing, over and over again, the object of anxiety. If particular thoughts or scenarios are feared, the therapist may talk the patient through the scenario repeatedly and even urge the patient to sit down every day for a half-hour and imagine the situation. If an action or setting is the source of phobia, the patient may best expose himself to it. Afraid of flying? Get on an airplane with a friend or therapist, and fly. Overcome by irrational fears of spiders? Go to a pet shop or zoo where spiders are safely contained, and make yourself observe them. The goal is to put the phobic fears and sources of obsessiveness into perspective—a perspective sensed in the body as well as accepted in the intellect. You will learn that the thoughts, even if they come, will not overwhelm you and spin you out of control. You will learn that you can face your fear and not be destroyed by it. And once, through practice and habituation, you learn this bone-deep, you will no longer be quite so afraid. Less afraid of the white elephant, you can drop exhausting efforts and strategies to avoid and suppress any hints of it. And less afraid of it, you may in fact stop thinking obsessively about it.

Classical Christian spirituality presents just such a therapy for the phobia of death. As Pastor Koelman noted, Scripture abounds with acknowledgments that a human life passes quickly.

> A mortal, born of a woman, few of days and full of trouble,
>   comes up like a flower and withers,
>   flees like a shadow and does not last. (Job 14:1–2)

> LORD, let me know my end,
>   and what is the measure of my days;
>   let me know how fleeting my life is.
> You have made my days a few handbreadths,
>   and my lifetime is as nothing in your sight.
> Surely everyone stands as a mere breath. (Ps. 39:4–5)

> You sweep [mortals] away; they are like a dream,
>   like grass that is renewed in the morning;
> in the morning it flourishes and is renewed;
>   in the evening it fades and withers.
>   (Ps. 90:5–6; see also Isa. 40:6–8)

> What is your life? For you are a mist that appears for a little while and then vanishes. (James 4:14)

The orthodox Christian tradition has held that this life is so fragile and fleeting that it makes little sense to put all our trust and hopes in it. St. Augustine observed the various ways mortals may grasp at significance and happiness. We seek power and prosperity. However desirable these may be, they cannot bring a real or lasting happiness. After all, the "happiness" of power and prosperity is constantly threatened by accident, disease, war, and death. No matter how much we accumulate, how much insurance of various sorts we acquire, the happiness gained has "the fragile brilliance of glass, a joy outweighed by the fear that it may be shattered at any moment." Better, counseled Augustine, to face the reality of death head-on. "I am certain of this, that no one has died who was not going to die at some time, and the end of life reduces the longest life to the same condition as the shortest." And: "There is no one, it goes without saying, who is not nearer to death this year than he was last year, nearer tomorrow than today, today than yesterday, who will not by and by be nearer than he is at the moment, or is not nearer at the present time than he was a little while ago." So "the whole of our lifetime is nothing but a race towards death." The one who lives longer does not avoid the ultimate destination of death but "merely has a longer journey" reaching it.

Of course, in the faith Augustine found courage and resourcefulness for facing death. Christ's defeat of death, the eventual renewal of heaven and earth, and bodily resurrection of the dead trump the transience of our ordinary, physical bodies and circumstances. A permanent and enduring happiness is made available by Christ's redeeming work. We need not, then, simply face the hard facts and stoically learn to live with them. In the final analysis, traditional Christian spirituality, unlike modern psychotherapy, is not about "adjustment" to what is—for what is now is not what will be in the end. It is not wrong or futile for us to desire deep, enduring happiness. Instead, says Augustine, if we desire only transient earthly joys, our desire is too small. It is insufficient to cling to uncertain, wispy joys "as though they were the only joys." Our desire must increase. We must look further, reach higher, toward the horizon of a mended and fulfilled world. We may then begin to be possessed by real happiness, the ultimate site of which is eternal life. Here is where we can reliably place our greatest trust and hope, where we can know joys that never end or fail.

Given such courage, we can admit the glimpses of death present in our everyday life. Fall leaves—at once fire-spangled and decayed, burning with color and dry as dust, beautiful and sad—speak of death. The quiet withering away of a friendship or movement from one job to another, simple goodbyes, episodes of forgetfulness, the realization that no moment or experience can ever be exactly duplicated: all these are little deaths. They demonstrate to us that, this side of our resurrection, all things change, melt, fade, or otherwise pass away. They are signs, like glints in a moving mirror or reflections in a passing car window, of our mortality and the mortality of everything and everyone we love on this earth. We can expend energy trying to ignore these reminders. But Christian spirituality presents another way. It calls us to recognize and acknowledge these little deaths, and in them larger deaths. It calls us to see them as they are, shot through with pain. And without pretending there is no pain, it calls us to see them in the light of their transformation in Christ and the lasting joys of resurrection happiness. The question then is not, How do we hold on to our earthly joys and try to keep them just as they are, as long as we can? Instead, the question becomes, How do we love these things in God and in hope of eternal life? How do we keep perspective and better fit ourselves—and our world—for enjoyment of the real, true, and final happiness that is to come?

Centrally, we learn the habits and ways of seeing that fit us for eternal life in gathered worship. There, in hearing the Scriptures and preaching, in harmonized singing, in prayer, and in the sacraments, we face death in the face of Christ. Gradually, with fits and starts, advances and setbacks, we are to a real degree freed of our debilitating denial of death.

And freed of that denial, we can practice a new kind of asceticism. Perhaps the asceticism most needed in our day is not the asceticism that emphasizes pain and self-denigration, like hair shirts and self-flagellation, but an asceticism of liberation from all kinds of addictions. Our addictions to substances or experiences—to speed, noise, frantic activity, alcohol, shopping—are among other things consuming distractions. We embrace these addictions to be distracted from boredom, from a nagging sense of shallow meaninglessness, and not least from the fact of our mortality. Asceticism for our day (not at all

unlike that of earlier eras of the church) would be a mortification of
our pervasive and profuse capacities for addiction. This mortification
would in turn be a liberation from our self-destructive addictions. It
would take us beyond ourselves, since even self-denial and self-hate
are ways of concentrating on the self. It would lead us to be caught
up by, to have our attention absorbed by, God's kingdom, and in that
kingdom the needs and hopes of our neighbors and the world.

As the twentieth-century Eastern Orthodox writer Paul Evdokimov
excellently puts it, such

> asceticism would be necessary rest, the discipline of regular periods of
> calm and silence, when one could regain the ability to stop for prayer
> and contemplation, even in the heart of all the noise of the world, and
> above all then to listen to the presence of others. Fasting, instead of
> doing violence of the flesh, could be our renunciation of the super-
> fluous, our sharing with the poor and a joyful balance in all things.
> . . . Modern asceticism serves the humanity that God assumed in the
> Incarnation. It is violently opposed to any diminution or abandoning
> of one's neighbor. . . . In the broader sense [and especially for today]
> an ascetic is a Christian who is keenly aware of the call of the Gospel,
> of the beatitudes, and who seeks humility and purity of heart in order
> to help his neighbor do the same.

Learning Death with Our Bodies

As we learn to acknowledge and admit the reality of death, rather
than deny it, we can prepare for our own death by familiarizing
ourselves with it while it remains (probably) at some distance. As
C. S. Lewis cleverly noted, it is easier to think about and prepare for
suffering when you are not already enduring the hurt of a toothache.
The aversion therapy I mentioned earlier works along similar lines:
If you're deathly afraid of snakes, it's best to view and encounter
them in safety, at some distance, and not wait until you've fallen
into a snake den. Martin Luther was also wise on this point. "We
should familiarize ourselves with death during our lifetime," he said,
"inviting death into our presence when it is still at a distance and not
on the move." Here I picture a lion—unthreatening at a distance,

rather than "on the move," already sprung and flying at us. "At the
time of dying, . . ." Luther says, "this is hazardous and useless, for
then death looms large of its own accord." In other words, the lion
sprung, about to land us, is big enough to block from our vision the
sun and sky and any other hope or perspective.

In an age gullibly wild for technique, I am loath to commend any
one-size-fits-all approach for how often we contemplate our death
or at what age our children should begin to face it. I am sure of this
much, however. We should not downplay or suppress the reality of
death in our worship. Every occasion of worship, after all, harks to
the death of Christ on a cross. Every baptism is a death, a drowning, and we should not gloss this. Our children will grasp what they
can as they can, and we should be alert to each child's questions and
probings as they arise. In any event, they (and we) are cushioned
or shielded in our approach to Christ's death on the cross, by the
understanding that through this death comes life.

The sacraments and other rituals of the church are particularly
powerful in our habituation to admit death, since they involve our
entire self, body as well as mind. At some level and in some way,
we all know in our body that we will die. Three years ago, I had a
cancer scare when I discovered a lump on my right collarbone. I was
writing at the keyboard when I paused and idly rubbed my neck. A
foreign, inch-and-a-half-wide knot immediately startled and scared
me. It turned out benign, a fatty tumor, but still from time to time
I find myself touching my neck or chest gingerly, my very fingers
reluctant and worried they may find a lump. Contemplation, reading, and thought are helpful in facing death. But we need means of
confronting death with our body, not just mentally or intellectually.
The sacraments and other rituals are such means.

A friend was an associate priest at St. Bartholomew's Episcopal
Church in New York City. St. Bartholomew's stands on prime real
estate, at the corner of Park Avenue and Fifty-first Avenue. Across
the street is the Waldorf Astoria Hotel. St. Bart's is not far from the
nexus of Manhattan's media, fashion, and business districts. The
church has a large and attractive building and often lets out meeting
space to nearby concerns. My friend, then, often rode the elevator
with celebrities, titans, or supporting players in the financial and

entertainment worlds. And sometimes such folk would show up for worship. That was the case one Ash Wednesday morning. Scriptures were read, the gospel was proclaimed, prayers were said; then my friend and another minister assumed posts behind the altar for the imposition of ashes.

The imposition of ashes is, among the church's rituals, perhaps the one that most starkly confronts each individual with his or her own mortality. The ashes are actual ashes, often burned down from palm leaves collected from the previous Lenten season, mixed with water into a black paste. At the imposition, one kneels before a priest; the priest dips a thumb into the paste, traces a small cross on the kneeler's forehead, and intones, "Dust you are, and to dust you shall return." It is solemn and potent: you not only hear the unsettling words but also feel the cold, grainy paste on your forehead.

On this particular Ash Wednesday, my friend proceeded at a stately pace, administering ashes deliberately on forehead after forehead. He was engrossed in the moment when suddenly he saw standing before him a preternaturally beautiful young woman, immaculately dressed and made up. She was obviously nervous and uncomfortable. She knelt hesitantly, leaning toward him with her forehead down, and he realized she wanted to speak. He bent over and she whispered, "Father, I am a model. I know I only have a few years, then I will be too old for this work. My body is aging, and I can hardly admit it to myself. I do it once a year, at this service. So rub the ashes on. Rub them hard."

Keeping Our Eyes on the Prize

But traditional Christian spirituality, as I have indicated, does not merely fit us to acknowledge death in body as well as spirit. It grants a perspective on death by shifting our primary focus away from ourselves, or death itself, to the real destination or end of our journey. Premodern Christians, I think, have much to show us on this count. They recognized that any home we now have on this earth is provisional. Our real home is a destination, the renewed heaven and earth. So the writer of the letter to the Hebrews noted that exemplars in the faith, such as Abraham and Sarah, recognized themselves "as strangers and foreigners on the earth." They "desire a better country," yearn toward their true homeland, and "indeed, [God] has prepared a city for them" (Heb. 11:13–16).

Historians tell us that it was as only as recently as the mid-nineteenth century that European Christians began to focus on the family dwelling as the model retreat or refuge—transferring the comfort and rest of heaven to the earthly home. Before then, Christians worked closer to the grain of the letter to the Hebrews. The family home, however warm it might sometimes be, was a way station on the pilgrimage of life. The true home was arrived at after death, and in its fullness after the resurrection from the dead. So the thirteenth- and early-fourteenth-century poet Dante expected the true and final homeland only in the eternity of the renewed creation, where every human resident would wear the "double raiment" of reunited body and soul. This picture was so strong and deeply engrained that even incipiently secularized Europeans desired eternity and sensed it as real to them as yesterday, today, and tomorrow are to us. Sir Thomas Browne, a Renaissance figure, could declare, "Think not thy time short in this world, since the world itself is not long. The created world is but a small parenthesis in eternity: and a short imposition, for a time, between such a state of duration as was before it and may be after it."

Of course, it is not easy to focus on home as a destination beyond death. We are in a spot similar to that of Europe before Columbus sailed and (despite himself) discovered the New World. The countrymen of Columbus and other early explorers were not sure there was a destination out there, far beyond the horizon. Perhaps the sailors would simply glide off the edge of the world into oblivion. But Columbus and others did return, with reports of an actual destination, and a wonderful one at that (although their discovery, and their lust for gold and other wonders of the New World, would not serve so well the already present occupants who knew it as an old world). Columbus had gone and come back to tell of it. Now many others, following, took courage and sailed themselves.

Similarly, the Christian confession is that an explorer or "pioneer of our salvation" (Heb. 2:10) has gone before us into uncharted

regions beyond life's border. Jesus Christ has gone ahead and come
back to tell of it. Columbus represented and substituted for Europeans
who could not themselves sail far west. More profoundly, Christ
represented and substituted for humanity, venturing into the region
of death not merely to explore it but to overcome it on our behalf.
As St. Athanasius put it,

> For the solidarity of mankind is such that, by virtue of the Word's
> indwelling in a single body, the corruption which goes with death has
> lost its power over all. You know how it is when some great king enters
> a large city and dwells in one of its houses; because of his dwelling
> in that single house, the whole city is honoured, and enemies and
> robbers cease to molest it. Even so is it with the King of all; He has
> come into our country and dwelt in one body amidst the many, and
> in consequence the designs of the enemy against mankind have been
> foiled, and the corruption of death, which formerly held them in its
> power, has simply ceased to be.

We take courage to face death, to cast our greatest energies in
service of a destination beyond it and any current "home," by focusing
on the powerful King who has come into our midst, the pioneer
who has gone before us. So, said Luther, it is a Christian spiritual
exercise not to "view or ponder death as such, not in yourself or in
your nature." Then death can only overwhelm—we will soon be in
despair or back to anxious denial. Instead,

> you must resolutely turn your gaze, the thoughts of your heart, and
> all your senses away from this picture and look at death closely and
> untiringly only as seen in those who died in God's grace and who have
> overcome death, particularly in Christ and then also in his saints. In
> such pictures death will not appear terrible and gruesome. No, it will
> seem contemptible and dead, slain and overcome in life. For Christ is
> nothing other than sheer life . . . The more profoundly you impress
> that image upon your heart and gaze upon it, the more the image
> of death will pale and vanish of itself without struggle or battle. . . .
> Thus you must concern yourself solely with the death of Christ and
> then you will find life.

Particular exercises for the searing, indelible imprinting of this image, the image of the death-conquering Christ, include hearing and reading the Scriptures, participation in the sacraments, and attendance to visual and tactile symbols that communicate the truth of salvation in Christ. To take but one such tactile symbol, an anointing with oil—as when we are sick—has us touched by another who represents Christ. The anointing itself is participation in Christ's anointing (the Messiah is and was the Anointed One). It is accompanied by words, which penetrate the mind and spirit, and it engraves its truth on our skin, marks our body, as well.

Practicing Resurrection

In worship and through the sacraments, and in other practices of Christian spirituality, we learn the story of Christ. We are, as it were, written into it—body and soul. Participating in this story, hearing and imitating parts of it like a child learning how to read, we learn a vocabulary, a grammar, and a plot line not otherwise available to us. Resurrection, as Christians and Jews understand it, cannot be learned apart from the traditions and ongoing practices of Christians and Jews. Christians learn to see the world in and through Christ; then we can see death truly. The "little deaths" of our everyday lives do not establish and give us the key to interpreting Christ's death and our mortality. It works the other way around. Christ's death is the key to seeing and rightly interpreting the little deaths. We can see that beyond death lies resurrection and a new creation, but only in Christ first and foremost. Springtime, with the blooming of flowers and profusion of new life, is not the reality reflected in the mirror of Christ's resurrection. Instead, Christ's resurrection is the most basic and all-encompassing reality; springtime is a reflection.

With priorities straight, we can from day to day look for "little resurrections" just as we recognize "little deaths." This is one way of practicing resurrection, impressing its reality on our imagination and reforming our hopes and emotions so that life eternal becomes to us as real as—even more real than—our temporal present or future.

On a bright day some summers ago, I went to the neighborhood swimming pool. As is my wont, I stretched out on a chaise lounge and read, absorbing the bright, warm sunshine. When I got hot, I jumped in the pool for awhile. Cooled and toweled off, I returned to my book. By and by, as the storytellers say, an elderly woman hobbled across the poolside tile in front of me. I do not want to dishonor the aged, but I will be honest and confess that she did not strike me as at all attractive. She leaned on a cane and moved grimacingly. Her milk-white face was drawn and ravaged by pains past and present. The skin on her upper arms and thighs sagged. Eventually she made it to the pool section where lanes were cordoned off by blue and white lines for lap swimming. She carefully eased into a sitting position. She laid the cane aside, cupped water up onto her arms and torso. She fitted goggles. Then she slid into the pool.

She stretched forward and used her feet to push away from the pool wall. Her strokes were fluid, full of grace. Her arms and feet churned economically, cutting the water smoothly with small, neat splashes. Her face lightened; she appeared to have lost herself somewhere beyond pain. She swam one, two, four laps before I stopped counting. Now she was, without any doubt, beautiful.

I had witnessed a little resurrection. Leaving the heedless medium of air, entering the buoyant, supportive medium of water, that good woman had her tired and beaten body transformed.

The Christian hope is something like that. We expect a renewed, transformed creation, a medium inconceivable by any earthly reckoning, a medium in which our bodies, themselves renewed, will thrive and be more themselves than ever before. Beautiful is just one word for it.

9

JESUS
AND THE
GROTESQUE

*The Earthiness
of Christian Spirituality*

I begin this chapter with two stories.

 The first involves the jazz musician and composer Charles Mingus. In his deliberately outlandish autobiography, *Beneath the Underdog*, Mingus details his rearing in the church at the hands of a fastidious, angry stepmother. She often quoted Scripture at the young Charles and just as often—in his eyes—treated him and other people hatefully. As a teenager, he is presented with her preachments once too often. He blurts back at her, "Did Jesus ever pee, Mama? Do the Scriptures say anything about that? And when he did Number Two did he use toilet paper?" His stepmother, outraged at what she regards as sacrilege, smacks him in response.

 The second story is set in the mountains above Santa Barbara, California. There, in a small, touristy town, my wife and I several years ago visited an old Spanish mission church. Touristy as the town was, most things in it (T-shirt and ice cream stores, for example) were easy for us to take in. But the mission was different. Wandering through it, we came across a crucifix. The Jesus on this crucifix had very clearly been flogged nearly to the point of death. Streaks of blood ran down his breast, thighs, and back. I could not help but wince: this was the most graphic crucifix I had ever seen. Walking around the display encasing it, I saw that the horror was even more pronounced. The back of this Jesus was flayed open, so open and deep that ribs were visible from behind.

What can Christian spirituality make of words like Mingus's, or of artifacts like the shocking crucifix? I am arguing for a bodily Christian spirituality, and these two incidents point up the awkwardness of accepting the body as fully an aspect of spirituality. The body is noble but also messy: we walk upright but carry within us bags of digesting food and excrement. The body is fragile; it can be broken and violated, so that its insides (blood, bones, guts) are repulsively exposed outside. If spirituality were about being angelic, ignoring bodily messiness and fragility, it would be easy to simply segregate blood, sweat, and excrement from the life of faith. But traditional Christian spirituality is emphatically bodily. Christian spirituality cannot ignore the incarnation, the truth that Christ was true man as well as true God; that his sanctifying work encompassed not only the soaring spirit but the torn flesh.

As we have seen, the body unsettles us because it ultimately dies. It also unsettles us because it changes constantly, and in its changing demonstrates that we in and as it are not permanent. It sheds hair and skin, emits fluids and wastes that remind us we are not angelic but mortal. In other words, the body can be grotesque. By *grotesque* here I do not mean primarily ugly or repulsive. I mean instead that the grotesque is a condition or object that is in between, that fits into no neat categories, that disturbs us with its ambiguity. Calves born with two heads, hermaphrodites, circus "freaks" of various sorts—all these are grotesque. They hover uncannily between states and bother us because they seem to upend an order we intuit as ironclad, tight, right, and obvious. People are either male or female: what to do with someone who possesses the genitals of both sexes? People are either children or grownups: what to make of a dwarf who is small as a child yet old as an adult?

But the grotesque is also much more mundane and prevalent than these examples. As human beings, as tortured wonders, we are each of us "in between." We think, we speak, we dream, we pray, so we set ourselves apart from animals and the rest of creation. And yet we are also animals—like them, we are embodied; like them, we are born, we eat and live for a spell, and we die. We humans, then, are liminal creatures, teetering on the threshold between the divine and the bestial.

It is true that humans are the only animals that build sewers, the only animals for whom the disposal of our feces is a problem. Yet this difference simultaneously reminds us how like animals we are—we may know to be embarrassed about our excrement, but like all other animals we inescapably produce it. The essayist Montaigne somewhere remarked that even on the highest throne in the world a man sits on his arse. Yet again, even the most powerful woman can bleed; even the most innocent child sweats. So in St. Augustine's estimation, the human is "an intermediate being," created and poised between the beasts and the angels. This in-betweenness, while not itself necessarily grotesque, entails that our lives, bodies, and selves are often marked by the grotesque. Godlike in some regards, animalistic in others, we can find our intermediate being incongruous, mysterious, and self-contradictory. It can appear monstrous as well as wondrous, and sometimes it is not easy to tell which.

It is central to the Christian confession that Jesus Christ entered and embraced our intermediacy. A truly Christian spirituality, then, must not flee from earthiness or deny the grotesque. It will make some sense of and help us inhabit our in-betweenness. In other words, we are spiritual creations not just in our churches and dining rooms but in our bathrooms and on our sickbeds. Christian spirituality comprehends not only the sparkle in our eyes but the grime under our fingernails.

Heaven in the Mud

Some may wonder if the Christian tradition really can fit us to embrace our earthiness, our grotesqueness. I expect many readers, for instance, share some of Mama Mingus's shock: we do not often consider Jesus of Nazareth with a digestive system and working bowels. Indeed, the church father Clement of Alexandria followed the gnostic Valentinus on just this point. Clement endorsed Valentinus's opinion that "Jesus endured all things and was continent; it was his endeavour to earn a divine nature; he ate and drank in a manner peculiar to himself, and the food did not pass out of his body. Such was the power of his continence that food was not corrupted within him; for he himself was not subject to the process of corruption." Though venturing no estimates of Jesus' digestive and colorectal system, St. John Chrysostom evinced a similarly severe aversion to human toiletry. Chrysostom counseled holy people not to be "lovers of luxury. . . . Food is called nourishment, to show that its design is not to injure the body, but to nourish it. For this reason perhaps food passes into [stinking, repulsive] excrement, that we may not be lovers of luxury." The saint would eat and drink very moderately. He or she would then still have to go to the bathroom, but not too often.

These attitudes, I think, fail to adequately embrace and comprehend human bodiliness. At worst, as Clement's appropriation of the gnostic Valentinus may indicate, they come close to denying the body as part of God's good creation. At best, they are an occasion of what I called earlier a realized eschatology, a grasping at an angelic, disembodied status that is not ours. We cannot consistently and fully affirm the rightness and goodness of our earthly bodies and at the same time reject their necessary, natural construction and functioning. While Scripture (unlike many recent movies) is not obsessed with what we do in toilets, it gives no hints whatsoever that humans did not urinate or defecate until after the fall or that Jesus, in order really to be holy, was free of these functions. There may have been purity issues with bodily wastes, but that did not mean the wastes were morally evil; it meant that they were impure if out of place and not handled rightly. (Similarly, in our culture it is not evil for me to dirty my hands at gardening. It is impure not to wash them after I am finished.)

The early-third-century church father Tertullian mined richer, more profoundly orthodox ore when he spoke out against the "heretical tenets" of those such as Valentinus, who held that Jesus the

Nazarene's body was not really, fully human but "had qualities peculiar to itself." Rather than regarding urinary and excretory organs as despicable sacks and straws of corruption, Tertullian saw them as "outlets for the cleanly discharge of natural fluids." He is closer to the more profoundly Jewish and Christian attitude expressed in "The Blessing of Asher Yatzar," a morning prayer that Jews may also recite after using the toilet:

> Blessed are You, HaShem, our God, King of the universe, Who formed man with intelligence, and created within him many openings and many hollow spaces; it is revealed and known before the Seat of Your Honor, that if one of these would be opened or one of these would be sealed it would be impossible to survive and to stand before You (even for one hour). Blessed are You, HaShem, Who heals all flesh and does wonders.

This remarkable blessing does not assume the digestive and excretory systems are repulsive accidents. Rather, they are the works of a Creator God "Who formed man with intelligence." The openings (mouth, nose, ears, and anus) and the "hollow spaces" (the heart, stomach, and intestines) work ingeniously and efficiently to allow the absorption, processing, and elimination of nutrients. These organs operate, some more humbly than others, to wondrously maintain health. They give life; if they fail "it would be impossible to survive." Furthermore, the toilet seat is juxtaposed to God's throne, says one commentary, "to teach us not to think that HaShem [God] does not concern Himself with lowly things such as the use of the bathroom, but that HaShem watches and knows everything."

With and as our bodies we sweat, weep, bleed, and defecate. These qualities may not show us at our most impressive or appealing. There is no edification in dwelling on them inordinately. It is good that we wash away sweat and blood, that we do our toilet business discreetly. But they are qualities of our creatureliness, goods that we need not, cannot, cast off and still bless our Creator with all that we are and have been made to be. So here I hope to dwell on the grotesque, our earthiness, in proportion and with an eye to edification. The physically grotesque can be incorporated into our Christian spirituality.

They are ways, and times, that we can draw closer to God by staying determinedly down to earth, when heaven is found in a grain of sand or a gob of mud.

Reweaving into the Earthy Web of Life

Acknowledging our in-betweeness—that we are "naked apes" as well as a "little lower than the angels"—can connect (or reconnect) us with the material creation of which we are a part. As the Genesis accounts have it, humans were created amid earth and its flora and fauna. Biblical rituals included thanksgiving festivals for harvests and their sustenance, so that plowing, planting, and reaping were not separated from spirituality. For the ancients, too little or too much rainfall was a matter of life and death. For us the weather is mostly a convenience or inconvenience, something we try to predict and exploit or compensate for, as with indoor sporting stadiums. Along similar lines, animal sacrifices strike us as "primitive," violent, and nasty. And (excepting those who are vegetarians) we still kill and consume animals, though at a sanitized distance. Affluent Westerners eat exponentially more meat than premoderns, including the biblical peoples. And except for the few persons who work on farms and in slaughterhouses, we encounter the flesh of cattle and chickens only in abstracted parts, slices wrapped in plastic, displayed in disinfected, odorless supermarkets. We never look the one-and-same animal that we will consume in the eye. We do not feed and doctor these animals to maturity or shovel their manure. Those who offered up animal sacrifices did all these things. So they could not, as we usually do, take these animals and their lives for granted. They honored the animals that were sacrificed and naturally included their food consumption in their spirituality.

My point is that modern or postmodern urbanites and suburbanites are removed or detached from creation and the "circle of life" in which we participate. So we can hide not only from death and disease but from the creaturely web of which we are a part and which gives us life and health. We are woven into this web, and we (and the rest of creation) suffer when we forget, ignore, or deny that. Admitting our

own animality can then be a spiritual exercise, an exercise of taking
the place we have been given under God with other creatures.

How can we admit or cultivate that awareness? We can take
seriously that we too live by eating and defecating. We can eschew
some of the conveniences that separate us from bodily messiness.
Though I do not pretend to undertake it with the same joy or intensity
with which I pray and sing hymns, I consider my household duty
of cleaning the bathroom a small Christian service. It needs to be
done, and it reminds me that I and my loved ones are—among other
things—mortal bodies. Try this: when working the final shift at a
homeless shelter, volunteer to clean the bathrooms. Or to take a final,
similar example: when our daughter was an infant, my wife and I
elected to diaper her in cloth. We hoped this was ecologically more
responsible than discarding cartons of disposable diapers weekly,
but we also wanted the necessarily messy work of rinsing out dirty
cloths to hold us down to earth. It was an act of love for our baby
just as she was, loaded diapers and all.

Yet another way to weave more fully into the web of life is to live
with animals. Having grown up on a farm, I know there is a drastic
difference between raising animals for a livelihood and keeping pets.
But making room for a dog or a cat (or one of each, as in our case)
highlights human kinship with all the living. The animals assume
their own roles in the family and household. They inhabit the world
in ways quite different from, but not entirely foreign to, ours. Our
dog, Merle, for instance, walks on all fours. I have never yet seen
him gaze into the sky. He would rather keep his nose to the ground,
and in his demeanor he is constant reminder that the dirt—not just
the stars—is worth pondering and investigating. Likewise, animals
in daily proximity never let us neglect, in our all human planning
and calculating, that life has to be taken one day at a time and finally
cannot be controlled, scheduled, and manipulated. It turns out we are
creatures too, and not gods. No matter how busy we are, the animals
must be fed, their hair must be vacuumed from the couch. And just
when we think we have at last devised a household routine that will
keep everything in order, the dog has an accident on the carpet or the
cat knocks a vase off the table. On the brighter side, Merle's simple
affection is a constant, and Sassy's purring contentment is a reliable

result of having her belly rubbed, no matter how complicated our human world gets.

Gardening, manual labor, and tending to the bedpans and sponge baths of the sick are additional ways we deliberately practice and acknowledge our physicality, our oneness with all earthly creation. There are surely many others, but you get the idea.

One Criminal under the Hat

Acknowledging the grotesque in our days and our being, in ways such as those hinted at above, can help put us in right relation to God and to our neighbors and enemies. Admitting that humans defecate, have dandruff, bad breath, and so forth not only reconnects us with the rest of earthly creation, but reminds us that we are not gods or God. We are not angels but creatures made from the same physical stuff of the ground we tread. I have already ruminated on how this earthy grotesqueness puts us in right relation to God, so here I turn attention to how it can also situate us rightly in relation to our neighbors and enemies.

Traditional Christian spirituality has constantly recognized the danger of thinking too highly of ourselves. It discloses and attacks the propensity to assume our virtue is greater than that of others. We tend to be hard on the sins of others yet look for excuses for our own. Our drive toward self-aggrandizement is pervasive. It takes many and subtle forms, including the deprecation of others. I stumble and fall, and one of the ways I may comfort myself is by recalling even bigger mistakes or sins on the part of a neighbor. I can get an even greater charge by identifying an enemy, then imagining him or her a devil. By comparison, at least, I am an angel. Christian spiritual exemplars have noted these tendencies and set guard against them. So Christ spoke dramatically about the peril of judging others (Matt. 7:1–5). The apostle Paul, according to tradition, offset the precipitous temptation of pride and self-deception by regarding as himself as the "foremost" or "chief" of sinners (1 Tim. 1:15). To consider later but still ancient Christian traditions of a self-wary spirituality, we can turn to the third- and fourth-century desert fathers.

The story is told of a desert father to whom a devil appeared, disguised as an angel of light. The devil dissembled, "I am the angel Gabriel, and I have been sent to you." The monk replied, "Are you sure you weren't sent to someone else? I am not worthy to have an angel sent to me." At this demonstration of authentic humility, the devil vanished.

In another desert tale, a hermit is casting an evil spirit from a demoniac. The demon agrees to leave the possessed but has a condition. The hermit must tell the demon who are the goats (destined for damnation) and who are the sheep (destined for salvation). The hermit responds: "The goats are people like myself; who the sheep are, God alone knows." The demon then can only scream, "Look here, I am going out because of your humility." In like manner, on through the centuries, the tradition over and over again insists that the true saint does not regard herself or himself as better than others.

The grotesque, as we will soon see, can be comic. But it can also take on darker shades. Evil can render us grotesque in sobering and alarming ways. The woman overcome by greed, in her constant, cold calculations, loses human warmth and connections. Another person, consumed by lust or jealousy, succumbs to beastly violence and commits murder. We can look at the most savage and grotesque criminals and wonder if they have lost their humanity. Are they now inhuman monsters? But again, classical Christianity sees a difference only of degree, not of kind, between the most admired saint and the most wanted criminal. The grotesqueness of evil, the warping ravages of sin, infect us all.

Recall G. K. Chesterton's fictional detective, Father Brown. In one insightful story, Chesterton reveals the "secret" that makes this diminutive Catholic priest such an extraordinary detective. Queried at a dinner party, Father Brown says that his adeptness at crime solving follows from a "religious exercise." Coming upon a crime, he works to think, imagine, and feel how a particular criminal has gotten so bent. The basis of this sympathy with the strikingly, darkly grotesque is Father Brown's faith. Harking back to orthodox Christian humility, the saintly detective realizes he is like the criminal "in everything except actual final consent to the action." Father Brown explains,

> I don't try to get outside the man [that is, the criminal]. I try to get inside the murderer. . . . Indeed, it's much more than that, don't you see. I *am* inside a man. I am always inside a man, moving his arms and legs; but I wait till I know I am inside a murderer, thinking his thoughts, wrestling with his passions; till I have bent myself into the posture of his hunched and peering hatred; till I see the world with his bloodshot and squinting eyes, looking between the blinkers of his half-witted concentration; looking up the short and sharp perspective of a straight road to a pool of blood. Till I really am a murderer.

Father Brown's aristocratic dinner companion is aghast and sniffs, "And this you call a religious exercise?" By all means, Father Brown answers, and again he explains:

> No man's really any good till he knows how bad he is, or might be; till he's realised exactly how much right he has to all this snobbery, and sneering, and talking about "criminals," as if they were apes in a forest ten thousand miles away; till he's got rid of all the dirty self-deception of talking about low types and deficient skulls; till he's squeezed out of his soul the last drop of the oil of the Pharisees; till his only hope is somehow or other to have captured one criminal, and kept him safe and sane under his own hat.

Chesterton follows Jesus, Paul, the desert fathers, and many other wise figures in the lineage of classical Christian spirituality. We are in true, right relation to our neighbors and our enemies when we learn to detect the twisted, grotesque marks of sin under our own hats and not just those of others.

A Spirituality That Breaks Wind

But of course, as I have been at pains to indicate, the humanly grotesque is not always or necessarily evil. It is often simply an entailment of our physicality and our creaturely limitations. The grotesque can be comic. Admitting that we are sometimes funny, despite our best efforts to be noble and suave, can be a spiritual exercise.

In the middle of delivering an eloquent, carefully composed public prayer, the pastor belches. The business executive thinks he has conducted a staff meeting with exquisite polish and élan, only to notice afterward that he stood in front of a roomful of people with his fly open. The expert saleswoman delivers a perfect pitch at a lunch, only to discover in a bathroom mirror that a piece of parsley had conspicuously pasted itself on her front teeth. These are embarrassments, not moral trespasses, and they happen to all of us. Our bodies are always, necessarily down to earth. They and their comportment are not completely under our control. We try to present them with appropriate dignity, but we cannot be human and always be graceful. We will track mud into the bishop's office, or doze off at an important ceremony, or trip in a parade. On such occasions we do best to cultivate an affectionate sense of humor, of the sort signaled in St. Francis's playful address of his body as "Brother Ass." I don't know if angels have (or need) the capacity to laugh at themselves, but holy people must.

Christians can be overly fastidious folk—but then they are trying to be angels, not people. The ostensibly holy can pretend never to belch or break wind. Some church buildings are redolent not so much of incense as of the antiseptic scent of a hospital clinic. The services of church custodians are important and sanctified, but do we seriously want to affirm that holiness must carry the ammoniac scent of Pine Sol?

Fortunately, there are luminaries of the tradition who embrace creaturely earthiness. The irrepressible Martin Luther may be chief among them. He could declare, "I resist the devil, and often it is with a fart that I chase him away." Hearing of a contemporary who "wrote blasphemously" against marriage, complaining about the "stinking, putrid private parts of women," the gritty Reformer responded with acidic humor. To "defile [women's] creation and nature is most godless," he said. "As if I were to ridicule a man's face on account of his nose! For the nose is the latrine of man's head and stands above his mouth. As a matter of fact, God himself must allow all prayer and worship to take place under his privy." Reflecting on the misguided zealousness of a minister who had himself castrated in his youth, Luther quipped, "For my part I'd rather have two pair [of testicles] added than one cut off."

Though not so gloriously earthy (or explicit) as Luther, St. Augustine was no stranger to anything human. Arguing that the sinless and perfected body will be at the complete control of the will, Augustine observes that we do in fact already, in ordinary, everyday experience, "find among human beings some individuals with natural abilities very different from the rest of mankind." These include people who can on whim, and without manual manipulation, move their ears, "either one at a time or both together." Then there are those who "produce at will such musical sounds from their behind (without any stink) that they seem to be singing from that region." We moderns may be tempted to dismiss this as but one among other fascinating legends Augustine recounts and presumes veracious, such as horses inseminated by the wind or the incorruptibility of peacock flesh. But then there are recurrent rumors of jazz trumpeter Bix Beiderbecke's ability to pass gas in tune, or the historically documented showmanship of the "fartiste" Le Petomane, a nineteenth-century cabaret performer who "could blow out candles with a well-aimed blast and break wind in tenor, baritone, and bass registers." (Who knew comedian Jim Carrey and his ventriloquized butt had such a venerable pedigree?)

Doubtless I have already said enough on this subject for some readers. But the point is important: the body is a good creation of a good God and remains good even in its less dignified propensities. To disown any part of our body and its functions is to grasp, presumptuously, at an angelism and angelic "spirituality" that is not ours. And that presumption is a real temptation in our modern Elvis World. In this modern setting, spirituality does not sweat.

As we have seen, Presley's vividly, undeniably physical performances were controversial especially on the sexual front. But Elvis midway through his career was also criticized for profusely, obviously sweating on stage. Critics considered his perspiration distasteful and unappealing and complained that audiences didn't want to see a performer in such a grossly physical state. This response had its roots in a view of the arts as an ennobling spiritual practice. Nineteenth-century English poet and critic Matthew Arnold first articulated such a position. Noting the decline of religion and the rise of secularism, Arnold said that modern men and women needed to look to the arts for a glimpse of the transcendent. He set the stage for an explicit dichotomizing of "low culture" and "high culture." Low culture was vulgar and spiritually unedifying. High culture was refined and spiritually elevating.

Classical music performed in a concert hall still ably represents this modern Arnoldian dichotomy. Orchestral concert halls are typically located in the arts and museum districts of our cities. Symphonic musicians dress in tuxedoes, and their audience does not typically wear jeans or other everyday clothing. Listeners participate in the performance only on a highly intellectual, unemotional plane—they do not respond to the music with their entire bodies (as in dancing, for example) but by polite applause at the end of each composition. This is high culture, meant to elevate its listeners spiritually, to take them out of the everyday into the transcendent. We do not pay to see classical musicians sweat. Orchestra halls dispense lozenges so that listeners can restrain their bodies and avoid inappropriate coughing. So have we been enculturated to perform and hear live classical music as a largely "spiritual" (nonphysical) exercise. On that enculturation, Elvis's sweating is a drag and a distraction—it pulls us back down to earth by a blatant reminder that the performer is a bodily, earthly creature. In modern churches, where the concern for (nonphysical, angelic) spirituality is more explicit, we may be apt all the more to ignore and downplay our bodies.

There is an interesting wrinkle. On the one hand, Elvis's sweat can offend modern sensibilities and reground us, put us consciously back in our bodies. On the other hand, Elvis's sweat represents a kind of postmodern spirituality. In 1966, Presley attended a concert of a favorite artist, the rhythm and blues singer Jackie Wilson. Backstage after the show, he told Wilson he loved the look of Wilson's heavy sweating on stage. Wilson agreed, commenting, "Man, the chicks really dig that." He informed Elvis that he hyped his perspiration by swallowing several salt tablets and copiously drinking water before a performance. Presley took note and adopted the trick for his own concerts. His sweat, then, was not entirely honest. It was admired for its effect: a heavily perspiring performer looks especially intense and hardworking. The sweat glittering under lighting is itself cinematic. (The sweating singer appears rain-drenched, and the frequent use of rain effects in film follows from rain's dramatic visual impressions.) Elvis, sweat rolling off him as heavily as off a ditch-digger in July, exploits sweat for its purely imagistic power and impression. The effect is mainly a surface effect, a virtual reality. He's working hard, but not physically so hard as the ditch-digger. Still, the chicks dig the effect, and this play on an imagistic veneer represents our postmodern Elvis World.

A traditional Christian spirituality of sweat does not fit comfortably into either the modern or the postmodern category. Unlike modern spirituality, it insists on embracing our physical creatureliness entirely, from head to toe and all in between. The spiritual and the scatological meet and, however odd, are not at odds. This spirituality sweats—and breaks wind. But Christian spirituality also takes the body more seriously than does postmodern spirituality. The body in all its physicality is real. It is not merely a sign or instrument to be manipulated for surface effect. It is a true, honest body inside as well as out. It is a body so true and central to human being that it will, transformed, be borne into eternity.

Deformations and Beauty Marks of Sanctity

But will we bear our earthiness and its sometime grotesqueness into eternity? Granted that we should not disrespect any part of the body in its earthly dispensation, including the "private" and sometimes embarrassing organs, will the resurrection body of our ultimate hope include not just eyes (of some sort) but digestive organs and genitals? Some church fathers thought not, but the thickest cord of orthodoxy affirmed that it will. Tertullian and Augustine are among those who noticed that Jesus in his resurrected body could consume fish. They imagined that all of the God-created body was wondrous and beautiful and would, however transformed, have a place in the renewed heaven and earth. Even more, they noted that even the evil grotesque might, in some respects, be redeemed.

No Christian of the remotest orthodoxy can say otherwise. For at the center of Christian faith and spirituality, endlessly recalled, hymned, and meditated on, is one of the most revoltingly grotesque human acts imaginable: the crucifixion of Jesus Christ. An actual crucifixion—unlike the pretty gold pendants we now hang from our necks—was horribly ugly and degrading. As is well known, crucifixion was the form of execution the Romans reserved for the lowest of the low, for slaves and base criminals. (No Roman citizen would suffer this form of execution.) It was meant to be extremely humiliating, lifting a naked, terribly agonized person up to public spite and ridicule. Crucifixion was grotesque in its diabolical violence, and in its intention to render the crucified someone or something less than human. And yet through this dirty travesty of human dignity, God acted to redeem and renew the world. Ironically, paradoxically even, Christians see the first century's goriest, most repulsive form of torture and execution as the highest revelation and work of glory.

Entire libraries are filled with books on the scandalous beauty that, backlit by the resurrection, shines through the cross. But, not least because of overfamiliarity and sanitization, we do not so often note that the cross and the rehearsal of Jesus' death fits Christians to be a people who can—who must—acknowledge the grotesque. Attention to the cross, and attempting to model our lives after Jesus' cruciform service, is an indispensable spiritual exercise.

Evil and grotesque as the crucifixion was, something good came out of it. But it is more than that. We can say that something good (stronger character, perhaps) comes out of an automobile accident or a bout with cancer yet not imagine the wreck or the disease as themselves in any way admirable or beautiful. The crucifixion is ugly, without doubt, but centuries of Christian art and devotion attest that it is not wholly or simply ugly. It is settled doctrine that Jesus' glory and divinity are climactically, most dazzlingly revealed at the crucifixion. There he is "lifted up" not only in degradation but in royal glory (John 3:14–15; 8:28; 12:31–33). Thus can the grotesque, sometimes even the evil grotesque, be made something edifying and beautiful.

It is remarkable that John's Gospel, surely the most "spiritual" (in the sense of nonphysical) of the four Gospels, is the one that most explicitly insists on the glory of the crucifixion. Also remarkably, it is John who takes account of the scars still borne by Jesus' resurrected body. In the famous story of "Doubting Thomas," that disciple sensibly refuses to gullibly accept that the selfsame Jesus he saw executed days before is now walking among the living. Thomas will not be satisfied of the veracity of these claims "unless I see the mark of the nails in his hands, and put my finger in the mark of the nails" (John 20:25). Later Jesus appears and invites Thomas to do exactly that, and Thomas, true to his word, believes. "My Lord and my God!" he confesses (John 20:28).

Somehow, then, the resurrected body of the Lord—the very definition of transformed physical perfection—is no less perfect for the presence of its raw scars. The scars themselves are no longer ugly, or merely something evil from which something good might result, but are themselves inherently beautiful. Does this suggest that our physical deficiencies will be carried into our resurrection bodies? What about the sufferer of cerebral palsy, the man who has had a leg amputated, the woman who lost a breast to cancer surgery? How would they be hopeful or glad of bearing these disfigurements into eternity? Classical Christian spirituality has been clear: such losses or lacks are grievous, such imperfections are flatly and finally imperfections. So Tertullian insisted, "To [perfect] nature, not to injury, are we restored. . . . If God raises men not entire, He raises not the dead." Likewise, St. Augustine argued that lost limbs would be restored, that the pristine nature of each individual would be held in God's memory and bestowed at the resurrection.

There is a single exception to this rule, and that is the Christlike scar. Augustine expects that "perhaps" the martyrs' bodies will bear the scars of their deaths, for these are marks incurred explicitly in witness to Christ, "the wounds they suffered in Christ's name." Consequently, "in those wounds there will be no deformity, but only dignity, and the beauty of their valour will shine out, a beauty *in* the body and yet not *of* the body." Any missing limbs or other functional deficiencies would be restored, but the scars of the martyrs' suffering "are proofs of valour" and "not to be accounted defects, or to be called by that name." Thus might the evil grotesque, like Jesus' suffering on the cross, be redeemed in toto, rendered an adorable example of perfection, a beauty mark of sanctity.

Footwashing and the Reclamation of the Grotesque

I want to end this chapter with some rumination on another earthy, bodily event presented only in John's Gospel—the ritual of footwashing. Ours is a day of hyper-cleanliness and virtual reality. I "partake" of the creation via a television nature show and suffer none of the crusted-sweat showerlessness or mosquito bites of an actual camping trip. Exactly in such a setting, I suspect footwashing is a bodily spiritual exercise we might profitably undertake more often. There are other bodily rituals in the Christian tradition, the Eucharist most significant among them. But footwashing uniquely forces us to directly confront the discomfort, even the grotesqueness, of our embodiment.

Meals, after all, can be quite dignified and dignifying occasions. The Eucharist is such a meal. It can be conducted, and usually is, without any attention to the less appealing aspects of our bodies. Furthermore, in eating, drinking, tasting, recitation, and seeing, the Eucharist involves the organs of mouth, tongue, nose, ears, and eyes—the head. The feet are humbler and simpler parts. When the apostle Paul contrasts the highest and lowest members of the body—recognizing a hierarchy while affirming the priceless value of both to the whole—he seizes on the head and feet. In Paul's words, "The eye cannot say to the hand, 'I have no need of you,' nor again the head to the feet, 'I have no need of you.' On the contrary, the members of the body that seem to be weaker are indispensable" (1 Cor. 12:21–22).

So long as we can stand, our feet are always the lowest parts of our body. Not only are they closest to the earth, to dirt and dirtiness, but with each step they touch and eat dust. Scripturally, the feet are euphemisms for the genitals, other organs Paul includes among the less "respectable" and "honorable" members of the body. In the Bible, "covering the feet" codes urination (as in 1 Sam. 24:3). And

Ezekiel denounces the seductive prostitute for "spreading her feet" (Ezek. 16:25, as rendered, e.g., in the KJV).

Consider, too, that Leviticus evidences special squeamishness about creatures closest to the soil, forbidding the consumption of animals that move on their bellies or all fours or have "many feet" (Lev. 11:41–42). Often dirty, always low, the feet are humble and humbling. To "tread underfoot" is a biblical figure for domination and subjection. Lifting and showing the bottom of the feet to another was an act of disdain. So the psalmist complains, "Even my bosom friend in whom I trusted, who ate of my bread, has lifted the heel against me" (Ps. 41:9). (Still today, showing the soles of the feet counts in many cultures as a scornful gesture. In *Black Hawk Down*, Mark Bowden explains what led up to the 1993 rebellion of the residents of Mogadishu against the U.S. soldiers intended to be peacekeepers in their country. Among other things, the Somalians were grossly offended by overflying helicopters with Marines on benches lining the skids, dangling the bottoms of their feet in the faces of the people they said they wanted to aid and protect.)

All of this helps us to appreciate the comparative humility and simplicity of footwashing. But it also underscores the shock and surprise of the disciples when Jesus, the Messiah and Lord, deigns to wash their feet. Footwashing was a task ordinarily consigned to slaves, women, and children. In John's Gospel, Jesus' footwashing of the disciples structurally and narratively foreshadows the ultimate humiliation and servanthood of the cross. Before shouldering the cross, Jesus could hardly have more dramatically demonstrated his radical love and friendship than by kneeling and touching the sweaty feet of his followers.

In the modern West, with most transportation by automobile or other technological means and only incidentally on foot, we have no daily customs of footwashing. Nor are we sensitive about flashing the soles of our feet. Yet it is no stretch for us to understand the biblical associations of the feet with lowliness and dirt. We don't walk on our heads, after all. Even if they stand mostly on suburban lawns or asphalt, our feet still touch the ground. Our restaurants forbid bare feet. We administer sprays and powders to prevent our feet from stinking. So it takes no involved scriptural hermeneutics to comprehend, at a visceral as well as an intellectual level, the discomforting symbolics of kneeling and washing another's feet. Putting one's head close to another's feet is inherently not a dominating position. The magnificent subversiveness of Jesus' washing the disciples' feet is not hard to grasp, especially when we recall that he washed Judas's feet too. It is difficult to imagine our masters behaving so with their mortal enemies today: try to picture George W. Bush washing the worn, dirty toes of Osama bin Laden or Saddam Hussein.

Notice, too, something a bit different about our concerns and associations with feet today. I can find no biblical hint that the "superiors" who routinely had their feet washed by their "inferiors" were ever embarrassed by their own feet. But for many of us, I suspect, one of the most unappealing aspects of a footwashing service is baring our feet to the gaze of others. Given the democratic morés of our day, unknown in ancient Palestine, we may be less humiliated by the act of touching another's feet. But we can urgently worry that our feet are ugly or smelly or otherwise degrading. It is not so much that we may be humiliated by touching another's feet as that we fear the humiliation of the other's seeing and touching and judging our feet. So on the receiving as well as the giving end, footwashing is a ritual of vulnerability and interdependence.

Yet here again the stretch from our world to the biblical world is manageable. In the stories of Scripture, taking off one's shoes is associated with powerlessness, mourning, poverty, and imprisonment. After Absalom's rebellion, David leaves the city weeping and barefoot (2 Sam. 15:30). Isaiah sees the captured Israelites shuffling into exile naked and shoeless (Isa. 20:2–4). Removing one's sandals can indicate the relinquishment of property, as with Boaz in the book of Ruth or Jesus' sending his disciples on mission barefooted, a sign of their renunciation of possessions, prerogatives, and protection (Luke 10:4). This signal of vulnerability and spiritual poverty is why shoes are removed in the presence of the holy, as did Moses at the burning bush. All these are important resonances to enrich and inform our practices of footwashing.

It is through attention to the gospel and Gospel stories that our feet, with the rest our bodies and lives, are transfigured. I have emphasized the lowliness and vulnerability—in some sense the grotesqueness—of feet. But as the apostle put it, the feet are not simply lowly. They are also indispensable and in their own way honorable and respectable. They are even rendered beautiful, as in Isaiah's exclamation, "How beautiful upon the mountains are the feet of the messenger who announces peace, who brings good news, who announces salvation, who says to Zion, 'Your God reigns'" (Isa. 52:7). The Psalms and other texts encapsulate the fullness of shalom in the figure of the feet: blessed are the feet that stand on firm places, that walk on right paths, that never slip or stumble (Pss. 18:33; 31:8; 40:2; 56:13). And of course feet are most immediately transfigured by the healings of lame persons by Jesus and the disciples.

Thus attending to our feet strikes chords not only of humility and vulnerability but of poignant tenderness and beauty. Once, at a halfway house that ministers to former prisoners moving back into society, I spoke with a man I will here call Marcus. The nearest thing to a mother Marcus could remember was a foster parent who sometimes tied him to a basement post and beat him. Yet among his fondest memories were those of this tired, angry woman offering up her hoary feet for him to rub and shave off calluses. That, he took it, was a form of love, care, and connection. On another occasion, I was at hand when a sickly, isolated eighty-five-year-old woman was taken by her family from her house and moved into a nursing home. She was not ready to go, but her children and grandchildren were as gentle as they could be. In a dim, dusty little bedroom, they lifted her legs from beneath the sheets and swung her feet onto the floor. Her toenails had clearly been unattended for months, probably years. They were thick, yellow, and so long they twisted and curled. They were Medusa's snakes transferred to the feet. It was a granddaughter who responded most adequately and appropriately. She dropped to both knees, took one of her grandmother's feet in her hands, caressed it like a lamp apt to produce a benevolent genie, and said, "Grandma, can I trim your nails?"

Are feet grotesque? Shaving the calluses or trimming the hoary nails of another's feet strikes me as just that. And yet, as is also true in both these cases, basic and beautiful are the feet and ministrations to them. Highlighting the wholeness of the physical body and the spiritual, corporate body of Christ, Luther insisted that a single member of the body "embodies" the whole. "This is obvious," he said. "If anyone's foot hurts him, yes, even the little toe, the eye at once looks at it, the fingers grasp it, the face puckers, the whole body bends over it, and all are concerned for this small member; again, once it is cared for all the other members are benefited." And, then, referring to the sacrament of the Table, Luther added, "This comparison must be noted well if one wishes to understand [the Eucharist]."

May we, tending to one another in body as well as spirit, be fitted to walk closer to the New Jerusalem, where at last we will, if not before, rest our feet together beneath the banquet table of the Lord.

10

You Wonder Why We're All Crazy

Making a Place for Sex in Christian Spirituality

I f you think that you could never like country music, that it's all predictable and hackneyed, come on over to my house and I'll show you otherwise. I wish I could demonstrate the resonance and beauty of country music on a guitar or my father-in-law's fiddle, but the only musical instrument I've mastered is the stereo. One of the CDs I might cue up, working toward your conversion, is a classic by the Flatlanders called *More a Legend Than a Band*. The Flatlanders were fronted by three longhair Texans, including the Lubbock-grown Butch Hancock. Once Hancock tried to explain himself to a journalist. "In Lubbock we grew up with two main things," he said. "God loves you and he's gonna send you to hell, and that sex is bad and dirty and nasty and awful and you should save it for the one you love. You wonder why we're all crazy."

You may want to recall Butch's take on hell and damnation when you read this book's final chapter. For now I am interested in the second part of his statement. When he talks about attitudes toward sex, he doesn't speak only for west Texans. Earlier, in chapter 2, I tried to be honest about orthodox Christian spirituality's ambivalence toward sexuality. We saw that much of the tradition was, at the least, uncomfortable with sex and, at the most, ready to regard it as always tainted with sin. As I also indicated there, modern Christians—even those of a traditionalist bent—have tried to embrace sex and, in its rightful place, sexual pleasure. But we frequently do so with confusion and some double-mindedness. I have repeated Hancock's wry observation to a number of Christian friends, and they often chuckle with recognition. Something like the message that sex is dirty and awful and you should save it for the one you love is what they gleaned from their upbringing. In fact, I don't think it's only Christians who go a little crazy about sex. (The double and triple messages postmodern commercial culture sends about sexuality are mind-blowing in their self-contradictions.) And I don't believe all the wrinkles and surprises of sex can ever be smoothed out, at least not on this side of the eschaton. When it comes to sex, one Christian philosopher has wisely and wise-acrely suggested, none of us are really or entirely straight. But I do believe classical Christian spirituality can make a place for sex and can encompass rather than merely cast out sexual desire.

Beatrice and the Affirmation of Sexual Beauty

Encompassing and embracing sexual desire begins, as I indicated in chapter 2, with a recognition that sexual pleasure should not be denigrated when it is well ordered and proportionate. For orthodox Christian spirituality, sexual pleasure is not an end in itself. It is not more important than our service to God and to our neighbors, service formed and lent substance by the kingdom of God revealed in Jesus Christ. Our sexuality, like all other aspects of our being, should be channeled to fit into and complement our witness to the kingdom. When we love and act faithfully and rightly, we should not be embarrassed or worried that enjoyment accompanies our loving and acting.

Our enjoyment of any real good is in fact a sign that our habits and character are shaped truly and rightly. A loyal mother should enjoy her children and achieve satisfaction when she parents them well. A dam builder who constructs a reliable, enduring dam should find pleasure in his work and accomplishment. Likewise, when sex is put to the service of its rightful ends and goals (in God's good order), it too should be enjoyed.

The direct biblical sources of such an attitude include Genesis 2 and the Song of Songs. In Genesis, woman is created as man's companion. Various animals pass before Adam, and he and God determine that none are really, fully compatible with the human. But when Adam first gazes on Eve, he is pleased at this "bone of my bones and flesh of my flesh." Woman and man are nakedly and unashamedly present each to the other (Gen. 2:23–25). They delight in one another, bodily as well as soulfully. The Song of Songs even more unabashedly exults in sexual beauty and desire. It is a straightforward celebration of a woman and man reveling in one another's attractiveness, rhapsodically cataloging the other's most favored physical attributes. Lips, skin, hair, eyes, breasts, legs—all are delighted in and enthusiastically celebrated. And this in a sensuous context including pleasure in food and drink, in pleasant scents and fabrics. At times, of course, later Christian tradition would attempt to "spiritualize" the Song of Songs, but the text is so resolutely physical that the earthly body can never be entirely be routed from it. In the context of the entire biblical canon, the Song of Songs' sexual desire may be taken up into and become a sign of a greater desire, the desire for God. But it is then made more, not less, than sexual desire. It is not eliminated or degraded but fulfilled, transformed, and lifted up.

Perhaps the Christian tradition's greatest celebration of eros so transformed, not destroyed but blossomed to its greatest end and potential, is Dante's *The Divine Comedy*. The great thirteenth- and fourteenth-century poet does not deny his love and desire for the beautiful Beatrice. Instead, putting it in right order and proportion, he celebrates and enriches it. Beatrice, at once subordinated to and made yet more glorious by the love of God, becomes the fictive pilgrim's guide out of the upper reaches of Purgatory and into the highest spheres of the heavens.

Dante, following Thomas Aquinas (who followed Augustine), is quite clear that human desire is easily disordered by sin. In the Inferno and in Purgatory he passes by parades of persons given up to distorted loves, bent and misshapen by greed, gluttony, lust, and so forth. It is the revelation of Christ that, like a sun, shines through the stained glass of our various human yearnings and clarifies them, showing their true colors. So cleansed, clarified, and purified as he passes through Purgatory, Dante as the pilgrim arrives at a place not where his desires are eliminated but where they are true and right. With his desire now rightly ordered and proportioned, he is told,

> From here on, let your pleasure be your guide. . . .
> Now it is your will upright, wholesome and free,
> and not to heed its pleasure would be wrong . . .

In other words, follow your bliss. But the bliss to be followed, the pleasure to be heeded, is not that of the autonomous person, the self-made man or woman. It is the pleasure of a will ordered to the designs of the trinitarian God, the Creator and Redeemer of humanity. Entered into Paradise, Dante is informed by an inhabitant that

> the essence of this blessed state
> is to dwell here within [God's] holy will,
> so that there is not will but one with His . . .
> In His Will is our peace—it is the sea
> in which all things are drawn that it itself
> creates or which the work of Nature makes.

Like the apostle Paul and St. Augustine, Dante expects that true human freedom is achieved not by the removal of all restraints—by being able to do "whatever I want to do"—but by being empowered to unimpededly serve and delight in the right end and Master.

> Sin is the only power that takes away
> man's freedom and his likeness to True Good,
> and makes him shine less brightly in Its light . . .

Straightened and clarified, ordered to and reflecting the originative and ultimate Desire who is Christ, human desire "shall be fulfilled." Arrived face to face with God, we will know, "like a wheel in perfect balance turning," our

> will and desire impelled
> by the Love that moves the sun and the other stars.

Return to the metaphor of stained glass. However attractive the pieces of glass and their arrangement, their splendor can be known only in the light. In the visual vacuum of darkness, the window can never be beautiful. The trinitarian God, Dante says, is the original and sustaining and most glorious Light that shines through and illuminates, displays, makes real the beauty of each piece of creation. With the stained-glass window, we may by our own feeble human attempts try to make it glow and brandish its beauty. But at best we muster a flickering, small candle, so that the window is still mostly shrouded in darkness. Or we muster something like a black light, which turns the colors of the glass garish and bizarre, even sinister. Only in full sunlight does the stained-glass window divulge and meet all its potential. Only in the true Light of God do the objects of human desire shine out in all their true beauty. In the sunlight the window is not obliterated but made most fully what it is, an artful portal. So in the Light of God, those we love and desire are not wiped out or pushed aside but become most truly themselves.

Along these lines, remember that the real-life Dante was captivated by the real-life Beatrice. She preceded him in death. In his extraordinary poetry, Dante as the pilgrim is reunited with Beatrice ten years after her earthly demise. Met by Beatrice in the highest realms of Purgatory, to be guided by her up and up through the heavenly spheres, Dante is overwhelmed by her beauty. First her eyes are unveiled to him, so that

> a thousand yearning flames of my desire
> held my eyes fixed upon those brilliant eyes.

Then her mouth is uncovered, dazzling the great poet beyond the limits of his skill with words. The beauty is Beatrice's, recognizably and enduringly so, but it is only more itself by virtue of taking its rightful place in relation to God.

> The glory of the One Who moves all things
> penetrates all the universe, reflecting
> in one part more and in another less.

So Beatrice's emerald eyes are the portals "from which [divine] Love once shot loving darts" at Dante. The magnificence of her mouth surpasses all description when "that harmonious heaven" remains as its "only veil." Similarly, as Beatrice ascends with Dante higher into the heavens, she only grows more and more beautiful. She remarks,

> My beauty, as you have already seen,
> becomes more radiant with every step
> of the eternal palace that we climb.

Dante the pilgrim travels with Beatrice's disembodied soul, and her soulful beauty stretches beyond the powers of his description. Yet even as he sees it unveiled and illuminated in the highest realms of heaven, he anticipates a greater beauty still—the beauty not just of the soul in God's presence but of the soul reunited with the resurrected body.

> When our flesh, sanctified and glorious,
> shall clothe our souls once more, our person then
> will be more pleasing since it is complete . . .
> [The heavenly] effulgence that contains us now
> will be surpassed in brilliance by the flesh
> that for so long has lain beneath the ground;
> nor will such light be difficult to bear,
> the organs of our bodies will be strengthened
> and ready for whatever gives us joy.

Such is the flesh affirmed and transformed—such is eros anointed, lifted, rendered not less but more intense, not shallower but deeper, not degrading but ennobling, not tawdry but true.

Sex and Its Christian Ends

So we can, in the light shed by orthodox Christian spirituality, bring our sexuality out of the shadows. Christian spirituality can affirm and embrace, rather than simply exclude and deny, sexual desire. But finding that there is a place for sexual desire and pleasure, can we be more specific? Here and now, in our earthly existence, how can we know our desire is rightly ordered and proportioned, that it is truly channeled and occupies its genuine place?

Classical Christian spirituality, happily, has been more specific. It has long and consistently set forth two primary ends or aims for human sexuality. Again, pleasure is not the final or highest end or goal of our sexuality. If it were, then indiscriminate promiscuity would exemplify the holiest "disciplining" of sexual desire. Sexual pleasure is good, but it takes its place when it serves generatively and companionably.

Sex's end or goal is generative in that it is intended to give life. Sex gives life most literally and obviously when it results in procreation, the birth and existence of new persons. It is also generative by joining lovers into "one flesh," a life that is greater than either single life and greater than the sum of its parts. Coupled and coupling, the couple is deepened, extended, enriched. In a sense, it and its members or mates know and embody more life, more love. In Christian spirituality, the couple exists not for itself, the mates not simply for one another, but so that their increased love will flow out from them as a couple. They will give life in such forms as hospitality, service to the poor, encouragement, social stability, and childrearing.

A second traditional Christian aim or goal of sexuality points to its unitivity, its creation and sustenance of companionship. Sex unites. Through and with intercourse, the two become one. So sex enhances companionship in a marriage. Committed to one another, and safe in that commitment, the mates through sex can completely reveal and entrust themselves to one another. The nakedness or vulnerability of sex is both physical and psychological. The lover unveils his or her body, in all its perfection and imperfection, to the gaze and touch of the other. But the most important sexual organ, contemporary sex therapists often insist, is the brain. As anyone raised on a farm knows, dogs and cats and cattle can couple randomly, brutely, free of memory or future expectations. But, all "open marriage" experiments to the contrary, humans recalcitrantly bring memories, hopes, expectations, insecurities, and much else to bed. Sex pursued primarily for pleasure is always marked by stratagems, guile, and game playing. Like the quarterback bootlegging the football, the sexual adventurer does not want to expose his or her true intentions, or true self, to the prospective or actual lover. Then the adventurer might not get what he or she wants, which is sex with this particular person and no accompanying entanglements. After all, the object of the sexual adventurer's game is to achieve the maximum pleasure at the minimum cost (rather as the Monopoly or Risk player attempts to accrue as much property as possible as cheaply as possible). Sexuality disciplined and practiced to the ends of Christian spirituality is quite different. It is intended exactly to more profoundly and completely expose the lovers, their intentions and selves, to one another and to bind them to one another more unreservedly in that trust-enhancing exposure.

The theological grounding of sex disciplined, aimed, destined to serve the ends of generativity and companionship is clear. Not all gods are faithful. The gods of Greek mythology deal with humans capriciously, according to the gods' whims. The goddess Fortuna, venerated in the modern and postmodern free market, also does not cultivate loyalty. As we have seen, consumer desire is free-floating and fickle, always ready to abandon commitment to a former brand, experience, or relationship when a newer and apparently better one comes along. But the God who is the subject and object of Christian spirituality is a God of constancy or fidelity. God covenants with Israel and the church, determined not to abandon them even when they are unfaithful. The married couple vows a lifetime commitment for better or for worse, in sickness or in health, in poverty or wealth—just as Christ will never give up on his bride, the church.

Christian marriage, then, is an icon, a sign of the true God's fidelity, a witness to this God's constancy. Classical Christian spirituality expects that sex most profoundly gives life and deepens companionship when it is both bounded and extended by fidelity. The couple is bounded in the obvious sense; committing themselves exclusively to one another, the mates forsake all others. The couple is extended in that its commitment, made publicly and supported by the Spirit and the church, can carry it through trials and into joyful surprises the mates never could have imagined when they took their first few steps down the path of wedlock. It is like the marathoner who knows the full joy of her race only if she commits to gutting it out and finishing it. Or it is like my long writing of this book—many have been the frustrating moments I would have liked to abandon it, but how much happier I am to have taken it this far, and how much happier yet will I be when I put the period on the last sentence. Only fidelity can finish a marathon or write a book. And only fidelity, orthodox Christian spirituality teaches, can complete and fulfill a marriage and allow sexual expression to reach its true destination.

The Difficult Case of Homosexuality

It is these profoundly theological ends of human sexuality that orthodox Christian spirituality uses to frame consideration of any particular sexual practice or custom. The fierce and important current debate over homosexuality points us all—"straight" or "gay," "traditional" or "progressive"—back to just such basic questions: Can actively homosexual relationships cultivate the Christian ends of generativity, companionship, and fidelity? To sharpen the point, consider that in scriptural terms the human is not whole and complete—not "one flesh"—except as male and female. It is in the difference yet complementarity of female and male that Scripture picks up as a profound running theme, seeing in it not only true humanity but a reflection of God's graceful, rock-steady relationship to humanity. God's covenant with Israel is witnessed to in marriage, as in the prophet Hosea's determination to stick with his whoring spouse and the frequent denunciations of idolatry as a kind of spiritual adultery.

And so the "great mystery" of wife and husband as "one flesh" becomes a sign of Christ and the church as his bride (Eph. 5:29–33). Can homosexuality, which by definition disallows this two-gendered union at least in terms of sexual activity, reflect and embody this bone-deep Scriptural and traditional theme? Such are the crucial questions the church is now working to sort out.

Since it pushes so far into the undergirding bedrock of our faith and spirituality, it is no wonder the sorting out over homosexuality arouses such intensity and strife. Yet we must care for the church's unity and for the welfare and honor of Christian brothers and sisters who find themselves homosexually inclined. Without pretending to do justice to this complex presenting issue—or having this discussion blossom into an entire additional chapter—I can here only make three brief suggestions.

First, we do well to recognize that one's stance or position on homosexuality does not necessarily determine whether or not one strives to be faithful to Scripture and the Christian tradition. Sexual orientation, though certainly significant, is not an item of the creed. Scripture does address the issue, but a crucial part of the argument is exactly what Scripture says and entails about what we now call homosexuality. There simply are orthodox biblical scholars and theologians (not to mention laypersons) who believe and argue that space can and should be made for certain homosexual relationships. They may be wrong, but they are not any less determined to honor Scripture and tradition than other Christians who proscribe all homosexual activity. So we need not—I believe we should not—cast this argument as one of simple faithfulness versus clear apostasy.

Second, we may promote both truer Christian faithfulness and a more constructive debate if we recognize that there really are not just two absolute Christian positions on homosexuality: the one utterly condemning it, the other totally allowing for it. For instance, even those taking the most "conservative" position today want to distinguish between homosexual orientation and homosexual behavior. At another place along the spectrum, others argue that there may be a place for committed, monogamous homosexual relationships among the laity, but that ordination to the ministry should entail a higher or stricter standard not allowing such relationships. Down yet another path of dispute, there is an intermediary position that would not put homosexual relationships exactly on par with heterosexual relationships, but counsels that the Christian discipleship of homosexually oriented people is best forwarded by supporting them in committed relationships. This is a remedial approach, analogous to Calvin's understanding of heterosexual marriage as itself therapeutic, containing and disciplining a sexual drive whose unruliness we might best be without but will not be and so must contain and moderate. Better to commit ourselves to one other than to burn, said Calvin, and be perilously tempted into more destructive and spiritually corrosive habits. Might something of the same be said for what we today regard as homosexuality? At the moment, such an intermediate position faces withering fire from the opposed positions at each of its flanks. But the long, often controverted history of the Christian tradition shows us that sometimes just such a complex or intermediate "solution" or position shines through in the long run.

Third, and last, we do well in the midst of any deep church controversies to recall that a signal virtue for Christian spirituality is patience. The church father Tertullian said, "Patience is the very nature of God," and accordingly put patience at the heart of Christian spirituality. He observed that we can hardly attain "the good health of faith and the soundness of the discipline of the Lord" without enduring patience. Ironically, and perhaps most significantly, it is likely that the most novel, and needed, witness a church debating and fighting over homosexuality can present to a watching world is patience. None of the orthodox tradition's important struggles of the past were decided in a few decades. If postmodern nations and media regard a long debate as one lasting a few weeks or months and regard the middle years of the previous century as ancient history, the church in the grand stretch of its history is not so attention-deficient or myopic. I, for one, am thankful for that much.

Sex in Heaven?

So we must consider homosexuality, along with all other sexual conditions and practices, in the light of the Christian ends or destinations of sex. But this talk of ends and destinations raises another kind of question. Resoundingly, traditional Christian spirituality expects the body to know no final end, in the sense of termination or cessation. The body will be resurrected and transformed, for eternity. But what of sex? Will we carry it into (and carry on with it) through eternity?

The key biblical text pertinent to this question is Matthew 22:23–30. Here we find Jesus in an argument with the Sadducees. The Sadducees did not believe in the resurrection from the dead; it was clear to them that Jesus did. Just like modern American political antagonists, they attempt to entrap Jesus with sex. They hustle out this scenario: Say that a woman has married a succession of seven men, one dying after the other. If she and her seven husbands are resurrected, whose wife will she be? The Sadducees, preening in their lawyerly canniness, expect that Jesus will have to jettison his confession of bodily resurrection. Either that or he will have to embrace heavenly polygamy—an unthinkable alternative. But Jesus surprises them with a third, entirely different answer. In the resurrection people will not marry but will be like the angels in heaven.

Since sexual activity in the Bible is sanctioned only within marriage, many have understandably taken this reply to mean there will be no sex in the new heavens and earth. Yet real complications arise if we rush to this answer and arrive at it flatfootedly. Something like sexual intercourse may or may not be entailed by bodily resurrection, but sexuality is much more than simply acts of intercourse. To be female or male shapes and informs our entire selves. Will there be no women or men in the afterlife, only some sort of androgynous transphysical bodies? Some luminaries, such as Gregory of Nyssa, have thought so. But if that is the case, we seem to be taking less seriously the bodiliness of the resurrection, radically downplaying any continuity between our earthly and our resurrected bodies. Jesus was resurrected recognizably male. In the main, Christian tradition has been too robust about bodily resurrection to countenance redeemed and transformed bodies that lose or eliminate their sexuality. Tertullian and Augustine explicitly affirmed that our bodies will be resurrected with their genitals. Much later Bonaventure expected resurrected bodies to possess genitals, hair, and intestines—and that "because of perfection." We will rise perfected and beautiful, and particularly male or female as an aspect of that perfection.

Biblical scholars and historians confirm this much: the Sadducees, in their time and place, would not have understood as marriage any sexual congress and partnership without procreation. (Just as we can still speak of a marriage as "consummated" once the newlyweds have copulated, so the Sadducees would have imagined a marriage consummated—real and complete—once children were born of it.) No one in the orthodox Christian tradition has expected there will be procreation in the afterlife.

We cannot determine exactly what more Jesus may be saying here, but at the least he is saying that just as angels don't procreate, neither will resurrected humans. Beyond that we can surely affirm that human relations in eternity will be marked by constancy and full trust, since constancy is a part of the eternal God's character. The fickleness and volatility of sexual desire can, in our earthly, imperfect condition, be reliably directed and contained only in the context of lifelong monogamy. If all our desires, including the sexual, are truly healed and purified in the transforming resurrection, might there be a place for some analogue to sexual intercourse in the afterlife—without an analogue to marriage as we now know it? How far dare we press Dante's language that at the resurrection "the organs of our bodies will be strengthened and ready for whatever gives us joy"?

I suspect we do best, like Dante, to remind ourselves that mortal language and imagination quickly fail us when we here and now dream of the resurrection. We simply do not have the words or concepts to speak in any detail or exactness about the renewed heavens and earth—even less than sixteenth-century Europeans had words and concepts to understand the "new world" and its inhabitants. What we can say is that if sexual desire can enrich life and companionship here, all the more will it, transformed and exceeded, enrich life and companionship following the resurrection.

A child at a certain age can conceive of no pleasure or satisfaction greater than eating chocolate. Any awareness of sexual pleasure (so much more beloved than chocolate by adults) is puzzling and distant. Sex may even appear wildly strange and repulsive to a child—how much better, decidedly, to allow a candy bar into your mouth rather than someone else's tongue. Likewise, we grownups may find it impossible to imagine something more intensely exciting and enjoyable than sex. And yet what we now know as sex will, in the consummated heaven and earth, be to us as chocolate is now compared to sex as we know it. In the building of constancy and fidelity, in the increase of life and companionship, in sheer enjoyment, it will be greatly surpassed, infinitely outdistancing whatever we might now be capable of imagining or predicting.

Sex and Justice

To this point I have tried to specify a Christian spirituality of sexuality as regards the physical body. But we can, heeding the tradition, also specify a Christian spirituality of sexuality by focusing on the social body. Of course, for Christians the physical body and the social body cannot be entirely or neatly separated. As I have indicated, for instance, the Christian disciplining of sexuality is social: Christians marry and sustain marriage in the context of the church. We make public vows and expect to be supported in those vows by the body of Christ. We can say more.

Following St. Augustine, I have spoken of the importance of rightly ordering and proportioning sexual desire. The socially minded word for right and proportionate order is *justice*. Justice concerns the proper, equitable arrangement and enactment of human relationships. Injustice occurs when relationships are disordered and people do not receive their just due. If I steal what is justly due you, whether it be property or your right to vote, I act unjustly.

Office and status help us to define justice. It is my child's just status that I care for her spiritually and financially, though your child does not have that same status in relation to me. To treat my wife justly requires that I love and care for her in many ways that would be disorderly and unjust if I so tried to treat another's spouse. The offices of police officers and mayors grant them a distinctive status, so that they can rightly demand certain things of me that others cannot. Justice demands that I pull over when the policeman catches me speeding and turns on his red light, though not that I pull over when you or a different officeholder (say, a dogcatcher) chases me down the street. Justice entails that the mayor's office can exact taxes from me but not that I must pay taxes directly to the schoolteacher (or that pesky dogcatcher). Justice can also mean that I tithe to my church but not to my Tuesday night reading group. In ways small and great, mundane and spectacular, communities and societies survive and function on the basis of justice. When right relationships and their proper ordering break down, social bodies can only disintegrate.

The thirteenth-century church doctor Thomas Aquinas approached sexuality and sexual behavior with exactly this understanding of justice and injustice. Illicit or disordered sex is, for Thomas, first and foremost a problem because it is an injustice. Granted, some instances of sexual injustice cited by Thomas evince the implacable patriarchy of his day. Since the female is under the guardianship of the male, it is an injustice to a father for another man to seduce his daughter and an injustice to a husband for another to rape his wife. (Thomas does not, of course, rule out the injustice against the women themselves in such cases.) Out from under the patriarchy of Thomas's world, we will not want to order just sexual relations by seeing women as the property of men. But we can still, with care, apply his point. Rape is an injustice to the woman attacked, most certainly. It is also an injustice to her husband and the couple as such, since it trespasses on territory exclusive to the married couple. It violently steals rights and privileges justly reserved only for the office or status of this marriage.

Similarly, Thomas can see sex outside marriage as unjust because it "rules out proper provision for bringing up any offspring of the act." Children need two parents: a mother to nurse them and a father to "protect and guide them interiorly and exteriorly." Thus Thomas can define promiscuity as an act that leaves offspring with only a mother to care for them. Again we will want to resist Thomas's strict, patriarchal allocation of gender roles. And the modern availability of generally reliable contraception means that in our day sex is more readily separated from procreation. But even modern contraception sometimes fails, and we do not need to look far to see the costs, socially and to children themselves, of sex pursued for pleasure and the sometime results of unwed parents who cannot support their "unwanted" children.

However we may exactly define and argue particular cases, Thomas's discussion helps us to see that sex and justice are related. Any enduring social body will need to define and by various means promote proper or licit sexual behavior and proscribe illicit sexual behavior. Exactly because sex is so intimate and so powerful, illicit or unjust sex hurts people and harms communities. Classical Christian spirituality guides the church in the necessary, crucial task of ordering sexual desire so that it may serve and build up, rather than enslave and tear down, the body of Christ. It is instructive that though Thomas certainly condemns what we might now call "personal sexual immorality," he worries first and foremost about sexual sin because it is an injustice that harms the social body. As one commentator puts it, "Careful study of the passage on sexual sin [in Thomas's *Summa Theologiae*] will show that his severity, and he is severe in his judgments, is based not on distaste for pleasure or even excess pleasure as such, but for the consequent injustice towards sexual partners, children and families that he believes it involves."

A Proper "Judgmentalism"

"And he is severe in his judgments," it is said of Thomas Aquinas on sex. Orthodox Christians have acutely recognized that sex is dangerous. Down through the centuries, they have taken it seriously and approached it with due caution. Our contemporary culture, on the other hand, wants sex both to be harmless, so freely indulged, and to retain an airbrushed frisson. Advertisers know, if they know nothing else, that sex sells. So sexual images and associations are used to sell everything from real estate to breakfast cereals. Seeking somehow to rise above what marketers themselves call the "clutter" of screaming, arm-waving media, fashion photographers sexualize twelve-year-olds and suggest bestiality. They and other media creators do a delicate dance or striptease—how to shock just enough to draw attention, yet not so much as to repel it?

But of course part of the frisson of sex remains its hiddenness, the mystery inherent to it by virtue of its privacy. How much less exciting would the bedroom be if we were already naked in the kitchen and the office? Magazines such as *Cosmopolitan* constantly promise to divulge the technical and imaginative "secrets" that will utterly win over and secure lovers. So even we if rarely talk of or want to sense shame, we esteem intimacy and its rewards. Intimacy requires privacy, a real and appropriate degree of hiddenness and guardedness. It recognizes that we are fragile creatures and that part of our beauty resides in this fragility. Something precious is unshielded, opened up, and given in the sexual act.

The language of intimacy, unlike that of shame, attempts to avoid the moral dimensions of sex but is never entirely successful. There can be no intimacy without vulnerability, and no vulnerability without the possibility of hurt. And morality just is the struggle to live together justly, to avoid or at least minimize our harm to others and to the whole of the social body. Such avoidance or minimization requires discernment and evaluation—it requires the making of judgments.

Naturally, then, actual judgmentalism about sex has not been eliminated from our culture. But since we want to tell ourselves we have absolutely stopped being judgmental about sex, we block from our view a nasty, hurtful, and hypocritical judgmentalism. In point of fact, our society pinballs between pervasive sexual display or indulgence and a hateful excoriation of the sexual activity of others who do indulge. Political culture perhaps most vividly discloses this schizophrenia. Divulging the sexual misdeeds of opposing officeholders has become the supreme political weapon. Partisan Democrats try to downplay or ignore the sexual adventurism of Bill Clinton while calling Republican adulterers to hard account. Likewise, partisan Republicans who impeached Clinton find various excuses or allowances for the adventurism of Newt Gingrich or Arnold Schwarzenegger. A saner sense of judgment and sexual morality would focus on how sex can be channeled and disciplined to build up and solidify the social body. Call it judgmentalism if you will, but this would be a constructive judgmentalism. In our setting, the sexual judgmentalism we will never call judgmentalism is used to tear the social body apart, then exacerbate its wounds.

Note that in modernity and postmodernity sex is being used, made to serve certain ends. In marketing, it is used to draw attention and to sell. In politics, it is used to humiliate and defeat. We want to say we are—in comparison to Victorians and Puritans and the church fathers—vigorously healthy in our sex and sexual attitudes. We want to say that sex is supremely fun and life-enhancing. Yet we often use it to brutally demand attention or to try to destroy other citizens and officers. Thus a central self-contradiction in our culture: it is at once hyper-sexualized and hyper-judgmental about sex.

In comparison, orthodox Christian spirituality may appear refreshingly straightforward. At least this spirituality does not try to pretend that it has nothing to do with morality, that it can avoid all judgment. Better to know what you're doing and name it accurately than to do it anyway and deceive and confuse yourself about the potential for pain you may create. The best surgeon knows that she may have to hurt to heal. She acknowledges that the knife incises and parts skin, that with it she inevitably wounds to heal. Then she is all the more careful in her cutting. If, on the other hand, she has been told and tells herself that what she does in the operating theater is entirely benign and bland—that the spilled blood is on par with watercolor paints—she is all the more dangerous and harmful to the patient beneath her scalpel.

Christian spirituality, then, admits there is a moral aspect to its approach and "handling" of sexuality. Judgments are unavoidable. Furthermore, at its best, it judges and uses sex to glorify God and build up the church. Its ends for sex are constancy, generativity, and companionship—not indulgence or drawing attention or destroying others. So I do not back off from the affirmation of orthodox spirituality's candid, clear admission that sex and sexuality must be organized, channeled, disciplined. Sexuality simply will be used to certain ends—the question is to what ends and how honest we can be about them.

At the same time, it is obvious that I have pushed and pulled within the tradition to happily and robustly affirm the pleasurable potentials of sex, to affirm those potentials more happily and robustly than have many past adherents of Christian spirituality. Just as I do not think we should forget the moral aspect of sexuality, I suggest that there are other aspects or dimensions to it. Our moral judgments about sexuality should be accompanied by recognitions that sex is also, often, constructively ecstatic (literally self-transcending) and that it can be comic (as we saw in chapter 7). Sometimes orthodox Christians can still act as if sex is about nothing but morality and focus exclusively on the dangers of sexuality. Instead, with the tradition's help, we might admit that sex and its consequences are not always and only sobering and direly serious. And we can admit that the sexual standards of classical Christian spirituality are high and demanding, so much so that none of us live up to them absolutely and many of us stumble along the way.

So we are called to our own delicate dance. There are solid reasons for the high standards—they beckon us to our greatest selves and ends, to a place where our own beloved Beatrices or Burts will reveal and share their most astonishing beauties. But we admit that, confused and partial as we are, surrounded by temptations and pervaded by insecurities, we in this life often and repeatedly fall short. We must hold up standards, but we must also (and even more) hold up grace. We must make judgments, but we must also be merciful and forgiving.

As in other regards, I find the desert fathers fascinating and instructive in their choreography of the delicate dance of sexual judgment and mercy. Certainly these ancient monks had severe sexual rules. They could, in ways I have already criticized, aspire to be more angels than people. Yet they did not pretend they were free of all sexual sin and temptation. They could be matter-of-fact about sexual shortcomings. The documents about them admit that monks were known to father children; older men sometimes harassed novices ("with wine and boys around," went one saying, the monks had no need of the devil to tempt them). There were even reported occasions of bestiality with monastery donkeys.

The desert fathers at their best emphasized that in this life they would never stop wrestling with sexual temptations and failings. In one story, a young monk comes to an old father and announces that he must forsake his desert calling because he is beset with lust. The old man replies, "Think it no strange thing, my son, nor despair of thyself. For I myself, at my age, and in this way of life, am sorely harried by just such thoughts as these. Wherefore be not found wanting in this kind of testing, where the remedy is not so much in man's anxious thoughts as in God's compassion."

In another such account, a younger brother, discouraged by his raging sexual drive, approaches an older brother with disappointment about himself eleven times in a row. The younger monk is ready to succumb to despair, when the older says, "Believe me, my son, if God permitted the thoughts with which my own mind is stung to be transferred to thee, thou wouldst not endure them, but wouldst dash thyself headlong." By so speaking, we are told, the old man "in his great humbleness did quiet the goading of lust in the brother."

Even more remarkable is the empathy of a fellow monk on another occasion. Two monks go to town to sell their handiwork. In the city, they separate and one falls into fornication. When they reunite to go home, the stumbler confesses, "I ran into temptation, and I sinned in the flesh." The other, "anxious to help him," says the same thing happened to him, though in fact he had conducted only his business and no sexual liaison. Then he counsels, "But let us go, and do penance together with all our might: and God will forgive us that are sinful men." They return to the monastery.

> The one began to do his penance, not for himself but for his brother, as if he himself had sinned. And God, seeing his love and his labour, after a few days revealed to one of the old men that for the great love of this brother who had not sinned, He had forgiven the brother who had. And verily this is to lay down one's soul for one's brother.

At least three factors of the desert fathers' attitudes are worthy of, and susceptible to, our twenty-first-century emulation. First, they weighted their disciplining of sexual desire not on anxious human willpower but on the compassion of God and the strengthening of the Spirit. Second, the desert fathers were honest about the presence and intensity of sexual desire. They did not pretend that in this lifetime they would ever entirely tame sex's volatility and mystery. They expected that the passions might be "in some sort bound" but not eliminated. Third, they maintained their standards and did not eschew judgment, but they consistently directed judgment first at themselves rather than others. Accordingly, their disciplining of sexuality was aimed at building up the community, not tearing it down. They recognized the socially damaging dangers of pride, resentment, and immoderate spiritual ambitions as greater and more hazardous than those of lust. For them, focusing first and foremost on the shortcomings of others did more harm—and hindered more witness to the kingdom—than sexual failings. In this regard, I cannot resist citing one last story, a favorite of mine among the sayings:

> Once a brother in Scete was found guilty, and the older brethren came in assembly and sent to the abbot Moses, asking him to come: but he would not. Then the priest sent to him, saying: "Come: for the assembly of the brethren awaits thee." And he rose up and came. But taking with him a very old basket, he filled it with sand and carried it behind him. And they went out to meet him, asking, "Father, what is this?" And the old man said to them, "My sins are running behind and I do not see them, and I come today to judge the sins of another man." And they heard him, and said naught to the brother, but forgave him.

11

EDUCATING
THE FLESH

Bodily Exercise
and Christian Spirituality

C ome with me to the nursing home where my Grandma Adams
now dwells. I am there for a birthday party, celebrating not
only Grandma's ninety-third but all the other July birthdays
of the home's residents. I am sharing cake and punch with Grandma.
With her close-cropped silver hair shining like a jockey's helmet,
she is her usual lively, slightly mischievous self. She tips her head
at a wheelchaired woman across the table and whispers in my ear,
"Watch. She always cleans out the paper cups and takes them back
to her room." Sure enough, moments later the woman across the
table glances about furtively, wipes her punch cup out with a napkin,
then secretes it down the side of the wheelchair's cushion. Grandma
gives me a sly smile.

Eva Sutton sits at my other hand. Eva's grandchildren were some
of my closest friends growing up, so I spent good time at her farm-

house. Eva was unfailingly sweet and solicitous of her grandchildren and their friends. In junior high, I tumbled out of a treehouse in her backyard and broke my arm. She fussed over me, nursed me with a glass of soda pop, and called my mother to hurry over. I always liked Eva's gentleness, her broad smile, and her wiry, resonant voice. (If she weren't a Southern Baptist, I would describe her voice as whiskey-soaked. But since she is a lifelong Baptist, I doubt whiskey has ever passed her lips, and I know she would not care for the metaphor.)

I want to visit with Eva. I mention her grandkids, but her mind is in another era. She talks about her mother and father as if they were alive and she were still a child. I never knew her parents, of course, so all I can do is smile back and occasionally squeeze her shoulder. The Eva I knew is gone—inaccessible even to herself.

Or is she? Later, when the party has ended and I have escorted Grandma back to her room, I see Eva as I depart the nursing home. She sits at the piano in the small foyer. Eva was the First Baptist Church's organist from before my birth across the span of my child-hood and well into my adulthood. The hymns she played for decades are now lodged in her bones. With age-bent fingers she plays "Softly and Tenderly." She sings, passionately if raggedly, in the old Eva voice. She gazes almost rapturously at the wall behind the piano, as if it were an icon transparent to the glory of God. Of course I stop to listen. She does two more hymns, and starts a third, before I leave.

Eva reminds me that the body learns, that it can be educated and deeply, resiliently marked by that education. Her fingers and tongue and lips remember the old hymns, even if her tattered mind doesn't.

Exercise and Diet Regimens

Early on in this book, I defined orthodox Christian spirituality as participation and formation in the life of the church, which is itself Christ's body, a social organism sustained by the Holy Spirit. I said that this participation and formation involves the whole person, very much including the physical body. Having unpacked that at some length and arriving now at the final chapters of this book, I can declare that Christian spirituality is a kinesthetic spirituality.

In straightforward dictionary terms, kinesthesia is sense and knowledge located in and stimulated by the body's muscles, tendons, and joints and by the practiced movements of those muscles, tendons, and joints. Kinesthesia is what athletes and dancers refer to as "muscle memory." Of course, in the strictest sense it won't do to oppose kinesthetic knowledge (muscle memory) to the knowledge of the mind (mental memory). The brain, after all, is also a part of the body, and it has something to do with all of the body's movements. But inasmuch as we think of the mind's special function as self-reflection and articulation by speech, there are things the body knows that the mind can't. My body knows how to ride a bicycle, though I could never (with my mathematically challenged mind) formulate the physics of keeping a bicycle upright and rolling. For most of us, it is the same with milking a cow, acting in a theatrical drama, doing calligraphy, painting, drawing, swimming, playing basketball, or making love. These are actions funded by kinesthetic knowledge. We are hard-pressed to describe in language the habituated actions that we undertake with our bodies. We don't ordinarily stop to analyze these activities, at least not while we're performing them. And if we do stop to think about the strokes while swimming, or the next step while dancing, we usually hinder or mess up those activities. Instead, we simply do what the body knows.

And what the body knows, it has been taught. The social and the physical bodies, as in so many other ways, work in tandem here. Eva had teachers who taught her how to play the piano, and hymn writers and singers who passed music down to her. My dad taught me how to milk a cow, kneeling beside me and guiding my fingers on the cow's teats. So, too, Christian spirituality. In and from the church we learn how to pray, how to partake of the Eucharist, how to sing in praise, how to make our bodies and thus ourselves present to the sick, the poor, the imprisoned. Along the way, in sermons and Sunday schools and seminaries, we do helpfully learn how to reflect on these actions. But first and foremost we learn kinesthetically, with our bodies. We are, for instance, coached in the postures and words of prayer long before we are taught any theories of prayer. And even

after at least some of us learn theories of Christian spirituality, we all
persist in kinesthetic practice and knowledge of spirituality. We learn
with, through, and as our bodies. We keep that learning fresh and
sharp by the ongoing, repeated workouts of our bodies. Christian
spirituality is exercise, even or especially *bodily* exercise.

I am afraid this is not well understood or appreciated in the current day. Christian spiritual disciplines, or exercises, are often not
very regularly observed even by many church attenders. There is
also a sense in which frequent prayer, Bible reading, works of mercy,
and other spiritual exercises are felt to be quaint, if not useless and
futile. What difference does it make if I pray daily or once a year?
And we are wary of being too strict about spiritual exercises. Pity
the pastor who might too strongly urge her flock to regularly pray,
read Scripture, and visit the sick. Anything approaching a guilt trip
is sternly to be avoided.

Indeed, we can look on our predecessors in the Bible and later
Christian tradition and think vaguely if not outright that they were
overwrought and extreme in their attitudes toward spiritual exercises
and the battle with sin. How, after all, can uptight St. Augustine
worriedly examine in minute detail his boyhood decision to steal
a few pears? Do a few expendable pieces of fruit really matter that
much? "Loosen up," we want to say. "Let it go. Don't take this stuff
so seriously." We think we are beyond such scrupulosity, such hyper-
sensitive consciences and severe views of God.

We may have largely jettisoned scrupulosity about spiritual matters, but notice that we affluent modern Westerners are scrupulous
and obsessive about other things. Consider our concerns for diet and
regular physical exercise. It is not at all unusual for us to speak in
life-and-death terms about eating and (the failure to) exercise. We
say that a "bad" diet is "killing" someone. We say that cigarettes are
murderous. Our physicians periodically, like clockwork, shout alarm
through our newspapers. They tell us that Americans are dying of
obesity, that we should exercise more often and longer. It is telling
that a prominent newsmagazine has now dropped its regular religion
section but includes a discrete health section—always reliably brim-
ming with warnings and exhortations and techniques for living longer.
In this climate, we approach even small, specific failures or lapses as

little short of lethal. It turns out that we worry as much—and in much the same way—about physical health as our Christian predecessors did about spiritual health and wholeness.

Yet it is not the case, unless you are acutely diabetic, that a single fudge sundae will literally kill you. Nor is it the case that failing to take a walk or to work out tonight will see me immediately stricken dead. Why, then, do we talk this way? Why do we talk in a manner that, soberly examined and in particular instances, can be seen as overwrought and extreme? We do so because we recognize that consistent, habitual eating of high-fat and super-sweetened foods will, and do, make us sick and clog our arteries. Over time, they do kill us. Any single dessert or deep-fried delectable will not drop us dead, but each is a "temptation" and a dabbling in "decadence" (as our restaurant dessert menus sometimes suggest). Made habitual, become characteristic of our eating, there really is "death by chocolate."

Similarly, the Christian spiritual tradition has worried over the potential of single sins, even apparently small ones, to tempt and groove us into habits that fatten and render sluggish the spirit (and the spiritual body along with it). Tertullian, Augustine, Luther, Calvin, and others call us to look toward lasting and permanent things. They want us to focus not just or even primarily on our physical body as it now is but on the shape and condition of the spirit and the resurrected, spiritual body to come. We moderns and postmoderns invert 1 Timothy 4:7–8, which reads, "Train yourself in godliness, for, while physical training is of some value, godliness is valuable in every way, holding promise for both the present life and the life to come." The habits and the character we build or neglect to build gradually and eventually leave us fit either for everlasting life (communion with God) or everlasting death (separation from God, the source of all life and good). To pray regularly, then, is akin to consistent physical exercise. Our doctors tell us that exercise once every two weeks is as good as nothing. The physical body needs frequent, regular exercise to keep the lungs and heart healthy, the body's muscles firm and supple. Praying once a month likewise has little effect on the conditioning of the spiritual person.

The same is true in terms of diet. To succumb to the small temptation of a deep-fried meal or heavy dessert can lead to slackened habits.

And we need—the health of our bodies requires—our vegetables, even if we find broccoli boring and less immediately attractive than, say, a chicken-fried steak. Again, our Christian forebears recognized that to indulge our spiritual appetites, to partake constantly of trivial or even harmful pastimes, led to analogously disastrous results. To neglect spiritual exercise and diet will surely detract from our spiritual health, our participation and formation in the life of the church. It will clog the arteries of our relations with God and our fellow creatures. And it can only, followed to its extreme, lead to our death and destruction.

So it may be silly for us to jibe at Augustine over a few pilfered pears, especially as we scrupulously read the nutrition labels on the canned pears in our supermarkets. "Physical training is of *some* value," Paul tells Timothy. But spiritual training is even more important, both in this life and for the life to come. If our bodies and selves need physical exercise, how much the more do they need spiritual exercise.

Patience and the Bodiliness of "Spiritual Worship"

To say it again, orthodox Christian spirituality is a kinesthetic spirituality. We learn and are maintained in Christian spirituality and character, in no small part, through the regular, habitual disposition and comportment of our bodies. I have already indicated the link between learning and bodily disposition and comportment, with examples such as milking a cow or swimming. These examples, however, do not disclose dimensions of character, morality, and spirituality. I would not consider you immoral or unspiritual because you do not know how to swim or milk a cow. So to get clearer on bodily habituation and comportment, and their relation to spirituality, we need other examples.

I suggest, first, the soldier's posture. Like me, you have probably known career soldiers who even after their retirement still stand straight and tall, their shoulders drawn high and straight. This posture has been drilled into them. They may forget any amount of military information, and they may blossom an impressive beer belly, but their body does not forget how to stand like a soldier. Of course, chiropractors tell us the soldier's regal bearing is healthy, salutary for the back. But that is not the point of the posture. The reason soldiers are made to learn it so that their bodies never forget it has more to do with character and morality. The erect stance embodies pride and strength. Standing tall communicates courage and vitality. More than this, it enacts and enables alertness, a readiness to action. The erect, alert soldier can move more quickly and powerfully than the slumped, slovenly soldier. Standing tall, then, does not simply communicate or signal the virtue of courage. It bodily instills and manifests it.

A second example indicates even more directly how the training and disposition of the body can hinder or enable spiritual practices and experience. Many long-distance runners have written of their sport explicitly in terms of spirituality. They testify that, well into a long run, endorphins and other bodily reactions put in them in a state of serene exhilaration. Some find this an excellent state for meditation or prayer. Others speak of it as a time of self-transcendence, with a deep sense of well-being, as well as the discovery of sources of energy and power that carry their body beyond what they thought capable. Of course, such spiritual states cannot be achieved or inhabited without arduous and ongoing training, the likes of which enable these runners to go the long distances that can open up into euphoria. So desire and spirit can mark and change the body (as my middle-aged spread and yen for Mexican food prove). But so can the trained or taught body mark and change, free and strengthen, the spirit.

In that light, let us consider a particular Christian spiritual fruit or virtue—patience (see Gal. 5:22). As I noted at the end of the last chapter, Tertullian and other early Christians saw patience as a signal virtue, lying at the very heart of Christian spirituality. Patience was especially crucial because our orthodox predecessors understood that we are in this life tortured wonders, in-between or intermediate creatures. We are in between apes and angels. We are also in between the times. Jesus has come, the kingdom of God is inaugurated on earth. Yet we await its fullness or completion, the renewal of the heavens and earth when all will be made whole and well and all creatures recognize the salutary lordship of Christ (Phil. 2:9–11).

As a twentieth-century commentator nicely puts it, the early church awareness of our status in between the times

> certainly did not mean that Christians must give up the idea of influencing history; it did not mean that they were resigned and defeated in advance. It rather was rooted in the Christian affirmation that there was another power besides that of brute force. . . . Such confidence rested on an all-embracing vision which saw God as the source of that power and anticipated its fulfillment in his eternal kingdom. The believers' contribution involved allowing God's power to act and placing trust in it; it involved enduring the present evil with the certainty of a final victory over it.

This meant (and means) that since God is in control, Christians must be willing to live out of control. Christian spirituality entails living out of control not in the sense of jettisoning self-discipline but in the sense of learning not to play God. It is the Triune God who makes and will make the kingdom of heaven a reality on earth. Christians cannot coerce or try to force others to behave as Christians should. Christians worry first about faithfulness and only second about effectiveness. We trust that God is alive and works in the world now and that ultimately God will effectively and fully—and to the real benefit of God's creation—rule. In the meantime, then, Christians are a people who must learn how to endure, how to suffer, how to remain faithful even if the world spurns or ignores the kingdom and its benevolent sway. In short, we must know how to be patient.

The nineteenth-century German father-and-son pastors Johann and Christoph Blumhardt exquisitely understood this Christian patience. In their understanding, the church and lived Christian spirituality are a witness to what God wants to become and do in the world. But there remains much resistance to God in the world and, inasmuch as it is a part of a rebellious world, in the church. So, the Blumhardts affirmed, "until all sin is checked, until the darknesses which have accumulated for centuries are dissolved and removed from among people, the community of Christ must suffer. Yet, thanks be to God, in this suffering we also discover a help that makes it possible to hold out." When we succumb to impatience and attempt to act on our own power and by our own devices, we often obscure rather than further God's work in and for the world. When we meet resistance and limitations, we are driven back to God, the great Creator-Redeemer God ready to do more "than we can ask or imagine" (Eph. 3:20). Accordingly, said the Blumhardts, "the kingdom of God comes not through logical concepts" and human cleverness "but through surprises."

To live in anticipation of God's surprises is to live joyfully and hopefully. But by the nature of the case, we cannot predict or control surprises—if we did, they would no longer be surprises. Thus in a broken and still hurting world we will often suffer, and we are called not just to suffer for ourselves but to embrace the hurt of our neighbors and enemies. "We who believe in the Savior can legitimately think of ourselves as people who, through our own suffering, help in the suffering of Jesus Christ by which the darkness is overcome. *Insofar as we are thinking of other people*, our suffering becomes a force which helps the Father in heaven in building his kingdom on earth."

The Blumhardts recognized that Christian patience in the face of suffering is communal. Of course, we are each of us inevitably faced with disappointments, anxieties, and pains—suffering to be endured in our "personal" lives. But God's kingdom and redemptive intentions are bigger than any one of us or our "private" selves. God in Christ, by the power of the Spirit, is determined to redeem the entire world. And this world, God's shattered creation, cannot be redeemed in a single lifetime. It is already a work of several centuries, calling for a patience that survives and is passed down through many generations. Given this, the Blumhardts counsel,

it is possible that the fruit of our prayers will first be experienced by later generations, by generations breaking forth in the songs of praise we ourselves would have liked to address to heaven in thanks for the granting of those prayers. Yet, how many attacks does it take before the walls of a well-entrenched city are breached? Our prayers, it might be said, are hammer-strokes against the bulwark of the princes of darkness; they must be oft repeated. Many years can pass by, even a number of generations die away, before a breakthrough occurs.

However, not a single hit is wasted; and if they are continued, then even the most secure wall must finally fall. Then the glory of God will have a clear path upon which to stride forth with healing and blessing for the wasted fields of mankind.

I need hardly comment how much this kind of patience goes against the grain in our contemporary setting, a world in which corporations can look ahead only so far as next quarter's earnings, a world in which we consume "fast food" and "instant" oats, in which insurance companies try to deny chronic illness, in which we expect our car's oil to be changed in fifteen minutes and our photographs to be developed within an hour. How can postmodern Christians, rushing from one disconnected task or novelty to the next, learn any degree of patience? Here I think the physical body, in all its sometimes exasperating slowness, stubbornness, and intractability, comes to our aid.

It is true, for instance, that modern technology (wonderfully) allows us to move across the country or globe at great speed. But the four-hour flight from Chicago to the West Coast is still four hours. As I sit for hours inside a cylinder thousands of feet in the sky, I must exercise restraint and patience. Even more, as often happens at O'Hare, while my plane sits on the runway an hour before taking off, I must be patient or be escorted off the plane by sky marshals brandishing zap guns. In my spirit or imagination, or with a telephone call or click of an e-mail message, I may commune instantly with a friend in Oregon. But to be fully and bodily present to that friend, I can only "suffer" and endure several hours of travel.

Likewise, I can in spirit or imagination see myself instantly twenty-five pounds lighter and back in excellent condition, able to run the mile just over five minutes as I did in high school. But to actually lose the weight or return to sterling condition, there is nothing for it but patience and consistent, ongoing dieting and exercise. This example also reminds us that patience is not simply or even primarily a matter of inactivity. We actively persist in difficult or demanding tasks, exercises, and practices only if we overcome impatience and keep at them long after there have been no instant results. Suffering (the airport delay, the diet, the workout, not to mention greater trials) produces patience, which produces character, which in turn produces hope—hope which, sustained, will not disappoint (see Rom. 5:3–5 KJV and NRSV). Of course, in classical Christian spirituality the stakes of our hope are much larger and more interesting than the success of my diet or the swiftness of my transportation. The hope the apostle Paul points to is the hope of salvation, the redemptive healing of a creation now groaning "in the bondage of its decay" (Rom. 8: 5). So we should hardly settle for the mere patience that will sustain us in our diet or keep us sane on stalled airplanes. Yet that mundane patience can be practice in a greater patience, a patience leaning forward toward a mended and new world.

As a Christian disciple I take the baby step of sitting quietly on a runway, or turning down a favorite dessert, ultimately to practice or exercise a grander patience, a patience that opens a path for the descent of God's Zion into a desperate world. "God so loved the world," and as a tiny part of it, me. I will be saved, if I am saved, only if and as the world for and to which God "sent his only Son" is saved. And I will be saved in and as my earthly body is saved, and that through patience as a gift of God's grace. As Tertullian put it, patience may begin in a commitment of the mind and will, but it "finds its fulfillment in the flesh. . . . If the 'spirit is willing, but the flesh'—without patience—'weak,' where is there salvation for the spirit as well as for the flesh itself?"

Regarding salvation and the integrity of body and spirit, it would be criminal for me to neglect another look at the apostle Paul's exhortation to "spiritual worship" in Romans 12 (even though we already considered this text, with St. Augustine, in chapter 6). Paul writes, "Present your bodies as a living sacrifice, holy and acceptable to God, which is your spiritual worship. Do not be conformed to this world, but be transformed by the renewing of your minds, so that you may discern what is the will of God—what is good and acceptable and perfect" (Rom. 12:1–2). What is interesting is how Paul's statement links and intertwines the disposition and comportment of the physical body with the "renewing of your minds" and "spiritual worship." The "living sacrifice" of bodies is not contrasted to "spiritual worship"—that sacrifice simply *is* "spiritual worship." Paul clearly speaks in the context of the formational social body that is the church, as the immediately following sentences indicate (12:3–5). From that context he refers to the tangible, material bodies of the members of the church, citing a number of practices that include visible, physical aspects—contributing to the needs of the saints, showing hospitality to strangers, rejoicing and weeping, associating with the lowly, feeding enemies (12:13–20). It does not occur to Paul to separate the body from the mind, the physical from the spiritual, let alone pit them against each other. Showing hospitality and feeding enemies, actions that must be done with and through bodies, are instances of "spiritual worship." The transformational "renewing of your minds" can flow or follow from these palpable, earthy exercises of Christian spirituality.

The letter of James speaks in a similar vein. "If a brother or sister is naked and lacks daily food, and one of you says to them, 'Go in peace; keep warm and eat your fill,' and yet you do not supply their bodily needs, what is the good of that? So faith by itself, if it has not works, is dead" (James 2:15–17). Here there is an interplay and complementarity between good intentions and salutations and the supply of bodily needs. Faith as mere intention, without act or deed, is incomplete, abortive, even "dead." Bodily disposition and comportment (here, feeding and clothing another) complete faith and bring it alive. More: there may be no real or actual intention apart from bodily action. The words "Go in peace; keep warm and eat your fill" may not be sincere. Apart from a determination to bodily enact them, they may simply be dismissive or mawkish piety. It is the determination to back or fund our words with physical, bodily involvement that makes any intention genuine intention. To borrow Paul's phrase, it is the living sacrifice of our bodies that renews our minds and makes our worship and faith true.

Prayer and the Body

Of course I can pray lying on my back, inert as a log. And that is a good thing, too, especially when I am sick. Yet classical Christian spirituality has paid close attention to the disposition of the body in prayer. In Scripture, the typical prayer posture involves standing, lifting up and spreading the hands and arms (as in Ps. 44:20–21 and Isa. 1:15). This bodily comportment—obviously originating in Judaism—was recognized and endorsed in later Christian tradition. (The First Ecumenical Council, at Nicaea in 325, gave canonical authority to standing for prayer on Sundays.) It is a posture that embodies and engenders authentic Christian prayer. We stand in respect, ready to do God's bidding. Our opened arms leave our chests unguarded, rendering us vulnerable to God and to others. The posture makes us receptive, as we hold up our hands to receive God's grace. Finally, this bodily comportment makes us free. We grasp or hold nothing in our hands and arms; our burdens are released. Standing with arms open and outstretched, our bodies are cruciform, like Christ on the cross. Our bodies thus disposed, our spirits are ideally positioned to follow the will and example of Jesus: "Let them . . . take up their cross and follow me" (Mark 8:34).

Other prayer postures have highlighted different but equally important dimensions of Christian spirituality. Kneeling in the body, or prostrating the body facedown, disposes the spirit to humility. There are more kinetic forms of prayer and praise, such as David's singing and dancing before the ark of the covenant (2 Sam. 6:16), a bodily disposition suitable to the spirit of joy and gratitude. The Greek Christian hesychasts looked to another biblical text for their prayer posture. They read of the prophet Elijah's ascending to the top of Mount Carmel, where "he bowed himself down upon the earth and put his face between his knees" (1 Kings 18:42). To pray, the hesychasts sat low to the ground, bowed their head, and rested their chin against their chest. (Hence arises the still popular, if denigrating, expression "navel-gazing.") These Byzantine Christians sought *hesychia*, or inner stillness, and found such a bodily position conducive to their contemplation. "Through our outward posture," said the fourteenth-century hesychast Gregory Palamas, "we train ourselves to be inwardly attentive."

So we can see that though there are various possible postures for Christian prayer, bodily comportment for prayer is always significant. Classical Christian spirituality forms the Christian through bodily participation in the worship of the church, including prayer per se but also various other rituals discussed earlier in this book, such as baptism, Eucharist, the imposition of ashes, and footwashing. All these rituals consist not only of words but of important bodily inclinations, positions, and movements. Christian spirituality is kinesthetic spirituality. We are sustained and grow as Christians through the exercise of our bodies as well as our minds.

Through creation, incarnation, and resurrection, the Holy Spirit works unrelentingly in history to esteem and exalt the flesh. Classical Christian spirituality never gives up on the body, social and physical. God comes to us bodily, that we might return to God in and as our bodies. Herein lies our hope, and the only and true hope of the world.

12

SAVED FROM DROWNING

The Generosity
of Christian Spirituality

In the opening pages of this book I discussed the pervasive appeal of spirituality in our day and world. I suggested that *spirituality* is a popular word now largely because it seems capacious, inclusive, nondogmatic, and nonjudgmental. To be spiritual, in this sense, is to care about "God" or the ultimate in a way that that is open and affirming of others, ready to live with and even appreciate their differentness. But of course as soon as we specify a particular community's or person's spirituality, as soon as we put an adjective (Jewish, Christian, Buddhist, or whatever) in front of the noun *spirituality*, that utter or unqualified openness evaporates. At a point in history where we can look back on episode after episode of brutality and slaughter of others in the name of Jesus Christ, the specified "Christian spirituality" can appear especially threatening. The threat ante, if we can call it that, is only upped when we further qualify this spirituality as

233

orthodox Christian spirituality. That further specification can appear all the narrower and more constricting to many outside the apostolic, traditional church. So we are left with the question: Can there be a generous orthodox Christian spirituality? Can those formed in classical Christian spirituality be open to differences in others? Or is traditional Christian spirituality necessarily prone to rigidity, even violence—figuratively if not all too often literally?

I will not for a moment attempt to deny the record, in which the church or various wings of it have acted with lethal violence. There have been the Crusades and the Inquisition. In the Reformation period, Protestants squared off against Catholics, and each against fellow adherents in their own communions. Nor is it hard to find such acts directly attributed to a motivation to serve the Christian God. Christopher Columbus spoke all too representatively out of such an attitude when he addressed his royal sponsors, "I hope in Our Lord that your Highnesses will determine to send [priests to the 'New World'] in great diligence in order to unite to the Church such great populations and convert them, just as your Highnesses have destroyed those who were unwilling to confess the Father, the Son and the Holy Spirit."

Yet as I have insisted throughout these pages, the church's faith is a living tradition. It has not always sanctioned violent or forced conversion. In its first three centuries it definitely eschewed any such approach—and now, in the last three to four centuries, it has once again done so. However orthodox or unorthodox any particular Christian argument for religious freedom may be, I believe classical Christian spirituality, at its best and truest to itself, is profoundly generous and emphatically nonviolent.

I can explain this assertion in terms key to this book. Christian spirituality is for people, not angels. The angels look directly on the face of God; they stand in God's immediate presence. In this they are both tremendously privileged and without any excuse. They are blessed to know and enjoy God directly and without doubt or confusion. This also means that if they choose not to stay in communion with God, they are once and for all separated from God. In Christian tradition, the angels before the commencement of time made a primal choice. Satan and his minions turned against the source of all life and good, which they clearly knew as true life and true good. Thus they, unlike the hosts of other angels, are forever separated from God.

The human circumstance is different. In this world and life, human creatures know God by faith, indirectly. In the Bible God reveals God's backside but not God's face (Exod. 33:17–23.). Luther talked about the "hiddenness" of God's glory. For orthodox spirituality, God's refusal to present God's self directly arises not from stinginess but from mercy and generosity. Not constituted like angels, we in our mortal fragility would be overwhelmed by a direct encounter with God. An unoccluded vision of God's face would blind and cripple us, much as would an unfiltered look at the sun. In addition, God desires our love, not our forced compliance. The trinitarian God calls people into the personal communion of Father, Son, and Holy Spirit. Personal, loving communion entails freedom. A tyrant might make a slave girl lie with him, live under his roof, and serve him. But we would not call this a relationship of love and personal communion. Love requires reciprocation, and there can be no reciprocation without an honoring of the other's free will. Another name for this relationship and condition is grace. By definition, grace is not imposed and scarce but free and generous.

Church fathers such as Irenaeus often commented on God's grace and human freedom. "For God made man free, " Irenaeus wrote. "From the beginning he has had his own power, just as he has had his own soul, to enable him, voluntarily and without coercion, to make God's mind his own. God does not use force, but good will is in Him always." Elsewhere Irenaeus affirms that the Word of God, to redeem humanity,

> did not use violence, as the apostasy [of the demons] had done at the beginning, when it usurped dominion over us, greedily snatching what was not its own. No, He used persuasion. It was fitting for God to use persuasion, not violence, to obtain what he wanted, so that justice should not be infringed and God's ancient handiwork not be utterly destroyed.

Accordingly, literal or physical violence of any sort—and certainly such violence in the name of Jesus Christ—awkwardly comports with

orthodox Christian spirituality. If God refuses to impose God's self on
people, it ill befits Christians to attempt to impose God on others.

Still, classical Christian spirituality purports to universal truth.
This spirituality just is participation and formation in God's work
in Christ, for all history, on behalf of the entire creation. The biblical story of salvation embraces the whole world, not merely certain
individual persons. It proposes and promises an encompassing end
or goal for all people, not only Christians. It is clearly not neutral
or blankly inclusive of all possible religions or spiritualities. Does
this lack of neutrality mean that, despite itself, it can finally not be
generous, noncoercive, and open to differences?

World Religions and Angelic Spirituality

We cannot answer this question adequately unless we interrogate
its terms. Again, I have suggested that we moderns and postmoderns
incline toward the term *spirituality* because it can appear uncondi-
tionally open and all-inclusive. In other words, it seems neutral: it
does not pronounce on the rightness or wrongness, the good or the
evil, the beauty or the ugliness of any specific spiritualities. It implies
that in general spirituality is a healthy, benign thing. It is salutary for
people to be "spiritual" in the sense of being nice, nonjudgmental,
tolerant, and centered on an ultimate good or ground of being in
such a way that no other person's spirituality is criticized or drawn
into question. Spirituality in this sense is neutral. With it, as the pop
psychologists would say, there is no right or wrong answer.

But notice that, in any real or actual sense, we can have no such
blank or neutral spirituality without great cost. We can have such
spirituality only by reducing all spirituality (or spiritualities) to a matter of taste or preference. I prefer Elvis to the Beatles and burritos to
sushi. You may prefer the Beatles to Elvis and sushi to burritos. There
is no harm done in our opposing preferences, and we can easily live
together despite these (comparatively minor or trivial) differences.
But I do not dedicate my life to Elvis and burritos (and I hope you do
not center yours on the Beatles and sushi). In other words, spirituality can be really neutral only if it is reduced and confined to mere

taste or preference. Such a spirituality can have little to do with the common good or what it means to be truly and most human. Such a spirituality is neutral by not mattering very much.

Orthodox Christian spirituality is not alone in its failure to fit within this reductive understanding of spirituality. The spiritualities of the great and venerable world religions all in one way or another look to the end or goal of life. Christian spirituality expects that the highest human end and aim is personal communion, shared with other creatures and the trinitarian God. Buddhism and Hinduism (in different ways) do not see the highest or truest human end resulting in communion. They teach that the basic and ultimate ground of reality is in a profound sense impersonal—so, in Hinduism, the classic metaphor of each being falling like a drop of water to be absorbed in the great, impartial, and undifferentiated ocean of being. World religions (or spiritualities) cannot be *world* religions without such global, all-encompassing expectations.

Accordingly, a Buddhist scholar writes that "the Dharma states with a precision and clarity . . . those universal laws in accordance with which the attainment of Enlightenment by a human being takes place . . . and the conditions upon which it depends and the means by which it must be achieved." This means that any truth in other religions can be "contained accurately" within Buddhism. From the Buddhist perspective and conviction, one can "plot with precision the various levels to which Hinduism, Christianity and Islam rise within the all-embracing thought of the Enlightened One [Buddha]." On the other hand, "it is not possible to fit Buddhism into the range of thought of others without distortions, prunings, abuse or persecution." As another writer, a Christian commentator on Buddhism, puts it, asking or telling Buddhists to let go of *buddhadharma*, the Enlightened One's teaching, as "the supreme expression of truth" requires "much more than simply tinkering with the system. It means an abandonment of almost everything that has been of key importance for Buddhist spirituality, intellectual life, ritual and ethical practice, and the rest. It is akin to asking a native speaker of English to please try and do without nouns."

Analogously, the same is true of other long-lived religious traditions, including Judaism, Islam, and, yes, Christianity. All these religions or spiritualities purport to know something about the true and final end of humanity. Just as Christian salvation as communion is by no means identical with Buddhist nirvana, these profound spiritualities do not agree on the ends for which they hope. Addressing such basic and ultimate realities as being and the salvation or enlightenment of the cosmos, they cannot help but arrive at some fundamental differences. So long as representatives of each spirituality believe their respective spiritualities really are concerned with the world, with true humanity, with true being or nonbeing, they cannot help but disagree—and disagree in significant (though not necessarily hateful) ways. Each will see the others' faiths as "contained accurately" within and in some sense surpassed by their own.

To assume otherwise is, in Christian terms, to pretend to an angelic status not possessed by human beings. It is to assume that all humans now gaze directly and immediately on the self-evident face of God (or whatever is ultimate reality). Such timeless and placeless angelic neutrality simply is not available to us. Since it is not, we can render a neutral human spirituality only by stipulating that spirituality cannot be about ultimate ends or supreme truth. This may be fine for a kind of unexamined dabbler's spirituality, spirituality as a hobby or personal interest (exemplified by some New Age approaches). It is not so fine for Islam, Judaism, Buddhism, Hinduism, Sikhism, and other longstanding religions of grander visions and more profound depth. We can embrace or promote this neutral spirituality only by doing violence to the specific and venerable spiritualities not merely of Christianity but of all the world religions.

Liberalism and the Illusion of Neutrality

Well, then, some might say and many have, so much the worse for religion. If spirituality cannot be neutral, it is innately divisive. Too many wars have been fought, too many people have been killed, in the names of various religions. Let us either tame and domesticate spirituality, making it a matter simply of private preference, or be done with it altogether. There is a name for this honoring of neutrality as the highest good, or at as least the pragmatically most-to-be-preferred arrangement of human affairs. That name is liberalism.

In a day and age when Liberalism with a capital L is often considered unmentionable, when liberal-baiting patriotism sometimes appears to be the *first* refuge of scoundrels, I want to be careful in defining what I here mean by liberalism. It is itself now a tradition a few centuries old. And this tradition has much to commend it. Furthermore, we late moderns in the affluent West are all to one degree or another liberals. Christian or otherwise, we affirm such liberal goods as religious freedom, the wide inclusion of as many persons as possible (female as well as male, black or brown or yellow or red as well as white, poor as well as rich, etc.) in the political process, and the aim to minimize human suffering.

Yet liberalism is a tradition, it has a history, and it is not in all its specifics friendly to orthodox Christian spirituality (and many other spiritualities). The proto- and early liberals constructed liberalism in response to the so-called Wars of Religion in sixteenth- and seventeenth-century Europe. Attributing this terrible violence to religion, they sought to neuter all religion or spirituality by privatizing and individualizing it. It would be fine for individuals, in their private lives, to hold religious opinions. But they must not be encouraged to think those opinions (or convictions, as orthodox Christianity would have it) could determine a common or public good. Instead, as Jean-Jacques Rousseau put it, they must be made to understand faith as "purely inward worship." Convictions about the common or highest good—especially theological convictions—were seen as divisive and harmful. On those terms, the classical liberal solution was elegant: confine any sense and pursuit of the highest good to the sovereign individual, thereby atomizing and disabling the critical masses that united might make for imposing political caucuses or murderous armies. Divide and disarm the potential conquerors. Pulverize them into their smallest and least threatening parts: autonomous individuals.

In the original liberal European context, this privatization of Christianity entailed dramatically changing it. It required thinning away and filtering out the thick particulars of apostolic, orthodox faith. Apostolic and orthodox Christian spirituality named the historical and social witness of a particular people in particular times and places. It pointed to the revelation of God to Mediterranean Jews and the first-century Palestinian followers of Jesus the Nazarene. Aspiring to neutrality not least of all, liberalism subordinated "religion" to "reason," a capacity thought available to all human individuals regardless of their historical and cultural contexts. Spirituality itself, in its highest or truest (and most acceptable) form, was made available to the individual immediately—that is, without the mediation of church, Scripture, or any other inescapably historical vehicle. Whatever of God's basic laws and purposes might have to do with anything other than the individual, such as the church or the national community, had to be only those believed available innately, by human nature, to any rational and decent person. So the specifics of biblical revelation and church tradition had to be curtailed and downplayed. Classical liberalism was willing to speak thinly and vaguely of "God" but not thickly and concretely of the trinitarian God the apostles encountered in Jesus Christ. (By principle, this same curtailment and reduction would be and has been applied to other religions.) Liberalism would focus all under its regime on what Thomas Hobbes called "mere life"—physical, earthly survival and comfort.

In the preceding I have necessarily spoken rather abstractly of liberalism as a political philosophy that would strive for neutrality. It would guard individual autonomy and concentrate publicly only on the provision of material needs. But it is important to note that liberalism was and is no mere philosophy. It has been put into practice, defining and structuring modern Western governments and economies. Modern government—from the military draft to regulations on the workplace and everyday taxations—seeps into all parts of all our lives. And the modern economy is a now pervasive consumer capitalism that has embraced nearly all aspects of life. Even those things formerly thought priceless, beyond the purview of the market, now face the belligerence of the bottom line. Human organs are up for sale, economists propose regulating adoptions via the stock market. The sick are no longer patients but healthcare consumers, Christian disciples are no longer worshipers but church-shoppers.

However happy or unhappy each of us is with such developments, it may occur to all of us to ask if liberalism really is neutral. In fact, as many contemporary liberals now admit, it is not. It turns out that liberalism has all along had its own conception of the good, its own biases. It sees the highest or ultimate personhood as the individual removed from and set against community and communal authority. William Galston, a liberal trying to be sympathetic to religion, writes that under liberalism "ways of life that require self-restraint, hierarchy or cultural integrity are likely to find themselves on the defensive." Stephen Macedo allows that liberalism "cannot help but shape people's lives broadly and deeply and relentlessly over time." The liberal society will, he says, be more hospitable to the artist, the entrepreneur, or the playboy than to the devoutly religious. For liberalism, human dignity is the open-ended capacity always and everywhere to choose but not to commit. Making open-ended and ongoing choice its highest good, liberalism is marked by a tendency to turn all human endeavor or discipline into matters of consumer preference.

These are very concrete ways in which we can recognize that liberalism—though hardly simply or entirely evil—is not neutral. From the standpoint of orthodox Christian spirituality, we can make this nonneutrality obvious from another angle. We might fairly and accurately say that liberalism substituted the nation-state for the church. In liberal nationalism, the individual or believer is dependent on the nation rather than the church for his or her identity and well-being. The nation-state becomes the messianic community, as when America is perceived as a city on a hill, the light shining the way for all nations. Nations, like the church and Christian spirituality, develop their own formative music, holidays, constitutive documents, heroes or "saints," and sacred places. And liberal nations demand sacrifices laid at their "altars." Their "tithes" are compulsory, in the form of taxation. More significant, they regularly expect sons and daughters to kill and die for them.

Realizing that modern "sovereign" nations are so constituted, act to preserve themselves at great cost, and often do attempt to impose their wills on other nations, we can note a telling irony. Orthodox Christian spirituality—seen as a threat to peace by the first liberals—can actually promote a much more inclusive and tolerant acceptance of the entire world than can the liberal nation-state. The church, after all, is not confined to any single nation. The kingdom of God is about the redemption of the entire world. So Tertullian, drawing on a kind of apostolic cosmpolitanism present in the church from its earliest days, could state: "One state we know, of which we are citizens—the universe." Basil of Caesarea said he as a Christian could know no exile, since "the earth I live on at the moment does not belong to me; but the land to which I might be banished is mine, or rather, it belongs to God, whose itinerant lodger I am."

Of course, some leaders and commentators believe the modern nation-state is now fading and dying, to be replaced by the global economy. Whether or not they are correct, the global economy is itself a creature of liberalism. As such, like offspring with its parents' genes, it carries the biases and preferences of liberalism. It is not and will not be neutral. And as multinational corporations now bend nation-states and their military apparatuses toward their will and contemplate "private armies," there is little indication the global economy will usher in a world free of lethal violence.

I do not believe these observations are harsh or unfair. They are judgments made not only by orthodox Christians but by many alert and dedicated proponents of liberalism. Modernity and liberalism, from the standpoint of this committed Augustinian, are neither uniquely evil nor utopian, the locus of salvation on earth. What attention to them proves, I think, is that liberalism is not neutral and by now (like the church) has blood on its own hands for which to account. Put more generally, it proves again that people are not angels. We can hide or disguise our biases and convictions about the ultimate good and what people are finally for or about. But we cannot escape them and their consequences. The question for any spirituality or way of life, then, is not, How can we achieve neutrality? It is how we can hold and embody our convictions without despising or attacking others with different convictions. So we return again more directly to classical Christian spirituality and its own capacity for generosity.

Three Sides to the Shape of Christian Salvation

I have already indicated the deepest theological basis for a generous Christian spirituality. Quite simply, the God met through Israel and in Jesus Christ is a God of grace and overflowing love. God's desire for people is our uncoerced participation in the celebratory song and dance that is the communion of Father, Son, and Holy Spirit. To cite a frequent biblical metaphor, the salvation to which God calls human beings is a wedding banquet, a party. God looks not for grudging or professional servants at that feast but for eager party-goers who readily and fully enter into the celebration. Just as true love is uncoerced and reciprocating, a true party cannot be peopled by unwilling attendees. (I think of reluctant children—such as myself at times—sulking off to the side of a family reunion. The celebration is only enhanced for child and older relatives alike when everyone freely enters into its spirit.)

There then can be no personal communion with the Triune God and one another (no salvation, in a word) without freedom. God's salvation—the ultimate and highest good or end for all creation—simply cannot be accomplished if human freedom is ignored and overpowered. If God simply wanted to rule like a tyrant or make creation function impersonally like a perfect machine, this could be achieved by wiping out all resistance, by retooling the machine and blithely disposing of any broken parts. But again, that is not salvation as orthodox Christian spirituality would have it. Salvation as Christian spirituality envisions and understands it must both change the world and preserve human freedom.

Let me put a finer point on it. Classical Christian spirituality and salvation, as the drift of this book makes abundantly clear, includes the body as well as the mind and spirit. As I have said, from creation through incarnation to the resurrection, God never gives up on the body. Our bodies, of course, are the locus of our particularity. When modern philosophers such as Descartes and Kant attempted to escape particularity, they focused on the mind over the body. Our minds can through memory and imagination jump immediately to distant places. Our bodies are always at any moment stubbornly in one place and one place only. With our minds we abstract and generalize; with and in our bodies we are always concrete and specific. So if God wanted to save only our minds, God might do no more than somehow communicate a disembodied message to us—depositing it in our brains just as money is dropped in a bank safe or an e-mail travels over phone lines and "into" computer servers. And just as an employer can functionally deposit hundreds of employee checks at once or a spamming advertiser send thousands of e-mails simultaneously, such salvation of the mind alone might be accomplished impersonally and by mass media. But such salvation would not be Christian salvation, since Christian salvation just is personal communion and never gives up on the body and its particularities. There are, then, three conditions for salvation as classic Christian spirituality envisions and understands it. This salvation must change the world, preserve human freedom, and reclaim the body as well as mind and spirit.

Of course, this series of conditions is nothing but a reversed rendition of the Father's work in Christ and the Holy Spirit. Willing to change the world, honor human freedom, and save body as well as spirit, God begins in a small and particular way, with the people Israel. This people mediates God's salvation by proclaiming and by embodying it. In Israel, and later in the church which is through the Jew Jesus adopted into the commonwealth of Israel, God creates a communion that can spread. It spreads personally, through persuasion and embodied witness. It creates and sustains communities that invite any and all to look and see, to listen and hear. The world is changed by the presence of a new people or culture, a "third race," a "holy nation" that knows no national boundaries. A new being—a being in communion with the Triune God—stands now on the face of the earth, as a sign and foretaste of creation's full and final redemption. Human freedom is honored. No one can be compelled to accept the grace and love of God; everyone is invited but no one dragged to the true party. They come out of curiosity, fascination, and anticipation arising from engagement with the (social) body of Christ. And all who enter into this salvation do so with and as their body. They have been touched and intrigued by the physical, tangible presence of actual communities. Neither now nor in the end will their whole self, including the necessary particularities of their body, be denied or rejected.

Destinations on the Other Side of Death

Exactly as communion with the Triune God, salvation then is personal and by invitation. If orthodox Christian spirituality is true—and here I mean nothing less than uniquely and finally true—then there can be no salvation except through Christ. So what of those who reject or apparently never receive an invitation to join the party? Does God's generosity, and the generosity of classic Christian spirituality, extend only so far then, and if spurned turn to spite and everlasting punishment?

Clearly the language of Scripture and the tradition can be dramatic and severe on this point. There is in both no little talk of hellfire and God's implacable wrath. Heard from some distance, such talk often terminates any consideration of God or Christian spirituality as loving, generous, and compassionate. But I would suggest that distance—and the church's own clumsiness and sometime vindictiveness—is exactly the problem. God's overflowing, trinitarian love and the importance of human freedom, as I have presented them above, are no modern or recent inventions. They go all the way to the core of classical Christian spirituality. They are as basic to the faith's understandings and teachings as any can get. So when we draw a little closer to the tradition, we may see that the (inescapable and significant) doctrines of judgment have a place but can take on a different light from the red glow of hate.

It is affirmed in most if not every quarter of orthodox Christianity that God desires the salvation—the willing and celebratory personal communion—of all. As we have just seen, this entails the preservation of human freedom. What this means is that God will never give up on any community or person, but God will not override the rejection of God by any community or person. In the kingdom of God, as in any party, the more the merrier. But full and ultimate salvation really is this personal communion, this divine party. Those who reject the invitation made in Israel and Christ cannot, by the nature of the case, enjoy the party. Thus the call or invitation to the party is enthusiastic and even urgent.

The Christian conviction on this count is like the modern rhetoric about diet and physical exercise I mentioned in the last chapter.

Exactly because our doctors believe we will be better and happier human beings for it, they and others often speak quite urgently and drastically about proper exercise and dieting. They tell us we must mount the exercise bikes and cut out the fatty foods, or die. Of course, we will not die immediately or lose any hope of happiness if we persist with couch vigils and pizzas. But we could have so much more—fit, energetic bodies and alert minds—that the couch and pizzas are death by comparison. On a much greater scale, the invitation to salvation is similar: life now and everlastingly in personal communion with the Triune God is true and full life. Anything short of it can only be death by comparison. The prophets and apostles speak urgently for a reason.

Drawing closer to the tradition of classical Christian spirituality, we can see that much of the talk of judgment is directed first and foremost at those who have definitely met God in Jesus Christ. In the Old and New Testament alike, the strongest condemnatory language is addressed to other members in the nation of Israel and in the church. Judgment begins "with the household of God" (1 Peter 4:17). The apostle Paul declares, "What have I to do with judging those outside [the church]? Is it not those inside who you are trying to judge?" (1 Cor. 5:12–13). Jesus says that the only unforgivable sin is rejection of the Holy Spirit, which the tradition has interpreted to apply to someone who has clearly and explicitly known the fruits and gifts of the Spirit, through Christ, but then perversely—willfully and deliberately—denounced and rejected that Spirit (Matt. 12:31).

As we have seen, salvation in Christ is mediated through Scripture, church, and sacraments. We know, to our sorrow, that not all mediations of Christ present him truly and winsomely. There is the case of the mid-twentieth-century European Jews who saw their parents or children hanged by Christian Nazis. There are those African-American slaves who were whipped by Christian masters. There are Muslims now who encounter supposedly Christian attitudes at the point of a gun barrel or through mass media entertainment that appears grossly hedonistic, violent, and greedy. Less dramatically, there are many just across the street from Western churches who often see the Bible wielded against them, as a club to beat them over the head. How fully and accurately have these people encountered Christ? It appears to me that many among them are rejecting not so much the real and true Christ as ugly and distorted representations of Christ—the Savior of the world obscured in a Frankenstein or Mengelian mask.

Orthodox Christian spirituality has accounted or allowed for the possibility (realized all too often) of these distortions. So the Bible speaks of God's patience in delaying the end and day of judgment (2 Peter 3:8–9). The tradition—never denying that Christ is the only true light—has conjectured that the light may get through to many people in some form (such as general revelation) without their knowing exactly how to name or identify it. (Similarly, imagine that you had never encountered the electric lamp. Then you do. Its light shines objectively, illuminating you and your surroundings, even as you know nothing about electricity and may be able to name it as nothing more accurately than "a really bright torch.") Yet other orthodox Christians, looking to such texts as 1 Peter 3:18–20, have wondered if there may be a postmortem evangelization or after-death revelation of Christ, with the dead meeting Christ perhaps for the first time and in any event more clearly and truly than during their earthly sojourn, and then being allowed to choose for or against communion with him.

Again, these are not newfangled or modern ideas: they arise from deep in the tradition and its commitment to a gracious God and, secondarily, to human freedom. As theologian George Lindbeck has recently observed,

> Christians in the first centuries appear to have had an extraordinary combination of relaxation and urgency in their attitude towards those outside the Church. On the one hand, they do not appear to have worried about the ultimate fate of the vast majority of the non-Christians among whom they lived. We hear no crises of conscience resulting from the necessity they were often under to conceal the fact that they were believers even from close friends or kindred. The ordinary Christian, at any rate, does not seem to have viewed himself as a watchman who would be held guilty of the blood of those he failed to warn (Ezek. 3:18). Yet, on the other hand, missionary proclamation was urgent and faith and baptism were to them life from death, the passage from the old age to the new. . . . So it is at least plausible to suppose that early Christians had certain unrecorded convictions about how God saves

unbelievers and how this is related to belief in Christ and membership
in the community of faith.

Theologians speculate that such "unrecorded convictions" may
include the sort I have just mentioned, general revelation and postmortem evangelization. In any event, we may rest assured that the
early Christians looked first to the love and grace of God and to
God's creation and sustenance of human freedom. Unlike some later
Christians, they were not ready to assume they knew all the details
of salvation and its extent. It is clear that in terms of assuming God's
judgment on anyone, they worried first and foremost about their
own shortcomings.

Nor does classical Christian spirituality assume that there are for
the dead only two entirely stark options: heaven and eternal bliss
or a hell of the greatest agony and pain. The doctrine of purgatory
demonstrates as much. Dante's rendering of purgatory is especially
instructive, allowing as it does a place for the pagan Virgil. Not only
does Virgil fail to suffer great punishment, but he reliably guides the
(Christian) pilgrim Dante on his spiritual path, leading him to the
threshold of Paradise. More recently the Anglican C. S. Lewis, who
like Dante drank long and deeply at the well of Christian orthodoxy,
rendered hell not as undifferentiated expanse of fiery torture but at
least in outer environs as a lonely place for those who want nothing
to do with God or others. Lewis's picture retains both the love and
mercy of a gracious God and the enduring reality of human freedom.
Those who insist on separating themselves from God live in isolation. It is hell, but hell as freely chosen isolation rather than hell as
torture chamber.

This is not to say such pictures as Dante's and Lewis's rule out a
hell of active agony. The residents of Dante's lowest circles of Hell,
or Lewis's farthest distance from heaven, are those who deliberately
habituated themselves to unmitigated evil. They have so distorted
their humanity that inescapably faced with final reality, they can
only suffer horribly. To again use the metaphor of light, it as if they
have intentionally and so thoroughly accustomed themselves to
darkness that even the faintest and most distant glow of truth burns
their eyes.

Mention of Dante's Virgil suggests yet another possibility, quite compatible with orthodoxy, for the eternal destiny of the great spiritual traditions other than Christianity. As I mentioned, Virgil's wisdom and goodness are not entirely denied. Virgil has something to teach the Christian pilgrim in the afterlife, even if Virgil himself does not attain the fullness of Paradise. Similarly, we need not pretend that the Buddhist or Hindu or holy person of another faith is after death necessarily stripped of all real wisdom and goodness. In earthly life the Hindu, for example, may through grace and discipline come to know something of the reality of God in Christ. She may finally reach an end that is not salvation—personal communion with the Triune God—but is another religious end. For the orthodox Christian, this can be seen only as a lesser end or arrived goal than salvation, just as the Hindu would see the Christian's personal communion as a less mature and full spiritual goal than a kind of monistic unity with the cosmic principle Brahman. But the traditional Christian can affirm real wisdom and insight in the devoted Hindu's intense awareness and pursuit of impersonal union with the cosmic principle underlying and sustaining reality. After all, Christians understand God not simply as personal and transcendent but also as immanent in creation, undergirding and upholding it by "natural law" or other impersonal means. Better, of course, from the Christian vantage point to know God more fully and triunely, yet the Hindu may—in this world and in the coming new world—have something to teach the Christian about meditation or about God's willingness to empty God's self (see Phil. 2:5–8).

Far from simply being generous, this strikes me as an occasion for Christian sobriety and humility. Although a Gandhi or a Dalai Lama might, if Christian salvation is true and ultimate, certainly go higher up and farther in, taking a path beyond that provided by their faith, they have traveled farther and more faithfully on their paths than many Christians have on the way toward Christ. Inasmuch as they have been drawn to a true vision of an aspect of the true God, they can be the Christian's worthy—if not final or only—teachers.

If Our Island Is Not the Whole World . . .

Along such lines, classical Christian spirituality is and can be generous, without relinquishing its convictions and worshipful practices
centered on Christ as the unique, only, and final Savior of the world.
It is the Creator-Redeemer God who sustains the cosmos, whether
or not every person in the world consciously knows it. The rain
falls and the sun shines "on the righteous and on the unrighteous"
(Matt. 5:45). Christ's death and resurrection saved and will save the
world from self-destruction. At history's end, the Christian faith and
hope could be proven wrong (just as other faiths and philosophies
will be proven wrong if creation is consummated in the kingdom of
God). But of course orthodox Christian conviction and practice is
not regarded by those committed to it as wrong or false. Classical
Christian spirituality is grounded in what its adherents take as objective reality—objective in the sense of being true whether or not any
given person subjectively thinks or feels it to be true.
    Imagine children raised in a cave, never allowed outside. Unless
told, they would know nothing of the sun. Yet the sun would remain
an objective reality—indeed a very important one—of their world.
Although the only light or heat the cave-reared children would be
consciously, subjectively aware of would be the light and heat of a
wood-burning fire, it would remain true that the heat of the sun affects the cavern's temperature. The light and heat of the sun would
enable the production of earthly oxygen, breathed by and sustaining
the children despite their cavernous ignorance.
    Likewise, the crucifixion and resurrection of Jesus Christ have in
fact changed the direction of the world, knocking it out of an orbit
of perdition into the orbit of life. All, whether they know it or not,
are affected by this changed reality. And all who are saved are saved
through Christ and Christ's work. Furthermore, Christians trust that
the God met in Jesus Christ is gracious and desires reciprocative love,
which means God honors human freedom (and which in turn entails,
among other things, that there is a hell). Finally, Christians believe
God alone is judge of any and all—the eternal destiny of persons is
not in human hands. For orthodox Christian spirituality, that much
is clear. What exactly happens after death to those who never hear

the name of Christ, or those who hear it in a distorted fashion and reject it, is not so clear. I have suggested some possibilities, each deeply rooted in the tradition, so that each honors all the basic, clear truths just mentioned.

I realize some Christians will suffer nervousness at anything short of a stark assertion that those who accept Christ as Lord and Savior in this life will go to eternal life with God while those who do not explicitly affirm Christ here and now will go to a hell of strict torment. Among other things, they will worry that any complication of this severely binary picture of human destiny may lessen Christian enthusiasm for evangelism and missions. As the reader might guess by now, I would answer that salvation is much more than a matter of what happens to the individual, disembodied soul after death. Classical Christian spirituality is bodily as well as soulful, social no less than individual, and arrives at eternity not by skipping history and time but by passing through them. If trusting in and following Christ is participation in the healing of the cosmos ("physical" and "spiritual") of a divided world, and of the whole person (body as well as soul), there is every reason to proclaim it immediately and enthusiastically and to invite others to ultimate life and health sooner rather than later.

Departing our cave kids, imagine another scenario. Fishing in a river, I am drawn into a current and hit my head against a rock. I fall unconscious and am drowning. A woman passing in a canoe sees me go under and rescues me. She saves my life. That is true, and quite eventful and significant to me, though I am unaware because unconscious. I am ashore and breathing and will live another day even though I do not know it at the moment. Now suppose that for one reason or another my rescuer cannot wait until I regain consciousness and must hurry away. When I rouse, I am alive and well, albeit with a knot on my head. This will remain a fact whether or not I ever learn the identity of my rescuer. My very life proves that I have been rescued. Footprints and mud flattened by a dragged body (as well as the knot on my head) prove that the accident and the rescue were no dream. Someone saved me. But who? Profoundly, I will want to thank my rescuer. It will only enhance my joy to see and know my rescuer. Here ignorance is not bliss—my gratitude will only be enlarged and completed if I know my rescuer. On this count I would rather not remain agnostic.

To get closer to the Christian understanding of salvation, we need to enrich the picture. Suppose that I come from a race of folk who dwell on an island. Suppose I and my people have known only this island. We have feared leaving it because the river surrounding it is huge, and we have thought that the whole world was only our island and the river. In our fear and fragmentary knowledge we have never learned how to swim or how to build canoes. There are vague rumors about sightings of unknown canoeists, who my people have seen as creatures with a single long, flat wooden leg gliding across the river's surface. Some dismiss these as delusional myths or hallucinations, while others wonder if the wooden-legged gliders on water are gods from another world.

Like a Hollywood screenwriter, let us add another twist or complication to the plot. Not only have my people believed our island is all the world. Not only have we failed to learn how to swim or build canoes. In addition to all this, the river is rising and our island is flooding. Some have responded to the rising of the river with fervent supplication to our gods. Others, the more fatalistic among us, simply try to live for today and today only. What is unknown to us is that there is, just beyond eyesight, not simply another island but an entire continent, and that there are dwellers on other (unknown) islands who discovered the continent and have learned how to swim, how to build canoes, and much else.

If all this is the case, knowing my rescuer is all the more urgent and worthwhile. Not only can I thank her and live in a manner worthy of her efforts, but she can teach me (and my people) how to swim, how to build canoes, how to navigate the river. She can even, from her people's advanced explorations, tell us of the teeming continent, an "island" bigger than our river, a whole other world. In our fears and limitations, it will be awhile before we can visit the continent. But following and learning from the rescuer, some of us, bold and most learned in canoe building and handling, occasionally catch glimpses of it—and of its stupendous promises and joys.

Christ and his salvation are somewhat like this analogy. Our world (our island) is sinking. Our rescuer enables all of us to escape to another island and live now. Our rescuer not only saves us to breathe another day but deepens and extends that salvation by teaching us how to swim and catch glimpses of another and greater world. Christ's salvation is eternal life ultimately for a renewed, perfected heaven and earth—a bounteous continent at which we may someday arrive. But it is also incipient eternal life now, in this day and age. Learning how to swim and build canoes will fit us for life on the continent and indeed enable us to arrive there. But it will also serve well and profoundly now, on the island of our limitations. Venturing to other islands before we arrive at the continent, the new and mended world, we meet others who can teach us a thing or two. Our community of life will grow and deepen and take on unanticipated shades of beauty. We will hope the best for all we meet, even if they do not join our community now. Above all, we will rejoice that we have been saved, body and soul. The birds fly in a bigger sky. The dappled fish drift in a river lapping on its other side against the banks of a renewed and undying world.

All this, because the Word became flesh and tented among us.

ACKNOWLEDGMENTS

Convict me of over-dramatization if you must, but the writing of a book is a long and often daunting pilgrimage. This author, at least, sometimes fears the mountains to be forded too high and treacherous for crossing to the other side of a completed manuscript and successful book. At times I find myself panicked, drowning in currents of competing thoughts, choking on inadequate comprehension or expression. At other points there are wonderful hours and days when I seem to stand atop a peak, with a chapter successfully launched and nothing ahead but an exhilarating rush down the slopes of happy momentum. Writing looks like and in some wise is a lonely business. But I know that I have not yet finished the journey of finding, carrying, and putting together the pieces of a book without great direction, correction, and encouragement along the way.

Robert Webber first pointed me beyond the foothills toward the higher ranges of the patristics, or the writings of the church fathers and mothers. Lauree Hersch-Meyer, an Anabaptist theologian, was my unlikely guide deep into the fascinating, vertiginous canyons of Augustine's grand thought and devotion.

A number of churches heard and responded keenly to reports from scouting expeditions, or early drafts of the book in development. I thank the pastors and layfolk at the First Methodist Church, Beaver, Oklahoma; the First Baptist Church, Lawrence, Kansas; and especially St. Barnabas Episcopal Church, Glen Ellyn, Illinois, my home parish of 22 years—currently so ably shepherded by Father Matthew Gunter. Similar scouting reports were given to attentive and sharpening listeners at venues for the Ekklesia Project, the Matthew's House Project, the graduate group of the InterVarsity Christian Fellowship at the University of Illinois, Middlebury College, and Grand Rapids Theological Seminary.

Seven theologically and pastorally astute friends read a late draft of the manuscript in toto. They knocked me off wrong directions, confirmed some right directions, and cheered me in their sharing of the intrinsic rewards of the common endeavor of serving God's kingdom through thought and word. I thank and celebrate the good company of Craig Barnes, Kyle Childress, Lillian Daniel, Stanley Hauerwas, Steve Long, Joel Shuman, and Jon Stock.

Chad Allen, Rebecca Cooper, B. J. Heyboer, and Don Stephenson are publishing colleagues and friends who read the manuscript, contributed to its improvement, and gave me courage from its start to its finish. They construct and maintain the vehicles that carry my explorations into the wide world. How wonderful it is to walk, work, and play every day alongside people of such ability, good humor, and commitment to excellent publishing that serves the church. Here, too, I must note the polishing and correction of an extremely talented copy editor, Ruth Goring.

Once more I am delighted to acknowledge the contributions of my closest co-travelers. Spouse Sandy sometimes picked up the slack when my (over)commitment prevented my due service to the functioning of our household economy. In myriad ways she continues to keep a bookish and dreamy husband tethered down to earth. My love and gratitude to my longtime and true companion. At the last, I have dedicated this book to the other member of our household, daughter Jesselyn. Growing up, she has forced me to grow up. We share an inordinate love of film and popular music, and few things give me more sheer pleasure than watching, listening to, discussing (and debating!) finds old and new with Jess. In these two and so many other ways she continues to stretch my imagination and expand my horizons. How sweet it is to present her with this palpable demonstration of my labor and passions, this abiding artifact of love and hope.

NOTES

INTRODUCTION

p. 15, "created and sustained by the Holy Spirit.": My formulation of a definition of orthodox Christian spirituality was especially sharpened by Ralph C. Wood, "Christian Spirituality: Inward Piety or Outward Practice?" *Christian Ethics Today*, October 2001, 3–6; and David S. Yeago, "The Bible," in *Knowing the Triune God: The Work of the Spirit in the Practices of the Church*, ed. James J. Buckley and David S. Yeago (Grand Rapids: Eerdmans, 2001), 60–66.

p. 17, "simply the Spirit's public": See Reinhard Hütter, "The Church," in *Knowing the Triune God*, ed. Buckley and Yeago, 23–47.

p. 18, "Christianly spiritual persons . . . 'are not bodiless spirits'": Irenaeus, *The Scandal of the Incarnation* (originally *Against the Heresies*), trans. John Saward (San Francisco: Ignatius, 1990), bk. 5, chap. 8.

p. 19, "The truly 'spiritual' disciple": Ibid., 4.32.

p. 21, sins "against myself": St. Augustine, *The Confessions of St. Augustine*, trans. John K. Ryan (Garden City, NY: Image, 1960), bk. 5, chap. 9.

p. 21, "What you take vengeance on": Ibid., 3.8.

p. 21, "For without you": Ibid., 4.1.

p. 21, "For it is certain": St. Augustine, *The City of God*, trans. Henry Bettenson (London: Penguin, 1972), bk. 13, chap. 21.

p. 21, "to protect from themselves": Augustine, *Confessions*, 7.18.

p. 22, "I was sure": Ibid., 8.5.

p. 23, ". . . and that of grace": George Herbert, "Affliction (IV)," in *George Herbert: The Country Parson, The Temple*, ed. John N. Wall Jr. (New York: Paulist, 1981), 208–9.

pp. 23–24, "You stand before God": Karl Barth, *Dogmatics in Outline* (New York: Harper & Row, 1959), 153–54.

CHAPTER 1

p. 29, "Gee, but the graveyard": Jimmie Rodgers, "T.B. Blues," as found on Rodgers, *America's Blue Yodeler, 1930–1931*, Rounder CD 1060.

p. 30, "In this regard St. Augustine": St. Augustine, *The Works of Saint Augustine: A Translation for the 21st Century*, part 3, vol. 8, trans. Edmund Hill (Hyde Park, NY: New City, 1994), sermon 277, quoting Wisdom 9:15.

p. 30, "So the third-century theologian Origen": Quoted in Caroline Walker Bynum, *The Resurrection of the Body: In Western Christianity, 200–1336* (New York: Columbia University Press, 1995), 64.

p. 30, "Mortality was much more visible and pervasive for premodern Christians": For information on urban conditions and mortality in the ancient world related in this paragraph, see Rodney Stark, *The Rise of Christianity* (San Francisco: HarperSanFrancisco, 1996), 149–60.

p. 32, "Sexual passion disrupted the serene": See Jack Miles, *Christ: A Crisis in the Life of God* (New York: Vintage, 2002), 57.

p. 32, "What about non-Western faiths and philosophies": For the following to the end of this paragraph, see Michael Saso, "The Taoist Body and Cosmic Prayer; Steven Collins, "The Body in Theravāda Buddhist Monasticism"; Paul Williams, "Some Mahāyāna Buddhist Perspectives on the Body"; Annemarie Schimmel, "'I Take Off the Dress of the Body': Eros in Sufi Literature"; and Eleanor Nesbitt, "The Body in Sikh Tradition," in *Religion and the Body*, ed. Sarah Coakley (Cambridge: Cambridge University Press, 1997), 239, 191, 210, 267, and 294, respectively.

p. 33, "Whatever you take, after all": Augustine, sermon 277.

p. 36, "soul 'persisted' after death": St. Augustine, *The City of God*, trans. Henry Bettenson (London: Penguin, 1972), bk. 13, chap. 2.

p. 36, "ensouled bodies and embodied souls": As in Karl Barth, *Church Dogmatics* 3/4, trans. A. T. MacKay et al. (Edinburgh: T & T Clark, 1961), 358–59.

p. 39, "It was not the corruptible flesh": Augustine, *City of God*, 14.3.

p. 40, "It is we [in our sin] who were the cause": St. Athanasius, *On the Incarnation*, trans. anonymous (Crestwood, NY: St. Vladimir's Seminary Press, 1953), chap. 1, para. 4.

p. 41, "'Rather,' said St. Athanasius, he sanctified the body": Ibid., 3.17.

pp. 41–42, God "has imprinted the form": Irenaeus, *Demonstration of the Apostolic Preaching*, in *The Scandal of the Incarnation* (originally *Against the Heresies*), trans. John Saward (San Francisco: Ignatius, 1990), para. 34.

p. 42, "Christ passed through all the ages": Irenaeus *Scandal of the Incarnation*, 3.18.

p. 42, "The knot of Eve's disobedience": Ibid., 3.22.

p. 42, "capable of consuming 'stronger nourishment'": Ibid., 4.38.

p. 42, "The truly 'spiritual' disciple": Ibid., 4.32.

pp. 42–43, "each cluster of grapes would produce": Irenaeus, *Against the Heresies*, ed. and trans. Cyril C. Richardson, in *Early Christian Fathers* (New York: Macmillan, 1979), bk. 33, chap. 3.

p. 44, "The soul in his view": See Dale B. Martin, *The Corinthian Body* (New Haven: Yale University Press, 1995), 11. The "physicality" of spiritual bodies, in the New Testament context, is corroborated by N. T. Wright, *The Resurrection of the Son of God* (Minneapolis: Fortress, 2003), 312–74.

p. 44, "bodies 'not yet spiritual but animal'": Augustine, *City of God*, 13.20.

p. 44, ". . . and yet was spirit, not flesh": Ibid., 22.21.

p. 46, "righteous will not need 'material nourishment'": Ibid., 13.22.

p. 46, "Science's net is not made": For an excellent treatment of science and orthodox Christianity, see Terence C. Nichols, *The Sacred Cosmos: Christian Faith and the Challenge of Naturalism* (Grand Rapids: Brazos, 2003); the Arthur Eddington parable is found on 203.

p. 47, "maturity is 'already latent'": Augustine, *City of God*, 22.14.

CHAPTER 2

p. 52, "Justin Martyr wrote with praise": Quoted in Mark D. Jordan, *The Ethics of Sex* (Oxford: Blackwell, 2002), 48.

p. 52, "dare to enjoy 'pastries and honey-cakes'": Clement of Alexandria, *Christ the Educator*, trans. Simon P. Wood (New York: Fathers of the Church, 1954), bk. 2, chap. 1, para. 4.

pp. 52–53, "natural and pure drink": Ibid., 2.2.1.

p. 53, "get out of control and become indecent": Ibid., 2.4.41.

p. 53, "laughter 'should be kept under restraint'": Ibid., 2.5.46.

p. 53, "shipwrecks us upon pleasure": Ibid., 2.7.60.

p. 53, "We must not think of bathing": Ibid., 3.9.46.

p. 53, "We must keep a firm control": Ibid., 2.10.90.

p. 53, "Pleasure sought for its own sake": Ibid., 2.10.92.

p. 53, "To indulge in intercourse": Ibid., 2.10.95.

p. 53, "the natural companionship between the sexes": St. Augustine, *On the Good of Marriage*, trans. Charles T. Wilcox (New York: Fathers of the Church, 1955), chap. 9, para. 9.

p. 53, "it is better not to marry": Ibid., 2.2.

p. 53, "Marriage and virginity are . . . two goods": Ibid., 23.29.

p. 53, "much more quickly would the City of God be filled": Ibid., 10.10.

p. 54, "without physical coition": Ibid., 2.2.

p. 54, "evil of lust": Ibid., 3.3.

p. 54, "'disgraceful' for a spouse to demand sex": Ibid., 5.5.

p. 54, "marital intercourse makes something good": Ibid., 3.3.

p. 54, "But to fairly represent St. Augustine's views": Ibid., 6.6.

p. 54, "In one of his sermons": See Mathijs Lamberigts, "A Critical Evaluation of Augustine's View of Sexuality," in *Augustine and His Critics*, ed. Robert Dodaro and George Lawless (London: Routledge, 2002), 187.

p. 55, "an adulterer toward his own wife": For the quotes from Calvin in this paragraph, see John Calvin, *Institutes of the Christian Religion*, trans. Ford Lewis Battles (Philadelphia: Westminster, 1960), bk. 2, chap. 41; bk. 2, chap. 43; bk. 2, chap. 44.

p. 55, "the 'remedy' of marriage": See Jordan, *Ethics of Sex*, 61.

p. 55, "God has created man and woman": Martin Luther, "On Marriage Matters," in *Luther's Works*, vol. 46, ed. Robert C. Schultz (Philadelphia: Fortress, 1967), 304.

p. 55, "Repeatedly plagued by depression": Richard Marius, *Martin Luther: The Christian between God and Death* (Cambridge: Harvard University Press, 1999), 439.

p. 56, "the necessities of this life": Jordan, *Ethics of Sex*, 58–59.

p. 56, "since the fall marriage has been adulterated": This and other 1519 quotes from Luther in this paragraph are from Martin Luther, "A Sermon on the Estate of Marriage," in *Luther's Works*, vol. 44, ed. James Atkinson (Philadelphia: Fortress, 1966), paras. 3–4.

p. 56, "a life of angels, the enamel of the soul": Quoted in Jordan, *Ethics of Sex*, 68–69.

p. 57, "the more perfect state": Quoted in ibid., 62.

pp. 58–59, "In every soul that surpasses": Quoted in ibid., 53.

p. 59, "For ancient physicians like Galen": Dale B. Martin, *The Corinthian Body* (New Haven: Yale University Press, 1995), 213–14.

p. 59, "who replied to someone asking him his attitude": Quotes from Clement in this paragraph are from *Christ the Educator* 2.10.94 and 2.10.95, respectively.

pp. 59–60, "an almost total extinction of mental alertness": St. Augustine, *The City of God*, trans. Henry Bettenson (London: Penguin, 1972), bk. 14, chap. 16.

p. 61, "Athanasius said . . . 'we possess upon earth'": Quoted in Peter Brown, *The Body and Society: Men, Women, and Sexual Renunciation in Early Christianity* (New York: Columbia University Press, 1988), 259.

p. 61, "Ambrose had declared, '[A virgin, Mother Mary] has brought from heaven'": Quoted in Jordan, *Ethics of Sex*, 66.

p. 61, "John Chrysostom sermonized, . . . 'These are our angels'": Quoted in Brown, *Body and Society*, 324.

p. 62, "did not become an angel but man": Barth quotations in this paragraph are from Karl Barth, *Church Dogmatics* 3/3, trans. G. W. Bromiley and R. J. Ehrlich (Edinburgh: T & T Clark, 1960), 475, 483.

p. 63, "A whole man is torn out": Clement, *Christ the Educator,* 2.10.94.

p. 64, Sometimes "desire abandons the eager lover": Augustine, *City of God,* bk. 14, ch. 16.

p. 66, "each seeks to satisfy his desire": Luther, "Sermon on the Estate of Marriage," para. 4.

p. 69, "Lust is not something wrong": Augustine, *City of God,* 12.8.

p. 69, "to reach the kingdom [of God] which has no end": Ibid., 22.30.

CHAPTER 3

p. 73, "I believe myself to be": William James, quoted in Carol Zaleski, "A Letter to William James," *Christian Century* 119, no. 2 (January 16–23, 2002): 32.

p. 74, "The microcosm of the physical body seemed most handily": Dale B. Martin, *The Corinthian Body* (New Haven: Yale University Press, 1995), 92, also 268n13.

p. 74, "The single physical body reflects": Ibid., 16–17.

p. 74, "Accordingly, as in Rome's Pantheon": Richard Sennett, *Flesh and Stone: The Body and the City in Western Civilization* (New York: W. W. Norton, 1994), 90, 102–6.

p. 75, "City planners built sewage systems": Ibid., 257–63.

p. 76, "In one example cited by the *OED*": *The Oxford English Dictionary*, 2nd ed. (Oxford: Clarendon, 1989), 16:259.

p. 76, "The church is the common mother": John Calvin, *Calvin's Commentaries: The Epistles of Paul the Apostle to the Galatians, Ephesians, Philippians and Colossians*, trans. T. H. L. Parker (Grand Rapids: Eerdmans, 1965), 181 (re Eph. 4:12).

p. 77, "Hence the early church saw individualization": Quotes from Maximus and Augustine in this paragraph are from Henri Du Lubac, *Catholicism: Christ and the Common Destiny of Man*, trans. Lancelot C. Sheppard and Elizabeth Englund (San Francisco: Ignatius, 1988), 33–34.

p. 78, "desire is wrong or distorted 'if the love'": St. Augustine, *The City of God*, trans. Henry Bettenson (London: Penguin, 1972), bk. 14, chaps. 6–7.

p. 78, "For you [God] have made us": St. Augustine, *The Confessions of St. Augustine*, trans. John K. Ryan (Garden City, NY: Image, 1960), bk. 1, chap. 1.

p. 79, "desire was not neutral but 'can only be understood'": Augustine, *City of God*, 14.6–7.

p. 79, "in love with being in love": Augustine, *Confessions*, 3.1.

p. 79, "What does it matter": Augustine, *City of God*, 18.41.

p. 80, "we have only succeeded in becoming a nuisance": Quotes from Augustine through this sentence in this paragraph are from ibid., 14.15.

p. 80, "In his view, it would in fact be better": Ibid., 19.15.

p. 81, "I was sure that it was better": Augustine, *Confessions*, 8.5.

p. 82, "A wise man's attitude toward industrial capitalism": G. K. Chesterton, *What I Saw in America* (San Francisco: Ignatius, 1990), 204.

p. 83, "Luxury, Augustine said, 'is more deadly'": Quotes from Augustine through this sentence in this paragraph are from Augustine, *City of God*, 3.21.

p. 83, "moral corruption far worse": Ibid., 1.31.

p. 83, "not the body but the character": Ibid., 1.32.

p. 83, "You seek security not for the peace": Ibid., 1.33.

p. 84, "evils 'which generally spring up'": Ibid., 2.18.

p. 84, "hustled out of hearing by the freedom-loving majority": Ibid., 2.29. For Augustine's God-centered understanding of justice, see Robert Louis Wilken, *The Spirit of Early Christian Thought* (New Haven: Yale University Press, 2003), 204–11.

p. 84, "Full publicity is given": Augustine, *City of God*, 2.26.

p. 84, "We have self-indulgence and greed": Ibid., 5.12; he here quotes, approvingly, the Roman Cato.

p. 85, "sensual pleasure is put above virtue": Ibid., 19.1.

p. 86, "we live in full community with the bodily presence": Dietrich Bonhoeffer, *Discipleship*, trans. Barbara Green and Reinhard Krauss (Minneapolis: Fortress, 2001), 213.

p. 86, "the church 'is a living witness'": Ibid., 232.

p. 87, Such an "exercise of the sex-act": Aquinas quotations through this sentence in this paragraph are from St. Thomas Aquinas, *Summa Theologiae: A Concise Translation*, ed. Timothy McDermott (Allen, TX: Christian Classics, 1989), 431–32.

pp. 87–88, "Adultery is 'not merely a sin of lust': Ibid., 253–54.

p. 88, "meant to 'serve the general good of mankind'": Ibid., 431–32.

CHAPTER 4

p. 94, "observe God in utter clarity": St. Augustine, *The City of God*, trans. Henry Bettenson (London: Penguin, 1972), bk. 22, chap. 29.

p. 95, "pass from this world into eternal life": Martin Luther, "The Blessed Sacrament of the Holy and True Body of Christ, and the Brotherhoods," in *Martin Luther's Basic Theological Writings,* ed. Timothy F. Lull (Minneapolis: Fortress, 1989), 259.

pp. 96–97, "*The Didache* includes careful instructions": *The Didache*, in *Early Christian Fathers*, ed. and trans. Cyril C. Richardson (New York: Macmillan, 1979), chaps. 7, 9, 10; eucharistic prayer, chap. 10, para. 3.

p. 97, "Ignatius exhorts": Baptism, *Letter to Polycarp* 6.2; Eucharist, *Letter to the Romans* 7.3, in *Early Christian Fathers*, ed. and trans. Richardson.

p. 97, "Justin calls baptism . . . and observes that the sacramental bread": On baptism, quoted in J. N. D. Kelly, *Early Christian Doctrines*, rev. ed. (San Francisco: Harper & Row, 1978), 194; on Eucharist, ibid., 198.

p. 97, "the Eucharist was 'the chief instrument'": Kelly, *Early Christian Doctrines*, 450.

p. 97, "the 'mother' of Christian faith and life": John Calvin, *Calvin's Commentaries: The Epistles of Paul the Apostle to the Galatians, Ephesians, Philippians, and Colossians*, trans. T. H. L. Parker (Grand Rapids: Eerdmans, 1965), 181 (re. Eph. 4:12).

p. 98, "not only to embrace with a believing heart": Quoted in John Williamson Nevin, *The Anxious Bench; Antichrist; and The Sermon on Catholic Unity*, ed. Augustine Thompson (Eugene, OR: Wipf and Stock, n.d.), 6.

p. 98, "Whoever therefore does not receive": John Wesley, quoted in Debra Dean Murphy, *Teaching That Transforms: Worship as the Heart of Christian Education* (Grand Rapids: Brazos, 2004), 192.

p. 101, "the Eucharist 'is too spiritual'": John Williamson Nevin, *The Mystical Presence: A Vindication of the Reformed or Calvinistic Doctrine of the Holy Eucharist*, ed. Augustine Thompson (Eugene, OR: Wipf and Stock, 2000), 134 (my emphasis).

p. 102, "Do you wish to instruct God": This and other Luther quotes in the paragraph are from Martin Luther, "The Sacrament of the Body and Blood of Christ—Against the Fanatics," in *Martin Luther's Basic Theological Writings*, ed. Lull, 323.

pp. 102–103, "You might as well tell me": Ibid.

p. 103, "Christians prayed to 'a baked God'": Ibid., 315.

CHAPTER 5

p. 107, "The sacrament '*first* lies outside'": Martin Luther, "The Sacrament of the Body and Blood of Christ—Against the Fanatics," in *Martin Luther's Basic Theological Writings*, ed. Timothy F. Lull (Minneapolis: Fortress, 1989), 314 (my emphasis).

p. 108, "seek him in creation 'apart from the Word'": Ibid., 321.

p. 108, "The unchanging Word of God": Luther, "Concerning Rebaptism," in *Martin Luther's Basic Theological Writings*, ed. Lull, 361.

p. 108, "If I am baptized on [God's] bidding": Ibid., 365.

p. 108, "We can and must constantly maintain": Luther, "The Smalcald Articles," art. 8, paras. 9–10, in *Martin Luther's Basic Theological Writings*, ed. Lull, 531.

p. 109, "into the depths of hell" and "in the midst of devils": *Luther's Works,* vol. 6, ed. Jaroslav Pelikan (St. Louis: Concordia, 1970), 131.

p. 110, "five-feet-two-inch": Jesus the Nazarene's probable height as adduced from archaeological study.

p. 110, "profitably think of it as 'transphysical'": N. T. Wright, *The Resurrection of the Son of God* (Minneapolis: Fortress, 2003), 476–79.

p. 110, "Even when I have left you": See Michael Welker, *What Happens in Holy Communion?* trans. John Hoffmeyer (Grand Rapids: Eerdmans, 2000), 89.

p. 112, "We are not set over into this new order": John Williamson Nevin, *The Mystical Presence: A Vindication of the Reformed or Calvinistic Doctrine of the Holy Eucharist*, ed. Augustine Thompson (Eugene, OR: Wipf and Stock, 2000), 152, 158.

p. 113, "*anamnesis* and its cognates carry the sense": See Dom Gregory Dix, *The Shape of the Liturgy* (New York: Seabury, 1983), 161.

p. 114, "When God remembers, God's answer creates": See Robert W. Jenson, *Systematic Theology*, vol. 2, *The Works of God* (New York: Oxford University Press, 1999), 258.

p. 116, "The force of the sacrament": Nevin, *Mystical Presence*, 173.

p. 116, "Deliver us from the presumption": "Eucharistic Prayer C," in *The Book of Common Prayer* (New York: Oxford University Press, 1990), 372.

CHAPTER 6

p. 123, "To receive this sacrament": Martin Luther, "The Blessed Sacrament of the Holy and True Body of Christ, and the Brotherhoods," in *Martin Luther's Basic Theological Writings,* ed. Timothy F. Lull (Minneapolis: Fortress, 1989), 244.

p. 123, "In times past" . . . "seek the betterment of the church and of all Christians": Ibid., 250.

p. 124, "Ancient Mesopotamian creation myths": See Richard Middleton, *The Liberating Image* (Grand Rapids: Brazos, forthcoming).

p. 125, "No one is going to say": St. Augustine, *The City of God*, trans. Henry Bettenson (London: Penguin, 1972), bk. 10, chap. 5.

p. 125, "wonderfully created, and yet more wonderfully restored": Collect "Of the Incarnation," in *The Book of Common Prayer* (New York: Oxford University Press, 1990), 252.

p. 126, "The true sacrifices are acts of compassion": Augustine *City of God* 10.7, 10.20.

p. 127, "Geologists now calculate that humanity": See Mike Davis, *Dead Cities* (New York: New Press, 2002), 361.

p. 127, "To 'fill the earth' is partly": See Middleton, *The Liberating Image.*

p. 128, "As kingfishers catch fire": "Inversnaid," in *Poems and Prose of Gerard Manley Hopkins* (New York: Penguin, 1969), 51.

p. 128, "Surely the playing of musical instruments": Karl Barth, *Church Dogmatics* 3/3, trans. G. W. Bromiley and R. J. Ehrlich (Edinburgh: T & T Clark, 1960), 472.

p. 131, the heart is "much more tenuous": Martin Luther, "The Sacrament of the Body and Blood of Christ—Against the Fanatics," in *Martin Luther's Basic Theological Writings*, ed. Lull, 320.

p. 131, "go joyfully to the sacrament": Luther, "Blessed Sacrament," 246–47.

p. 132, "the medicine of immortality": Quoted in Paul Evdokimov, *Ages of the Spiritual Life*, trans. Sister Gertrude et al. (Crestwood, NY: St. Vladimir's Seminary Press, 1998), 124.

p. 133, "when they partake of the Eucharist": Quoted in ibid., 124.

CHAPTER 7

p. 140, "The credit card was introduced": Thomas A. Bailey and David M. Kennedy, *The American Pageant* (Lexington, MA: D. C. Heath, 1991), 913.

p. 140, "In 1956, the average teenager": See James Miller, *Flowers in the Dustbin: The Rise of Rock and Roll, 1947–1977* (New York: Fireside, 1999), 144.

p. 140, "In 1939, the National Broadcasting Company": For this and other information about television in this paragraph, see Bailey and Kennedy, *American Pageant*, 913, and Mitchell Stephens, *The Rise of the Image and the Fall of the Word* (New York: Oxford University Press, 1998), 46.

p. 141, "Early in 1955, Florida devotees": For information and the quotation in this paragraph, see Peter Guralnick, *Last Train to Memphis: The Rise of Elvis Presley* (Boston: Little, Brown, 1994), 190, 223, 279, 167.

p. 142, "performance on *Ed Sullivan* was watched": Ibid., 338.

p. 142, "there were at least fifty Elvis products": Ibid., 354.

p. 142, "When we went out on Elvis's motorcycle": Ibid., 355.

p. 143, "His second was in that exotic city in the Mojave Desert": On Vegas and the statistics in this paragraph, see Mike Davis, *Dead Cities* (New York: New Press, 2002), 86–90, and Sally Denton and Roger Morris, *The Money and the Power: The Making of Las Vegas and Its Hold on America* (New York: Vintage, 2001).

p. 144, "Years later, at Presley's funeral": Peter Guralnick, *Careless Love: The Unmaking of Elvis Presley* (Boston: Little, Brown, 1999), 655.

p. 144, "I think I became a dollar sign": Ibid., 609.

p. 144, "Elvis is a man whose task": Greil Marcus, *Mystery Train: Images of America in Rock 'n' Roll Music* (New York: Plume, 1997), 123.

p. 145, "He was no longer the man": St. Augustine, *The Confessions of St. Augustine*, trans. John K. Ryan (Garden City, NY: Image, 1960), bk. 6, chap. 8.

p. 147, "I lose myself in my singing": Guralnick, *Last Train*, 430.

p. 147, "He first witnessed the mannerism": Ibid., 48.

p. 148, "Enterprising publicists first labeled him": Presley's early monikers and descriptions of his style are found in Marcus, *Mystery Train*, 129, 133, and in Guralnick, *Last Train*, 163, 182, 203.

p. 148, "laboriously constructed out of a series": Marcus, *Mystery Train*, 149.

p. 149, "In its studios, he could spend two hours": For information on Presley's work ethic while recording, see Guralnick, *Last Train*, 336, 298, 300, 239.

p. 150, "Presley's experience offers an analogy": For information in this paragraph, see Guralnick, *Careless Love*, 102–3, 122, 128.

p. 150, "We live by faithful improvisation": See Samuel Wells, *Improvisation: The Drama of Christian Ethics* (Grand Rapids: Brazos, 2004).

p. 151, "I hadn't been around anyone who was [that] religious": Guralnick, *Last Train*, 337.

p. 151, "We used to read the Bible": Ibid., 376.

p. 151, "I read my Bible, sir": Ibid., 352.

p. 151, "I know my mother approves": Ibid., 322.

p. 152, "Humbard later reported, 'took both his hands in mine'": Guralnick, *Careless Love*, 617.

p. 152, "I am not trying to build a brief": The information in this paragraph comes from ibid., 173–225, and Paul Simpson, *The Rough Guide to Elvis* (London: Penguin, 2002), 36.

p. 153, "As for racism": The quotes following in this paragraph are from Guralnick, *Last Train*, 384, 484.

p. 153, "The June Taylor Dancers": Dave Marsh, *Elvis* (New York: Thunder's Mouth, 1992), 100.

p. 154, "1956 performance of 'Hound Dog' on the *Milton Berle Show*": This and several other performances are available on the DVD set *Elvis: The Great Performances*, Rhino R2–976096.

p. 155, "It catches the comic elements": For corroboration, see Miller, *Flowers in the Dustbin*, 135; note also 80, where a Presley musician remarks on the laughter of an early concert audience—Elvis thought the crowd was "actually making fun of him."

p. 155, "a famous shot from New Orleans": The photo can be found in Marsh, *Elvis*, 67–68.

CHAPTER 8

p. 159, "he counseled parents, 'from time to time'": This and the following quotes from Koelman are found in Jacobus Koelman, *The Duties of Parents*, trans. John Vriend (Grand Rapids: Baker Academic, 2003), 154–55, 158, 133.

p. 161, "seen life spans increased, on average": Jane Spencer and Cynthia Crossen, "Why Americans Are So Scared," AOL News, April 16, 2003 (not archived).

p. 166, "the fragile brilliance of glass": St. Augustine, *The City of God*, trans. Henry Bettenson (London: Penguin, 1972), bk. 4, chap. 3.

p. 166, "I am certain of this": Ibid., 1.11.

p. 166, "There is no one": Ibid., 13.10.

p. 166, "as though they were the only joys": Ibid., 15.15, 15.17.

p. 168, "asceticism would be necessary rest": Paul Evdokimov, *Ages of the Spiritual Life*, trans. Sister Gertrude et al. (Crestwood, NY: St. Vladimir's Seminary Press, 1998), 64–65.

p. 168, "We should familiarize ourselves with death": Martin Luther, "A Sermon on Preparing to Die," in *Martin Luther's Basic Theological Writings*, ed. Timothy F. Lull (Minneapolis: Fortress, 1989), 640–41.

p. 171, "the 'double raiment' of the reunited body and soul": Dante Alleghieri, *The Divine Comedy: Paradise*, in *The Portable Dante*, ed. and trans. Mark Musa (New York: Penguin, 1995), canto 24, lines 92–93.

p. 171, "Think not thy time short": Quoted in John R. Gillis, *A World of Their Own Making: Myth, Ritual, and the Quest for Family Values* (New York: BasicBooks, 1996), 46; on the true home as eschatological destination, not earthly arrival, see 109–29.

p. 172, "For the solidarity of mankind": St. Athanasius, *On the Incarnation*, trans. anonymous (Crestwood, N.Y.: St. Vladimir's Seminary Press, 1953), chap. 2, para. 9.

p. 172, "you must resolutely turn your gaze": Luther, "Sermon on Preparing to Die," 643.

CHAPTER 9

p. 175, "Did Jesus ever pee": Charles Mingus, *Beneath the Underdog* (New York: Vintage, 1971), 111.

p. 176, "the grotesque is a condition or object that is in between": See Mark Dery, *The Pyrotechnic Insanitarium: American Culture on the Brink* (New York: Grove, 1999), and Julia Kristeva, *Powers of Horror: An Essay on Abjection* (New York: Columbia University Press, 1982).

p. 177, "the human is 'an intermediate being'": St. Augustine, *The City of God*, trans. Henry Bettenson (London: Penguin, 1972), bk. 9, chap. 1.

p. 178, "Jesus endured all things and was continent": Clement, *Stromata* 7.59. Found in English translation at www.earlychristianwritings.com/text/ clement-stromata-book3–english.html.

p. 178, "lovers of luxury": St. John Chrysostom, *The Homilies of S. John Chrysostom on the Epistles of St. Paul the Apostle to Timothy, Titus, and Philemon* (Oxford: John Henry Parker, 1853), homily 13, para. 4.

p. 179, "outlets for the cleanly discharge": Tertullian, "On the Resurrection of the Flesh," in *The Ante-Nicene Fathers: The Writings of the Fathers down to A.D. 325*, vol. 3, ed. Alexander Roberts and James Donaldson (Grand Rapids: Eerdmans, 1978), chaps. 2, 61.

p. 179, "the Blessing of Asher Yatzar": The translation of and commentary on this Orthodox Jewish prayer may be found at http://members.aol.com/ LazerA/asheryatzar.htm. My thanks to Lauren Winner for drawing it to my attention.

p. 183, "The story is told of a desert father": The two stories related in this paragraph are found at *The Desert Fathers: Sayings of the Early Christian Monks*, trans. Benedicta Ward (New York: Penguin, 2003), 164–65.

p. 184, "No man's really any good": G. K. Chesterton, "The Secret of Father Brown," in *The Father Brown Omnibus* (New York: Dodd, Mead, 1982), 638, 640.

p. 185, "He could declare, 'I resist the devil'": Quotes from Martin Luther in this paragraph are found in his *Table Talk*, ed. and trans. Theodore G. Tappert, vol. 54 of *Luther's Works* (Philadelphia: Fortress, 1967), nos. 122, 2807b, 2865b.

p. 186, "in ordinary, everyday experience, 'find among human beings'": Augustine, *City of God*, 14.24.

p. 186, "cabaret performer who 'could blow out candles'": Dery, *Pyrotechnic Insanitarium*, 111.

p. 187, "Man, the chicks really dig that": Peter Guralnick, *Careless Love: The Unmaking of Elvis Presley* (Boston: Little, Brown, 1999), 239.

p. 190, "To [perfect] nature, not to injury": Tertullian "On the Resurrection of the Flesh," 57.

p. 190, "'perhaps' the martyrs' bodies will bear the scars": Augustine, *City of God*, 22.19.

p. 192, "In *Black Hawk Down*": See Mark Bowden, *Black Hawk Down: A Story of Modern War* (New York: Signet, 2000).

p. 195, "This is obvious": Martin Luther, "The Blessed Sacrament of the Holy and True Body of Christ, and the Brotherhoods," in *Martin Luther's Basic Theological Writings*, ed. Timothy F. Lull (Minneapolis: Fortress, 1989), 245.

CHAPTER 10

p. 197, "In Lubbock we grew up": Quoted in Nicholas Dawidoff, *In the Country of Country: People and Places in American Music* (New York: Pantheon, 1997), 299.

p. 198, "none of us are really or entirely straight": See Richard Mouw, "Hanging in There," *Christian Century* (January 13, 2004): 24.

p. 200, "From here on, let your pleasure": Dante, *The Divine Comedy: Purgatory*, in *The Portable Dante*, ed. and trans. Mark Musa (New York: Penguin, 1995), canto 27, lines 131–32, 140–41.

p. 200, "the essence of this blessed state": Dante, *Divine Comedy: Paradise*, canto 3, lines 79–81, 85–87.

p. 200, "Sin is the only power": Ibid., canto 7, lines 79–81.

p. 201, "ultimate Desire who is Christ, human desire 'shall be fulfilled'": Ibid., canto 23, line 105; canto 22, lines 61–63.

p. 201, "will and desire impelled": Ibid., canto 33, lines 142–45.

p. 201, "a thousand yearning flames": Dante, *Divine Comedy: Purgatory*, canto 21, lines 115–45.

p. 202, "The glory of the One Who moves": Dante, *Divine Comedy: Paradise*, canto 1, lines 1–3.

p. 202, "the portals 'from which [divine] Love'": Dante, *Divine Comedy: Purgatory*, canto 21, line 117.

p. 202, "that harmonious heaven": Ibid., canto 31, line 144.

p. 202, "My beauty, as you have already seen": Dante, *Divine Comedy: Paradise*, canto 8, lines 13–15; canto 21, lines 7–9.

p. 202, "When our flesh, sanctified and glorious": Ibid., canto 14, lines 43–45, 55–60.

p. 206, "They may be wrong, but they are not any less determined to honor Scripture": See, for example, A. K. M. Adam, "Disciples Together, Constantly," *Homosexuality and Christian Community,* ed. Choon-Leong Seow (Louisville: Westminster John Knox, 1996), 123–32; David S. Cunningham, *These Three Are One: The Practice of Trinitarian Theology* (Malden, MA: Blackwell, 1998), 299–303; Stephen E. Fowl, *Engaging Scripture: A Model for Theological Interpretation* (Malden, MA: Blackwell, 1998), 119–27; Eugene F. Rogers Jr., *Sexuality and the Christian Body: Their Way into the Triune God* (Malden, MA: Blackwell, 1999); and Rowan Williams, "The Body's Grace," in *Our Selves, Our Souls and Bodies,* ed. Charles Hefling (Cambridge, MA: Cowley, 1996), 58–68.

p. 207, "there is an intermediary position that would not put homosexual relationships": This position, so far as I am aware, was first argued by the

German theologian Helmut Thielicke. See his *Theological Ethics*, vol. 3, *Sex*, trans. John W. Doberstein (Grand Rapids: Eerdmans, 1964), 269–92. For a more recent examination by a biblical scholar arriving at this position, see Mark Allan Powell, "The Bible and Homosexuality," in *Faithful Conversation: Christian Perspectives on Homosexuality*, ed. James M. Childs Jr. (Minneapolis: Fortress, 2003), pp. 19–39.

p. 207, "Patience is the very nature of God": Tertullian, *Patience*, in *Disciplinary, Moral, and Ascetical Works*, trans. Rudoph Arbesmann et al. (New York: Fathers of the Church, 1959), chaps. 3, 1. For an excellent treatment of Tertullian on patience, see Robert Louis Wilken, *The Spirit of Early Christian Thought* (New Haven: Yale University Press, 2003), 283–85.

p. 208, "Some luminaries, such as Gregory of Nyssa": See Sarah Coakley, "The Eschatological Body: Gender, Transformation, and God," at www.bostontheological.org/colloquium/bts/coakley.htm. I am grateful to Father Matthew Gunter for drawing this article to my attention.

p. 208, "Much later Bonaventure": Quoted in Caroline Walker Bynum, *The Resurrection of the Body: In Western Christianity, 200–1336* (New York: Columbia University Press, 1995), 99, 255.

p. 209, "Biblical scholars and historians confirm this much": See Jack Miles, *Christ: A Crisis in the Life of God* (New York: Vintage, 2002), 61.

p. 211, "Similarly, Thomas can see sex outside marriage as unjust": For the material in this paragraph, see St. Thomas Aquinas, *Summa Theologiae: A Concise Translation*, ed. Timothy McDermott (Allen, TX: Christian Classics, 1989), 431–32.

p. 212, "Careful study of the passage on sexual sin": Ibid., 375.

p. 215, "They could be matter-of-fact about sexual shortcomings": For this and the following information in this paragraph, see Peter Brown, *The Body and Society: Men, Women, and Sexual Renunciation in Early Christianity* (New York: Columbia University Press, 1988), 230.

p. 215, "The desert fathers at their best": The accounts in this and the following paragraphs are found in *The Desert Fathers*, trans. Helen Waddell (New York: Vintage, 1998), 80, 83–84.

p. 216, "the passions might be 'in some sort bound'": Ibid., 194.

p. 217, "Once a brother in Scete": Ibid., 101–2.

CHAPTER 11

p. 226, "certainly did not mean that Christians must give up": Jean-Michel Hornus, *It Is Not Lawful for Me to Fight: Early Christian Attitudes toward*

War, Violence, and the State, trans. Alan Kreider and Oliver Coburn (Scottdale, PA: Herald, 1980), 214.

p. 226, "This meant . . . Christians must be willing to live out of control": Stanley Hauerwas, *The Peaceable Kingdom: A Primer in Christian Ethics* (Notre Dame, IN: University of Notre Dame Press, 1983), 105–6.

p. 227, "The Blumhardts recognized that Christian patience": Quotations are from *Thy Kingdom Come: A Blumhardt Reader*, ed. Vernard Eller (Grand Rapids: Eerdmans, 1980), 84–85, 97.

p. 229, "As Tertullian put it, patience": Tertullian, *Patience*, in *Disciplinary, Moral, and Ascetical Works*, trans Rudoph Arbesmann et al. (New York: Fathers of the Church, 1959), chap. 13.

p. 231, "The First Ecumenical Council": Andrew Louth, "The Body in Western Catholic Christianity," in *Religion and the Body*, ed. Sarah Coakley (Cambridge: Cambridge University Press, 1997), 113.

p. 231, "Through our outward posture": Kallistos Ware, "'My Helper and My Enemy': The Body in Greek Christianity," in ibid., 105–7.

CHAPTER 12

p. 234, "I hope in Our Lord": Christopher Columbus, journal, November 6, 1492, as quoted in Tzvetan Todorov, *The Conquest of America* (New York: HarperPerennial, 1982), 50. For historical and theological exploration of Christianity and violence, see Kenneth R. Chase and Alan Jacobs, eds., *Must Christianity Be Violent? Reflections on History, Practice, and Theology* (Grand Rapids: Brazos, 2003).

p. 235, "did not use violence": Irenaeus, *The Scandal of the Incarnation* (originally *Against the Heresies*), trans. John Saward (San Francisco: Ignatius, 1990), bk. 4, chap. 37; bk. 5, chap. 1.

p. 237, "Accordingly, a Buddhist scholar writes": Phra Khantipalo, as quoted in J. A. DiNoia, "Pluralist Theology of Religions: Pluralistic or Non-pluralistic?" in *Christian Uniqueness Reconsidered: The Myth of a Pluralistic Theology of Religions*, ed. Gavin D'Costa (Maryknoll, NY: Orbis, 1990), 120.

p. 237, "requires 'much more than simply tinkering'": Paul Griffiths, "The Uniqueness of Christian Doctrine Defended," in *Christian Uniqueness Reconsidered*, ed. D'Costa, 168.

p. 239, "purely inward worship": Jean-Jacques Rousseau quoted in William T. Cavanaugh, "The City: Beyond Secular Parodies," in *Radical Orthodoxy*, ed. John Milbank, Catherine Pickstock, and Graham Ward (London: Routledge, 1999), 189–90.

p. 240, Hobbes called "mere life": Thomas Hobbes quoted in Ashley Woodiwiss, "Christian Economic Justice and the Impasse in Political Theory," in *Toward a Just and Caring Society*, ed. David Gushee (Grand Rapids: Baker, 1999), 120.

p. 241, "under liberalism 'ways of life that require self-restraint'": Galston and Macedo are quoted by Ashley Woodiwiss, "Rawls, Religion, and Liberalism," in *The Re-enchantment of Political Science*, ed. Thomas A. Heilke and Ashley Woodiwiss (Lanham, MD: Lexington, 2001), 74–75.

p. 241, "Making open-ended and ongoing choice its highest good": See Ronald Beiner, *What's the Matter with Liberalism?* (Berkeley: University of California Press, 1992), 22–24.

p. 241, "And liberal nations demand sacrifices": See Timothy Fitzgerald, *The Ideology of Religious Studies* (New York: Oxford University Press, 2000), 104. Also Carolyn Marvin and David W. Ingle, *Blood Sacrifice and the Nation: Totem Rituals and the American Flag* (Cambridge: Cambridge University Press, 1999).

p. 242, "So Tertullian, drawing on a kind of apostolic cosmpolitanism": Tertullian and Basil are quoted in Jean-Michel Hornus, *It Is Not Lawful for Me to Fight: Early Christian Attitudes toward War, Violence, and the State*, trans. Alan Kreider and Oliver Coburn (Scottdale, PA: Herald, 1980), pp. 106, 104.

p. 244, "Willing to change the world . . . God begins in a small and particular way": On the necessary particularity of Christian faith, I draw from Gerhard Lohfink, *Does God Need the Church? Toward a Theology of the People of God*, trans. Linda M. Maloney (Collegeville, MN: Liturgical, 1999), 27, 46–47.

p. 247, "Yet other orthodox Christians, looking to such texts": For an excellent survey of traditional Christian understandings of salvation and its extent, see John Sanders, *No Other Name: An Investigation into the Destiny of the Unevangelized* (Grand Rapids: Eerdmans, 1992).

p. 247, "Christians in the first centuries appear": George A. Lindbeck, *The Church in a Postliberal Age*, ed. James J. Buckley (Grand Rapids: Eerdmans, 2002), 82.

p. 248, "More recently the Anglican C. S. Lewis": See Lewis's *The Great Divorce* (New York: Macmillan, 1946).

p. 249, "Mention of Dante's Virgil suggests yet another possibility": On thought behind this paragraph, see S. Mark Heim's extraordinary book *The Depth of the Riches: A Trinitarian Theology of Religious Ends* (Grand Rapids: Eerdmans, 2001).

INDEX